The International Library of Psychology

THE PSYCHOLOGY OF ECONOMICS

Founded by C. K. Ogden

The International Library of Psychology

GENERAL PSYCHOLOGY
In 38 Volumes

I	The Neurosis of Man	*Burrow*
II	Creative Imagination	*Downey*
III	The Caveman Within Us	*Fielding*
IV	Men and their Motives	*Flugel*
V	The Mind in Sleep	*Fortune*
VI	The Mind and its Body	*Fox*
VII	Practical Psychology	*Fox*
VIII	Man for Himself	*Fromm*
IX	The Law Within	*Fuller*
X	The Nature of Laughter	*Gregory*
XI	Readings in General Psychology	*Halmos et al*
XII	The Psychologist at Work	*Harrower*
XIII	The Psychology of Philosophers	*Herzberg*
XIV	Emotion	*Hillman*
XV	The Foundations of Common Sense	*Isaacs*
XVI	The Psychology of Consciousness	*King*
XVII	The Sciences of Man in the Making	*Kirkpatrick*
XVIII	The Person in Psychology	*Lafitte*
XIX	Man's Unconscious Passion	*Lay*
XX	Psychological and Biological Foundations of Dream-Interpretation	*Lowy*
XXI	Nervous Disorders and Character	*Mckenzie*
XXII	An Historical Introduction to Modern Psychology	*Murphy*
XXIII	Modern Theories of the Unconscious	*Northridge*
XXIV	The A B C of Psychology	*Ogden*
XXV	The Psychology of Thought and Feeling	*Platt*
XXVI	Introductory Psychology	*Price-Williams*
XXVII	Empirical Foundations of Psychology	*Pronko et al*
XXVIII	Psychotherapy	*Schilder*
XXIX	The Psychology of Time	*Sturt*
XXX	The Origins of Love and Hate	*Suttie*
XXXI	Art and the Unconscious	*Thorburn*
XXXII	The Elements of Psychology	*Thorndike*
XXXIII	Telepathy and Clairvoyance	*Tischner*
XXXIV	Human Psychology as Seen Through the Dream	*Turner*
XXXV	The Psychology of Self-Conciousness	*Turner*
XXXVI	The Psychology of Economics	*Weisskopf*
XXXVII	The Measurement of Emotion	*Whately Smith*
XXXVIII	How to be Happy Though Human	*Wolfe*

THE PSYCHOLOGY OF ECONOMICS

WALTER A WEISSKOPF

Routledge
Taylor & Francis Group
LONDON AND NEW YORK

First published in 1955 by
Routledge and Kegan Paul Ltd

Reprinted in 1999, 2001, 2002 by
Routledge

2 Park Square, Milton Park, Abingdon, Oxfordshire OX14 4RN
711 Third Avenue, New York, NY 10017

Routledge is an imprint of the Taylor & Francis Group, an informa business

First issued in paperback 2013

With the kind permission of University of Chicago Press

Transferred to Digital Printing 2006

The publishers have made every effort to contact authors/copyright holders of the works reprinted in the *International Library of Psychology*. This has not been possible in every case, however, and we would welcome correspondence from those individuals/companies we have been unable to trace.

These reprints are taken from original copies of each book. In many cases the condition of these originals is not perfect. The publisher has gone to great lengths to ensure the quality of these reprints, but wishes to point out that certain characteristics of the original copies will, of necessity, be apparent in reprints thereof.

The Publishers give thanks to the University of Chicago Press for giving permission to reprint this work.

British Library Cataloguing in Publication Data
A CIP catalogue record for this book
is available from the British Library

The Psychology of Economics
ISBN 978-0-415-21048-5 (hbk)
ISBN 978-0-415-86886-0 (pbk)

General Psychology: 38 Volumes
ISBN 0415-21129-8
The International Library of Psychology: 204 Volumes
ISBN 0415-19132-7

Preface

THIS book is a study of the psychology and philosophy of social thought, exemplified by the analysis of certain economic ideas. The method is briefly sketched in the first part and then applied in a series of case studies to crucial concepts in economics. The emphasis lies as much on the approach as on the results of its application. It is contended that, without the help of the psychocultural method, socioeconomic thought often remains incomprehensible. It is sometimes necessary to go beyond its traditional framework because the immanent approach does not lead to a meaningful interpretation. I have tried to listen 'with a third ear' to economists, to uncover what lies below the surface of their thoughts. As in art, one can detect a 'style' in the writing of economists and social scientists. The analysis of this style often throws more light on the meaning of their thought than can be gathered from its obvious content. The hidden undercurrents rather than the truth value and factual accuracy of economics are the subject of this book. I have not tried to debunk economics as 'unscientific'. But I have attempted to show that, like other sciences, economics has an instrumental character and performs, perhaps unconsciously, an ethical and fiduciary function.

This book is the result of many schools of thought. I owe a great debt not only to traditional economic theory and philosophy but to psychoanalysis and to sociology, anthropology, and social psychology, in so far as they centre around the concepts of culture and personality. I have been deeply influenced by the writings of Sigmund Freud, Erich Fromm, and David Riesman. The materials used in this book have been provided by various social sciences; the novelty, if any, lies in their combination and application to economics. Therefore this book is addressed not only to economists but to all social scientists.

The writing of this book was facilitated by two grants-in-aid from the Social Science Research Council; the second grant was received upon recommendation from Roosevelt College.

The courtesy of the following publishers, journals, and copyright-holders in permitting the use of copyrighted material is gratefully acknowledged:

American Economic Association, *American Journal of Economics and Sociology*, Miss Phyllis Bottome (for the heirs of Alfred Adler), Cambridge University Press, J. M. Dent, *Ethics*, Faber and Faber, Harcourt, Brace and Company, Harper and Brothers, Harvard University Press, W. Heffer and Sons, Hermitage House, The Hogarth Press, *The Journal of Political Economy*, Alfred A. Knopf, The Macmillan Company, W. W. Norton and Company, Princeton University Press, Public Affairs Press, G. P. Putnam's Sons, Rhinehart and Company, Sigmund Freud Copyrights Limited, William Sloane Associates, The St. Martin's Press, Yale University Press.

All direct quotations are used by permission of the publishers.

Contents

PART IV

Male and Female Symbolism in the Thought of Ricardo, Malthus, Engels, and Marx

PART V

Alfred Marshall's Value and Equilibrium Theory

PART VI

The Disintegration of Economic Rationalism

Part I

Introduction

Chapter I

THE APPROACH

DISSATISFACTION with certain aspects of economic theory is as old as the discipline itself. Almost as soon as the classical founders completed their edifice, the antagonists began to undermine the newly erected structure. Economic theorists built a close-knit system of economic laws logically derived from certain philosophical and psychological premises.[1] The heretics tried to puncture this system by criticizing its assumptions and its methods for its lack of realism, its neglect of sociological and political factors, its faulty interpretation of human behaviour; for its use of metaphysical and normative concepts; and for its essentially static and mechanistic approach to economic phenomena. Almost before the ink was dry on Ricardo's *Principles*, Sismondi complained that economic science ' is so speculative that it seems divorced from all practice.'[2] The criticism of the socialists, nationalists, romanticists, historicists, and institutionalists accompanied the development of orthodox economics.

Professor Mayo has blamed Ricardian economics for the social ailments of our civilization.[3] He denounces the 'chronic divorce' of economic theory from practice and questions 'the original clinical and practical adequacy of economic theory' to the facts it studied. Similarly, the uselessness of economic theory because of its self-imposed limitations is deplored by Professor Walker.[4] He characterizes the present state of economic theory as 'theoretic blight'. 'The familiar features of the concrete world are left out of account altogether or are definitely misrepresented.' Economists themselves have expressed grave misgivings over the possibilities of the discipline.

1 I am referring to the dominant theoretical trend as expressed mainly in the writings of A. Smith, Ricardo, J. S. Mill, Jevons, the Austrians, A. Marshall, J. B. Clark, and F. H. Knight. The objects of my analysis, however, are not the entire systems developed by these writers but certain central ideas which have become part and parcel of our common beliefs.

2 *Nouveaux principes*, I, p. 57.

3 Elton Mayo, *The Social Problem of Our Civilization*, chaps. i, ii, esp. p. 38.

4 Edward Ronald Walker, *From Economic Theory to Policy*, esp. chaps. iii and iv.

INTRODUCTION

> After almost two centuries of development economists still do not have anything better to offer than a promise for the future. Meanwhile the optimistic economists are working out their analyses on the simple assumption [of economic rationality] and resolutely refusing to despair of evolving in the future a technique which will allow them to assume the existence of whatever human motives have an influence on the economic sphere.[1]

The sad state of economics has frequently been admitted by Professor Knight, one of the outstanding exponents of orthodox economics as well as one of its most penetrating critics. He clearly states that economic theory, based on utilitarian premises, is purely abstract and without content and that the formal principles of economy are without reference to what is to be economized and how.[2]

It would be possible but superfluous to multiply such critical quotations from old and recent literature *ad infinitum*. But, in spite of the constant criticism and the admission by economists that much of it is justified, some of the basic assumptions and methods have not been changed. Why did economists retain certain concepts and methods which were considered scientifically inadequate? Why is it that such obviously untenable concepts as omniscience, which human beings do not possess, or equilibrium, which admittedly is never reached, or economic rationality, which, as generally recognized, is not the only motive of human behaviour—why are such concepts and analytic tools still used in economic analysis? One gains the impression that these ideas and methods must fulfil certain psychological requirements and that possibly on this account they are retained in spite of their insufficiency on purely scientific grounds.

This book represents an attempt to answer some of these questions and to explain the function and meaning of some economic ideas with the help of the psychocultural method. In order to explain this approach, some remarks about the nature of science and knowledge are in order. In the form in which it has developed in modern Western civilization, science is a method of acquiring knowledge through factual observation and logic. The facts are procured through sensory experience and processed into systems of laws and regularities by logic. The most important results of science have been achieved in the field of the natural sciences, especially in physics. The social sciences, including economics, have been greatly influenced by the outlook of the natural sciences.

[1] Joan Robinson, *Economics Is a Serious Subject*, p. 10.

[2] F. H. Knight, *Risk, Uncertainty and Profit*, Preface, p. xii.

For centuries the truth value of science has been an open problem. In various formulations the fight between realism and nominalism has been carried on since the Middle Ages. Whereas realism believes in the fundamental identity of thinking and being, nominalistic or hypothetical thinking negates this identity and repudiates the belief

> that the human mind is capable of arriving directly at an insight into the order of the universe; all concepts are held to be purely hypothetical and to be based on assumptions.[1]

The trend of modern thought has, since Kant, been away from realism, toward a hypothetical approach. This has made it legitimate to raise the question: On what basis are thought-constructs developed? If they are not reflection of reality, what determines their content?

Attempts have been made to answer this question with the help of the transcendent approach and its most important application, the sociology of knowledge. The extraneous, transcendent, extrinsic method, in distinction from the immanent approach, does not analyse systems of thought from the point of view inherent in the system but from a frame of reference external to it.[2] The immanent interpretation inquires whether a system of thought is logically consistent and whether its findings are in conformity with observed facts. The transcendent interpretation of thought involves the application of a new frame of reference to systems of thought. It is in itself a system of thought and requires, therefore, certain assumptions which are foreign to the intentional, conscious presuppositions of the system to which they are applied.

Actually, the extraneous method, as used, e.g., in the sociology of knowledge, may be considered a special version of hypothetical thinking, the concepts and constructs of which are also supposed to be extraneous to the reality to which they are applied. In both cases the constructs used are taken from 'outside' the phenomenon under consideration. They include elements not contained in the object: the hypothetical method is already essentially an extraneous method. Therefore, the difference between hypothetical thought and the extraneous method is not so much a contrast between two different methods as it is a difference in the choice of the frame of reference.

The transcendent method, however, was only one step in the

1 K. Pribram, *Conflicting Patterns of Thought*, p. 2.

2 Otto H. Dahlke, in *Contemporary Social Theory*, ed. Barnes and Becker, p. 64; A. H. Child, 'Problems of Sociology of Knowledge'; Karl Mannheim, *Ideology and Utopia*; Ernst Grunwald, *Das Problem einer Soziologie des Wissens*.

direction of a broader outlook toward systems of thought. In some of the modern social sciences it has been superseded by the *holistic approach.* Holism requires that the whole be grasped as an entity which is more than, and different from, its parts. The basic experience stems from the feeling of a person of being one and the same, of being an entity of some permanence. The experience of wholeness can also be involved in the contemplation of a work of art. A tree can be grasped as a totality which expresses an underlying pattern; each of its branches and leaves reflects the pattern of the whole. The essence of this experience is summed up in the German concept of *Gestalt.* The concepts of personality and culture, as used in the modern social sciences, are holistic ones. A person is a Gestalt, a total configuration, the parts of which cannot be understood in isolation; a change in a part necessarily changes the entire character of the whole, and the part, separated from the whole, becomes a different being. Most data in the sciences of man are of such a complex, holistic nature. In contrast to the atomistic world view, which looks for basic, simple units out of which more complex entities are composed, the holistic approach does not try to 'reduce' wholes to their parts but to comprehend them as wholes.[1]

In this book the attempt is made to approach economic thought from the holistic point of view. We view man as enmeshed in the totality of the universe, of his society, culture, and environment, and within the entity of his own self, as a *cosmion,* a person. Every element within these entities is interrelated with every other element. The entire network of mutual interrelations cannot be fully grasped by the human mind; and this lack of complete insight and knowledge is an essential of the human situation. Only in rare exceptional moments of intuition can the totality of world and man be perceived. The limitations of the human intellect make it necessary to dissect this totality and to confine one's self to the uncovering of certain specific and one-sided relations and uniformities. However, the human intellect, aware of this situation, tries forever to transcend its own limits; and the transcendent and, even more so, the holistic method are manifestations of this endeavour.

Within this totality, man is beset with inner conflicts which are unavoidable concomitants of human existence. These conflicts cause tensions which give rise to needs; their satisfaction consists in the elimination of tension. The existential, primeval conflict is founded in the fact that man is part of nature, subject to necessities as a biological organism and a social animal, yet able to transcend nature and society through his consciousness, reason, and spirit. This con-

[1] A. H. Maslow, 'Dynamics of Personality Organisation', pp. 514 ff., 571 ff.

flict causes anxiety, and the need arises to ward it off with the help of harmonizing thought-constructs. Inner conflict may be of social origin. The individual depends upon his environment for his livelihood, and he needs social recognition as a prop for his self-respect. The desire to be accepted is one of the most effective motives for social adaptation, of moulding man according to the social ideals of his society. Social acceptance is impaired by impulses which run counter to the value attitudes of the environment. If such impulses arise, the fear of being rejected by society leads to the danger signal of anxiety. This can be alleviated again by intellectual constructs which try to deny the anxiety-creating conflicts.

This discussion of the human situation forms a necessary background for the understanding of socioeconomic thought. The latter deals, consciously or unconsciously, also with general human conflicts but mainly with those caused by the cultural and socioeconomic situation. These conflicts may be brought about by cultural change, such as conflicts between old and new world views and ethical systems. Other conflicts arise between the essential needs of human nature and the specific value-attitude system to which civilization tends to subject individuals.

In order to understand how socioeconomic thought helps in alleviating such conflicts, a functional, instrumental theory of thought has to be developed. Man is confronted with anxiety-creating dichotomies and conflicts; his thinking is a reaction to this situation, an instrument for dealing with these problems of existence. Man could not live without synthesizing and organizing his experiences. In order to make life livable, he has to interpret it in such a way that conflicts are settled by compromise and unbearable factors are eliminated, so that he can live in relative harmony with himself and with his environment. The function of socioeconomic thought is to enable man to live under the socioeconomic conditions under which he is forced to live. The puzzling aspects of economic thought can often be understood from the functional viewpoint. What appears incomprehensible to logic and factual observation may become meaningful in view of the function which thought has to perform in the psychological structure of the individuals confronted with common external and internal problems.

In this book the holistic method is applied to some aspects of economic thought in the form of the *psychocultural approach*.[1] We

[1] The term is borrowed from G. Gorer, *The American People—a Study in National Character*, p. 18. Although he does not use the same term, E. Fromm has provided the theoretical foundation for the analysis of ideas in their psychological interrelations with cultural processes, in *Fear of Freedom*, Appendix, pp. 277 ff. For the

believe that thought in general and socioeconomic thought in particular deal with conflicts of a psychological nature, created by cultural conditions; hence the term 'psychocultural'. The meaning of this term and of this method will be elaborated in the remainder of Part I. We would, however, like to stress here that all types of conflicts are reflected in the psyche and can, in a sense, be called 'psychological', even if their roots lie in other spheres. However, our approach is not merely psychological but also transcendent and holistic; transcendence, holism, and psychoculturalism are the pillars on which this method is based.

The psychological aspect of our analysis is obvious in the emphasis on the 'unconscious' function of thought. It seems, at first, that 'unconscious thoughts' are an impossibility, a *contradictio in adjecto*. Thinking is usually considered to be the acme of consciousness. However, ideas can play a psychological role without the individual's being aware of it. Here some of the findings of psychoanalysis can be used, without accepting its entire frame of reference. The belief in the existence of an unconscious mind implies that there are inner phenomena, unknown to the individual. It implies further that, like all human behaviour, conscious thought is imbedded in an unconscious matrix (Erich Fromm) and that its entire meaning and function cannot be understood without considering its unconscious motives. Thoughts may have two 'meanings': a conscious, intentional one and another of which the thinking individual may not be aware. The latter is often derived from its harmonizing, anxiety-avoiding, conflict-eliminating function. The psychoanalytic distinction between a 'manifest' dream text and a 'hidden', 'latent' dream content can also be applied to thought. Dreams are reactions to sleep-disturbing external or internal stimuli. As in neuroses, the disturbance usually stems from a past or present conflict situation. Dreaming consists in a processing of the elements of the conflict situation in such a way as to provide for a momentary solution by which the sleep-disturbing conflict is overcome. This is done by the so-called 'dream work', which not merely reproduces the conflict situation symbolically, but elaborates it, fits it into a new context, or replaces it by something analogous but slightly different, so as to weaken the disturbing conflict or eliminate it for the time being. This is true not only of night dreams but also of daydreams and fantasies, which also help the individual to overcome disturbing conflict situations. There is only a short step from daydreams and

application of this method to economics see the author's 'Psychological Aspects of Economic Thought', p. 309; 'Individualism and Economic Theory', p. 317; and 'Hidden Value Conflicts in Economic Thought', p. 195.

fantasies to conscious thinking; both extrapolate inner experiences, and both have the function of alleviating conflicts. Their existence has to be denied through suppression or repression[1] of the anxiety-creating facts. This is done in night- and daydreams and also in conscious thought. Under these circumstances, thought becomes an instrument of the unconscious mind; it would be incomprehensible unless interpreted in the light of this function. This requires the uncovering of the underlying conflict situation. In this respect the psychocultural method resembles psychoanalytic therapy; both try to establish an awareness of unconscious processes.

Psychoanalysis has paid attention mainly to those unconscious conflicts which have their origin in the biological, the instinctive, and the libidinal. We would like to go further and postulate that basic human conflicts are not only of a biopsychological but also of a social, intellectual, and spiritual nature. However, the parallel between our approach and the one of psychoanalysis consists in the basic role attributed to conflict. Psychoanalysis has rediscovered the antinomic and dialectical structure of human existence. Other schools of psychology, especially those concerned with the Gestalt aspects of personality, opened the way for an insight into the totality which underlies these conflicts and antinomies. Both approaches, taken together, prepare the way for a 'realistic' understanding of human phenomena.

So far, we have talked about thought as one of the instruments of the individual in dealing with the ineluctible conflicts of his existence. We have pointed out, however, that these conflicts and the concomitant anxiety can arise for cultural and social reasons. In so far as this is the case, the individual shares with his contemporaries the problems posed by these conflicts. The way he deals with them may be of importance for his contemporaries as well as for himself. This is especially true of the way in which socioeconomic thought deals with certain intellectual and cultural conflicts of Western civilization. The conflicts are, as we shall see, common ones, emerging from a particular historical situation. It is, of course, possible that an author may find a way of interpreting and structurizing these general conflicts which is useful only for himself. However, if systems of socioeconomic thought are widely accepted, one can assume that they represent a solution of problems not only for the author but also for those who were influenced by his thought. A system of social philosophy may originate in the mind of one individual; if it

[1] The former is conscious denial; the latter takes place if something is pushed outside the limits of consciousness for unconscious reasons. The individual is not aware of the causes and results of the process of repression.

influences the beliefs, attitudes, and behaviour of many others, if it becomes institutionalized, the individual answer to common problems is of social importance.

It is not only the system and the concepts of socioeconomic thought but also the underlying conflict situations which are of supra-individual, social importance under such circumstances. The psychocultural analysis of socioeconomic thought will uncover its interrelation with cultural conflict situations. If certain ideas represent a generally accepted way of dealing with those conflicts, it can be assumed that not only the solution but also the conflict situation are of general importance. Thus the psychocultural approach, by uncovering the harmonizing function of economic thought, can also throw some light on the underlying cultural conflicts.

Chapter II

THE ECONOMIC VALUE COMPLEX

ONE of the functions of social thought is to fortify people in their moral beliefs and to eliminate value conflicts. The modern social sciences do not perform this function openly but only implicitly and unconsciously. Social scientists try to be ethically neutral, and economists are no exception. One of the reasons for the reluctance to acknowledge ethical elements in economics is the emphasis of our time on science. Scientific reasoning has laboured to find a place for the normative element in its universe of discourse. In a world of facts and logic the normative seems to have no place. Openly ethical considerations were relegated to theology and philosophy, both fields which hold a secondary place in the thought of our age. The social sciences were overwhelmed by the success of the natural sciences, which were supposedly free of value judgments. However, man cannot live without guiding norms for his conduct. Action, confronted with alternatives, requires the awareness of an 'ought to' as a basis for decision. Moreover, people cannot believe in any norms, values, and ideals without rooting this belief in some basic idea which is part of the world outlook of the period. In the Middle Ages this was the divine will disclosed by revelation; in modern civilization, it is the laws of reason uncovered by science. The sciences aim to be free of value judgments; our time, however, wants to justify everything by science, including ultimate values. Thus the logical demand for ethical neutrality in the sciences conflicts with the psychocultural need for an ultimate basis for values.

For this reason the social sciences are a mixture of factual and value statements. Ethical neutrality could be maintained only if we could find an extra-scientific basis for values such as revelation or faith. All this, however, makes a discussion of economics and ethics difficult and confused. It is almost impossible for anyone who still accepts the value system which underlies economic thought to admit that many findings of economics are, in reality, value judgments, because such an admission deprives these values of their validity in a culture where science alone can prove anything. Only in a period in which these economic value attitudes are on the decline can the normative character of the science which propagates these values be discovered. Because of this peculiar situation, the unveiling of the normative character of a science thus assumes the character of a debunking process; however, one does not necessarily debunk a system of thought by showing its normative character; one merely debunks the thinking of those who refuse to acknowledge the existence of this normative aspect.

The fact that the normative element in economics has been often overlooked may also be due to what could be called the 'pro-conscious bias' of modern science. With the exception of certain schools of psychology, the social sciences have confined themselves to an examination of conscious thought and behaviour. Dynamic psychology, however, has discovered that men are not only guided by consciously adopted norms; normative systems can become internalized and guide behaviour without the conscious knowledge of the actors. Such unconscious value systems show the following characteristics: (1) normative rules, values, and attitudes of social origin are internalized and become part and parcel of the individual's personality; (2) these internalized normative systems can become partly or wholly unconscious and influence a person's thought, feeling, and action without his being aware of it; (3) the internalization of such systems of values and attitudes is a process which enables the individual to conform in his thoughts, feeling, and actions to the demands of his environment. It facilitates his doing what he is expected to do; (4) such internalized normative systems, in spite of the fact that they are part of an individual's psychic apparatus, have a supra-individual, collective content and a continuity in time. The value systems of the parents mould those of the children. Members of the same group, civilization, and subculture have internalized normative systems with the same content. Thus we can call such a system a 'value complex' and describe it as a largely unconscious part of an individual's character structure, moulded by sociocultural influences and representing internalized sociocultural norms.[1]

In his famous essay *The Protestant Ethics and the Spirit of Capitalism*,

[1] These internalized systems have been analysed by Erich Fromm, *Fear of Freedom*, pp. 22 ff., as the 'social character'; by A. Kardiner, *The Psychological Frontiers of Society*, chap. ii, as the 'basic personality structure'; by S. Freud as the 'superego' (see *Group Psychology and the Analysis of the Ego*, chap. xi, and *The Ego and the Id*, chap. iii). The term 'value complex' is borrowed from R. K. Merton, *Social Theory and Social Structure*, p. 329. R. Linton in A. Kardiner, *op. cit.*, chap. viii, uses the term 'value attitude system'.

Max Weber has described what may be called 'the economic value complex'.[1] This system of attitudes and moral precepts is characterized by the following value orientations:

1. Accumulation: the striving for acquisition of wealth and riches, for the increase of possessions, is felt to be a duty. The individual must continually prove that he is chosen, successful, valuable; he can never relax, never tell himself that he has accumulated enough and reached his goal.
2. Quantification: the tendency to account for success in quantifiable terms, to carry on a sort of moral-economic bookkeeping.
3. Labour: work and labour in an occupation within the framework of the existing economic order is considered a duty and the only acceptable way of life; it acquires the dignity of an ultimate end.
4. Individualism: the individual is supposed to strive for this—worldly success in isolation alone.
5. Competition: the main driving force is to prove one's value through success. 'Successful' members of the middle class, like the 'elect' of Puritanism, consider themselves an élite group; they must distinguish themselves from the unsuccessful or 'damned'. This attitude requires that success be accomplished by competition, at the expense of somebody else, to set apart the 'blessed' from the 'rejected.
6. Rational conduct: economic success should be pursued in a conscious, rational, systematic way, based on constant motives, on a life-plan, in a purposive, consistent fashion. Spontaneous, emotional, impulsive, capricious, sentimental, or enthusiastic behaviour is considered to be morally reprehensible.
7. Asceticism: enjoyment, especially of the senses and of sex, is more or less repressed. In respect to economic conduct, this results in a high evaluation of saving and a rejection of luxurious consumption.

This syndrome of value attitudes has been traced back by Max Weber to the Calvinist and Puritan ethic. The Puritan ethic was first an ethical system which met with rejection. It was accepted only by members of the respective churches. After it had led to the economic success of many of its adherents and after the market economy developed which fostered these attitudes, this value system became divorced from its religious framework. It was adopted as a value attitude by most middle-class groups in Western countries.

[1] Max Weber calls it the 'spirit of capitalism', in the book with the above-mentioned title, trans. T. Parsons. We have chosen a different term because we want to stress the fact that it has become an inner, often unconscious, normative system.

It became the goal of moral education; and it became an unconscious part of the character structure of middle-class individuals.

Some important ideas in economic thought can be understood as intellectual and ethical justifications of this value-attitude system, as will be shown later. One of the historical reasons why this value complex had to be justified was that it developed against the fierce resistance of an anti-chrematistic ethic. Moneymaking for its own sake, the taking of interest, buying cheap and selling dear, exploiting the vagaries of supply and demand for one's advantage, etc.—all these and other activities which form the daily routine of economic life today were considered morally reprehensible throughout Western civilization more or less until the sixteenth century of European history. Aristotle had already distinguished between household management, which provided for the necessities of life, and the reprehensible art of moneymaking, which consists of the illegitimate accumulation of riches as an aim in itself. It is legitimate to procure the necessities of life through trade, but it is reprehensible to trade with the sole aim of making a profit.[1] According to the *Corpus juris canonici*, property is sinful. Tertullian states that if covetousness is removed, there is no reason for gain, and if there is no reason for gain, there is no reason for trade. The Fathers of the Church used a moral approach to economic problems and looked at them from the point of view of the salvation of the individual.[2] The economic ethic of the medieval church is summarized in the statement: 'homo mercator vix aut numquam potest Deo placere' ('the merchant can never, or hardly ever, please God').

Against this attitude the new economic spirit had to develop. The phases of this development have been the object of outstanding scholarship and can therefore be summarized briefly.[3] In the writings of the medieval Schoolmen, in the thought of Luther, and in the economic thinking of the Anglican Church, economic conduct was subjected to religious ethics, and the pursuit of economic gain as an end in itself was still rejected as immoral. However, Calvin and the English Puritans, after the Revolution, considered the economic attitudes—such as thrift, diligence, sobriety, frugality, work in a calling—as Christian virtues. Yet in the practice of the communities dominated by their precepts, life in general and business activity in particular were still subject to the rigid discipline of an almost totalitarian church régime. The religious element began

1 Aristotle, *Politics*, Book I, in Monroe, *Early Economic Thought*, pp. 13 ff.

2 W. A. Ashley, *English Economic History and Theory*, Part I, chap. iii, pp. 1–25.

3 See the writings of Max Weber, Schultze-Gaevernitz, Cunningham, Troeltsch, Tawney, Sombart.

to disintegrate in the eighteenth century; the individualistic work-and-success ethic, however, remained victorious in a secularized form. In the writings of the classical economists the religious cloak was completely dropped, and economic thinking emerged in its autonomous form.

This development has cast a shadow on the overt relations between economics and ethics until the present time. Ethics was and is interpreted as religious, anti-chrematistic ethics. The secularization of economics included its conscious emancipation from ethics. Because the religious approach—indeed, the approach to economic problems from the days of Aristotle onward—had been ethical, the new science of economics tried to eliminate all traces of its antecedents by eradicating from its explicit, overt system of thought all conscious, normative, ethical aspects.

This, however, did not prevent important remnants of the old approach from surviving, although in a hidden form, in the thinking and writings of the new generations, who regarded economic aims as ultimate, positive values. The emancipation was never completely successful. Both attitudes—the religious Christian, anti-chrematistic attitude, on the one hand, and the new economic value complex on the other—became internalized value systems of Western middle-class man. This was especially true during the periods of transition from precapitalist to capitalist times. The two conflicting value-attitude systems were, and still are to some extent, the source of a basic conflict in our civilization. This conflict found its reflection in economic thought. Some of the elements which are present in economic thought almost throughout its entire history can be interpreted as a symptom of the largely unconscious conflict which raged in the minds of economists and their contemporaries, between the Christian precapitalist ethic and the economic value complex. This will be discussed later.

Part II

Classical Value Theory and Adam Smith

Chapter III

THE PSYCHOCULTURAL BACKGROUND OF CLASSICAL VALUE THEORY

IN Part I we described the nature and origin of the economic value complex. We have seen that value systems are interrelated with cultural and social conditions and that they can become internalized and unconscious. Certain aspects of economic thought can be interpreted as manifestations of and reactions to the economic value complex. We shall now examine the interrelation between this complex and classical value theory.

Value in Use versus Value in Exchange

Both Adam Smith and Ricardo, after briefly mentioning the concept of value in use, neglect it completely, to devote themselves exclusively to the discussion of value in exchange.

> The word value . . . has two different meanings, and sometimes expresses the utility of some particular object, and sometimes the power of purchasing other goods which the possession of that object conveys. The one may be called 'value in use'; the other, 'value in exchange'.[1]

Adam Smith, after mentioning the fact that 'the things which have the greatest value in exchange have frequently very little or no value in use', concentrates on exchange value, ignoring value in use.

Ricardo proceeds along similar lines. He begins by quoting Adam Smith's statements about the two types of value and concludes that

> utility then is not the measure of exchangeable value, although it is absolutely essential to it. . . . Possessing utility, commodities derive their exchangeable value from two sources: from their scarcity, and from the quantity of labour required to obtain them.[2]

[1] Adam Smith, *Wealth of Nations*, Book I, chap. iv, p. 28. All quotations from the *Wealth of Nations* refer to the 'Modern Library' edition.

[2] David Ricardo, *Principles of Political Economy and Taxation*, chap. i, Sec. I, p. 5. All quotations from the *Principles* refer to the 'Everyman' edition.

He then shifts immediately to a consideration of exchange value, leaving aside value in use.

The dichotomy of value in use and value in exchange reflects the conflict between the precapitalist attitude and the economic value complex. By rejecting the concept of value in use, the classical economists declared themselves implicitly as partisans of the new mode of life and the economic value complex. The market economy required that the individual strive toward acquisition, accumulation, and riches, without limit, as ends in themselves. The use of wealth was originally not the main purpose of acquisition. Thus use value could not play a predominant role in the determination of economic values. Value in exchange is the important concept in an economic order in which people are supposed to exert themselves to the utmost in order to accumulate capital. Need satisfaction is only an incidental aim.

The main problems of early capitalism were related to production: how to increase the production of physical goods through technological and mechanical improvements and how to procure a sufficient surplus of capital to put new inventions into effect. This economic situation was reflected in the approach of the classical economists to economic conduct and economic welfare. They looked for the best way of getting the largest possible amount of produce with a limited amount of land and an increasing supply of labour. Production was, to some extent, an end in itself. Nevertheless, classical thought contains important utilitarian elements. Adam Smith had the choice between the doctrine of utility and the labour theory of value.[1] Pufendorf took as the foundation of 'the proper and intrinsic price, the aptitude of things or actions to minister to the needs, comforts or pleasures of life, that is to say their utility.'[2] Hutcheson, the teacher of Adam Smith, followed Pufendorf and mentions demand and use as determinants of price. Adam Smith, however, followed Locke and based exchange value on labour. The reason for this rejection of utility was that the classical economists tried to justify the market system and the economic value complex, for which exchange value, based on work effort, is the decisive magnitude, and value in use of only secondary importance.

The fact that Smith mentions the paradox of value in connection with the distinction between the two types of value supports our interpretation. This 'paradox' implies that utility cannot be used to explain exchange values because very useful things, such as

[1] E. Halévy, *The Growth of Philosophical Radicalism*, trans. M. Morris, p. 96.
[2] 'Devoir de l'homme et du citoyen,' in Halévy, *op. cit.*, p. 96.

water, are cheap, and less useful ones, such as diamonds, are expensive.[1]

The psychological meaning of this statement becomes clearer when compared with Pufendorf's treatment of this problem.

> Nay, we generally find the most necessary things are cheapest, because, by the peculiar providence of God, nature affords a greater increase of them.[2]

After stating that the price of goods often rises if goods are scarce, he remarks:

> The ambition of mortals esteems those things most which few men have in common with them; and think meanly of those which are seen in the hands of everyone. But generally we set a great value upon nothing but raises us in some measure above the rank and conditions of others; . . . this stems from the corruption and depravity of human nature; for my goods are never the worse because others possess them, nor better because others want them.[3]

It is of interest to compare this statement with Adam Smith's discussion of the paradox of value. Pufendorf (1632–94), living in a period and in a country (Germany) where the market system was hardly developed, did not feel compelled to become its apologist. Like the classical economists, he looks for an ethical basis of economic value and finds it in utility. The difference between Pufendorf and the classical economists, however, is that he does not feel the necessity to justify market prices. If prices do not reflect the utility of goods, it is because human beings are too unreasonable to grasp the objective value scale of the laws of nature and reason. His objective value scale is the same as the one of the classical economists: necessities should, on the basis of utility, have a high value, luxuries a low one; but then he explains the inverse variation of the market prices with use values as a consequence of human depravity.

The classical economists also recognize that prices and utility move in opposite directions: necessities are useful but cheap, luxuries are less useful but expensive. The statement that necessities are more, luxuries less, useful implies a belief in an objective value scale. The value system underlying this line of thought is the Puritan one; it is the idea that luxurious, conspicuous consumption is morally reprehensible; money should be spent only for the necessities of life and

[1] *Wealth of Nations*, Book I, chap. iv, p. 28.

[2] *Of the Law of Nature and Nations*, Book II, chap. iii, p. 115, quoted from H. R. Sewall, *The Theory of Value before Adam Smith*, p. 39.

[3] *Ibid.*

should otherwise be saved. Parsimony is a virtue, and the spendthrift who throws his money away on diamonds is morally condemned. The classical economists implied that prices should conform to these evaluations. Being unable to establish such a parallelism, Adam Smith and Ricardo reject utility as a determinant of value and price and accept the market prices; Pufendorf accepts utility as a basis of value and arrives at an ethical condemnation of market prices. In this way, the two types of value—value in use and value in exchange—become symbols of two world outlooks. The children of emerging capitalism, in which the striving for gain has become an end in itself, cannot explain prices by utility. Usefulness is a necessary, but insufficient, value determinant. To be useful to the individual is not the predominant aim of the market system. It took about a century befure utility conquered a dominant place in economic thinking.

The Labour Theory of Value[1]

The labour theory of value has, for centuries, presented to its students a series of puzzling problems which could not be resolved merely by taking the theory at its face value and by criticizing it from the point of view of logic and factual verification. One has to probe deeper into the interrelations between unconscious tendencies and socioeconomic patterns in order to understand why this theory was the prevalent economic doctrine for almost a century after Adam Smith. Its essence has been expressed by Adam Smith in the statement that 'labour is the real measure of the exchangeable value of all commodities.'[2] Ricardo calls labour 'the foundation of the exchangeable value of all things.'[3]

The labour theory of value provided an ethical justification of market prices and connected ethical and economic values with the central ideas of the world outlook of the period. These results were accomplished in the following way:

1. Both private property and economic value were traced back to personal, individual labour. Thus individualism, private property, and market values were intellectually unified into a closely related system.

2. With labour as the foundation of property and economic value, one of the most important elements of the new ethic—the sanctification of labour and work as moral obligations—became the pivot on

[1] Part of the following material has first appeared in *The American Journal of Economics and Sociology*, Vol. 12, No. 1, October 1952.

[2] *Wealth of Nations*, Book I, chap. v, p. 30.

[3] *Principles*, chap. i, p. 7.

which social philosophy came to rest. Ethical, social, and philosophical thought was thus unified.

3. The theory conformed to the style of thought of the period. It took over from scholasticism the idea of a substance behind the vagaries of real phenomena. Furthermore, like Newtonian physics and mechanics, the theory looks for ultimate, indissoluble, simple, homogeneous, quantifiable units which underlie all sensory phenomena. Such a substance and final unit were found in human labour.

However, the application of this theory to the reality of the market and its use in the explanation of price movements was beset with difficulties. Adam Smith was forced to relegate the validity of the theory to the early and rude state of society before appropriation of land and accumulation of stock took place. Ricardo was induced to develop his theory of rent, which eliminated the influence of rent on prices by demonstrating that there is no rent at the margin and that prices determine rent and not vice versa. With the help of an ingenious system of assumptions and definitions, he also tried to eliminate or to minimize the role of capital and profits in price determination. By this type of model-building, the labour theory of value was 'saved'. It had to be saved because it satisfied a psychocultural need of the time for intellectual unification and for the ethical justification of the basic institutions of the new social system —private property and market prices. By explaining them in a way that conformed to the scientific method of the period, a central idea and formula were found for the comprehension of the physical and social universe. The tenacity with which classical economists and their followers clung to the labour theory of value shows their unconscious fear of losing this instrument of intellectual and ethical unification. We shall later elaborate these statements with reference to the writings of Adam Smith and Ricardo.

The Lockian Antecedent

In a brilliant study, Gunnar Myrdal has answered the question why labour was chosen as the foundation of value by the classical economists.[1] Myrdal's explanation is that the classical economists and their followers wanted to find a common ground for the ideas both of private property and of economic value. John Locke had established an inseparable connection between individual freedom, labour and property:

> Though the earth and all inferior creatures be common to all men, yet every man has a 'property' in his own 'person'. This

[1] G. Myrdal, *The Political Element in the Development of Economic Theory*, trans. P. Streeten, pp. 56 ff.

> nobody has any right to but himself. The 'labour' of his body and the 'work' of his hands, we may say, are properly his. Whatsoever, then, he removes out of the state that Nature hath provided and left it in, he has mixed his labour with it, and joined it to something that is his own and thereby makes it his property. It being by him removed from the common state Nature placed it in, it hath by this labour something annexed to it that excludes the common right of other men. For this 'labour' being the unquestionable property of the labourer, no man but he can have a right to what that is once joined to, at least where there is enough, and as good left in common for others.[1]

This paragraph shows the intellectual double face of the seventeenth century and is an excellent example of an intellectual compromise. The concept of common property is a medieval one. It can be traced back to Stoic and Neo-Platonic ideas. This medieval tradition, still alive in the minds of people in Locke's time, was considered an ideal. Locke took over this dogma, but he tried to derive it in the first place from reason and only in the second place from revelation. Through reason, and through reason alone, however, he tried to justify private property.

> God, who has given the world to men in common, hath also given them reason to make use of it to the best advantage of life and convenience.[2]

How could man use this common property unless he could appropriate it to himself in some way? The logical links between the common property of land and nature and the exclusive right to private property necessary for the functioning of the market system are man's property of his own person, from which is deduced the right to private ownership of the work of his hands. Property is not simply created by taking possession. When somebody is nourished by apples gathered from trees, they become his property only

> with the first gathering. . . . That labour put a distinction between them and common. That added something to them more than Nature, the common mother of all, had done and so they became his private right. . . . The labour that was mine, removing them out of that common state they were in, hath fixed my property in them.[3]

This entire line of reasoning is a compromise between the world views of two different periods. The traditional, medieval concepts

[1] John Locke, *Of Civil Government*, Book II, chap. v, p. 130.
[2] *Ibid.*, p. 129.
[3] *Ibid.*, p. 130.

of common property of land and nature is combined with the idea that every person owns himself exclusively, a manifestation of the new individualism. The conclusion that common property has to be appropriated individually to be of any use represents an attempt to justify private property, the cornerstone of the new economic and political system. Through the idea of labour, individualism and private property are linked together. Labour is an activity of a person; he creates the product which thus becomes a part of his personality and thereby his exclusive, private property. All this, however, is combined with the idea of originally common property; with the help of reason, private property is justified and derived logically from the traditional idea of common property. The Middle Ages and modern times, the organic traditional type of society and the modern, individualistic one, are harmonized, at least in theory; and thus the individual who partakes of both can rest his intellectual conscience in peace.

The following quotation from Adam Smith reads like a paraphrase of the Lockian theory:

> The property which every man has in his own labour as it is the original foundation of all property so it is the most sacred and inviolable. The patrimony of a poor man lies in the strength and dexterity of his own hands; and to hinder him from employing his strength and dexterity in what manner he thinks proper without injury to his neighbour, is a plain violation of the most sacred property.[1]

This theory of property, based on labour, satisfied the need for intellectual synthesis. The classical economists tried to unify their view of society by founding economic value upon the same principle as private property. According to Locke, private property is based on labour as a part of the personality. According to the classical economists, economic value is also based on labour. Labour thus becomes the focus of the political and economic theory of the time; it makes things economically valuable, and it provides the moral and philosophical justification for the institution of private property.

The Religious Work Ethic

We have already pointed out, in our discussion of the economic value complex,[2] the central importance of labour and work in the value system of the market economy. It seems plausible that this

[1] *Wealth of Nations*, pp. 121, 122.
[2] See above, pp. 13 ff.

sanctification of work also motivated the choice of labour as a determinant of value.

The idea that work justifies economic value can already be found in the Middle Ages. Quoting Chrysostom and Jerome, Aquinas condemns the pursuit of gain for gain's sake and the merchant's activity in so far as it consists in buying cheap and selling dear; but he condones this procedure if the higher selling price is caused by a change in the product made by the merchant or if it is charged for an improvement: 'for if he charges a higher price for a thing that has been improved, he seems to receive a reward for his effort.'[1] In these words of a theologian, a basic principle of economic ethics is expressed: that reward should be proportional to effort. This principle is the historical and psychological root of the labour theory of value.

In Luther's thought the idea of sanctification of labour in a vocation, which was previously restricted to the clergy and to socially exalted positions, is 'now extended to all, which involves the direct incorporation of the idea of the calling into the very heart of Christian ethics.'[2] Working in one's occupation thus becomes a duty ordained not only by the secular institutions but also by religious commands.

Calvinist thought took one further step toward the sanctification of labour and toward the establishment of the work-and-success ethics. To prove his election and for the greater glory of God, the Calvinist is 'impelled . . . to a life of unceasing, penetrating, and formative *labour*.' The individual was required to produce actively within the economic sphere, to devote himself to unceasing labour, not for the sake of need-satisfaction, but for the greater glory of God. Calvinism contributed to the emergence of an attitude which considers 'the ideal of hard work, of the prosecution of work for its own sake, as a duty in itself.'[3]

The entire ethical system of Puritanism centred around the idea of labour and work.

> The rational order of the universe is the work of God, and its plan requires that the individual should labour for God's glory. . . . The only genuine faith is the faith which produces works. . . . The

[1] Thomas Aquinas, *Summa theologia secunda secundae*, Qu. LXXVIII, Art. IV; see Tawney, *Religion and the Rise of Capitalism*, pp. 38 ff., who calls the labour theory of value 'the true descendant of the doctrines of Aquinas', and Karl Marx the 'last of the schoolmen'.

[2] E. Troeltsch, *The Social Teaching of the Christian Churches*, trans. O. Wyon, II, p. 561.

[3] *Ibid.*, pp. 589, 611.

> second duty of the Christian is to labour in the affairs of practical life.[1]

The Puritan is called by God to work in some worldly employment for his own and the common good. Conscientious discharge of the duties of business becomes a religious obligation. The maxim: 'laborare est orare' was revived 'with a new and intenser significance'.[2]

> Labour is a kind of ascetic discipline . . . not merely an economic means, to be laid aside when physical needs have been satisfied. It is a spiritual end . . . an ethical duty. . . . There must be no idle leisure . . . bodily employment and mental labour should not be neglected. . . . God hath commanded you some way or other to labour for your daily bread.[3]

Max Weber has pointed out that the religious idea of a calling was consciously anti-capitalistic. The main interest of the religious reformers was 'the salvation of the soul and that alone' and never socioeconomic reform. However, Max Weber mentions the indirect effects and 'unforeseen and even unwished for results of the labours of the reformers.'[4] These indirect, unforeseen, and unwished-for results of thought may have been preformed in the unconscious minds of the authors as unconscious tendencies of the times. Neither Luther nor Calvin nor any other of the religious reformers who contributed such important strands of thought to the development of the spirit of capitalism knew consciously what they were doing; but they accepted at least certain aspects of it unconsciously, under the impact of institutional change. Their problem was to combine this acceptance with the traditional ethical and religious philosophy of their times. The result was the economic teachings of the reformed churches. Their attitude toward work survived in a secularized form, especially in the ideas of Locke. The ethical importance of work remained a main tenet in the value system of capitalism throughout the eighteenth and nineteenth centuries. It is not unreasonable to assume that it has influenced the choice of labour as the basis of economic value.

1 Tawney, *op. cit.*, p. 199; see also De Grazia, *The Political Community*, pp. 59 ff. who gives an excellent survey of the development and importance of the labour-and-work ethic in modern civilization.

2 Tawney, *op. cit.*, p. 200, quoting Bunyan, *The Pilgrim's Progress*, and Richard Steele, *The Tradesman's Calling* (1684).

3 Tawney, *op. cit.*, p. 201 (condensed).

4 Max Weber, *The Protestant Ethic and the Spirit of Capitalism*, trans. T. Parsons, p. 90; also Troeltsch, *op. cit.*, p. 578: 'for the most part, however, the [capitalist] civilization is entirely unconscious of its original connection with Calvinism.'

Chapter IV

ADAM SMITH

The Meaning of Labour in the Wealth of Nations

IT does not seem as though Adam Smith evaluated labour as a morally desirable type of activity when he identified it with 'toil and trouble'. This does not sound like an exhortation to people to consider work as an ethical duty. It seems rather that he considers labour as a disutility in the sense in which the term was used by the marginalist and neoclassical schools:

> The real price of every thing, what every thing really costs to the man who wants to acquire it, is the toil and trouble of acquiring it. What every thing is really worth to the man who has acquired it . . . is the toil and trouble which it can save to himself. . . . What is bought with money or with goods is purchased by labour, as much as what we acquire by the toil of our own body. That money or those goods indeed save us this toil. They contain the value of a certain quantity of labour which we exchange for what is supposed at the time to contain the value of an equal quantity.[1]

The same idea is expressed in the statement that:

> . . . equal quantities of labour, at all times and places, may be said to be of equal value to the labourer. In his ordinary state of health, strength and spirits, in the ordinary degree of his skill and dexterity, he must always lay down the same portion of his ease, his liberty, and his happiness.[2]

Here labour is the expression and measure of subjective sacrifices, of 'ease, liberty and happiness', a measure of subjective disutility. Undoubtedly, we find here a utilitarian element in Adam Smith's thought which survived in spite of the explicit rejection of utility as a basis of value. This utilitarian element, however, was superseded by the labour theory of value, which, at least in the Ricardian version, avoided any such element and assumed a rather mechanistic character. Even in Adam Smith's version, labour has the character of

[1] *Wealth of Nations*, p. 30. [2] *Ibid.*, p. 33.

a force and substance which create economic value. In the remark that 'money or goods contain the value of a quantity of labour which we exchange against . . . an equal quantity,' it becomes quite clear that the exchange process is viewed as an interchange of two equal substances, propelled by equal forces.

Did Adam Smith want to depreciate labour by talking about it in terms of 'toil and trouble' and in terms of a sacrifice of 'ease, liberty, and happiness'? This may be a compromise formation in which two conflicting attitudes toward labour and work are combined. If need-satisfaction and subjective utility were the ends of economic activity, then labour and work are means toward these ends. If labour and work are considered as ends, need-satisfaction and subjective utility become mere by-products of work. Adam Smith shows ambivalence in this matter. By rejecting utility and choosing labour as a basis of value, he implicitly accepts the work ethic. By defining labour in terms of toil and trouble and of sacrifice of happiness, he shows a utilitarian attitude. This reflects a basic conflict of the period, the conflict between the attitude of the traditional subsistence economy, aiming merely at need-satisfaction, and the new acquisitive work ethic, with labour and accumulation of wealth as ultimate ends. The duality of definitions and assumptions in the theory of value thus mirrors the duality of modes of life.

Productive and Unproductive Labour

That Adam Smith is more openly in favour of the work ethic is clearly shown by the moral evaluation of labour expressed in his distinction between productive and unproductive labour in Book II, chapter iii. Labour is productive if it

> . . . adds to the value of the subject upon which it is bestowed, . . . [if] it realizes itself in some particular subject or vendible commodity, which lasts for some time at least after that labour stocked and stored up to be employed. . . . That subject . . . can afterwards . . . put into motion a quantity of labour, equal to that which had originally produced it.[1]

The labour of the manufacturer is productive; the work of all those who merely render services, from the menial servants to navy and army personnel, churchmen, lawyers, physicians, men of letters, players, buffoons, musicians, etc., is unproductive because it 'does not fix or realize itself in any permanent subject, or vendible commodity.'

[1] *Ibid.*, Book II, chap. iii, p. 314.

Adam Smith interrelates productive labour with the accumulation of capital. This is already indicated in his definition: only labour which produces something lasting is productive; the element of durability and of future use for further employment of labour is stressed. Productive labour produces capital and durables. When it is stated that 'that part of the annual produce which replaces a capital never is immediately employed to maintain any but productive hands',[1] another relation between capital and productive labour is established.

The moral nature of the distinction becomes obvious in the following discussion of economic virtues, such as industry and parsimony, and vices, such as idleness and prodigality. The virtues are directly connected with productive labour and the vices with unproductive. The link in this chain is formed by capital accumulation. The more the total product is used for the formation of capital, the more productive labour will be employed; capital formation, however, is a direct consequence of industry and parsimony. The economic virtues of saving and industry, the Puritan work ethic, and its worldly asceticism promote the employment of productive labour. The greater the industry, the greater the funds destined for the maintenance of industry.

This discussion culminates in a moral apotheosis of industry and parsimony and in a condemnation of idleness and prodigality:

> Our ancestors were idle for want of sufficient encouragement to industry. It is better, says the proverb, to play for nothing than to work for nothing. In mercantile and manufacturing towns . . . they are in general industrious, sober and thriving. . . . In those towns which are principally supported by the . . . residence of a court . . . they are in general, idle, dissolute and poor.[2]

The distinction between economic virtues and vices is here tied in with class distinctions. The virtues are those of the mercantile groups in industrial towns; the vices belong to the aristocracy and the courts. English and Dutch towns are economically virtuous, and therefore prosperous; French towns, supported by courts, cause idleness and thereby poverty. It has been pointed out that the this-worldly asceticism of the Roundheads and Puritans was in part a reaction formation against the conspicuous and hedonistic consumption habits of the aristocracy, against which the middle-class revolutions were directed.[3] This is clearly reflected in the foregoing

[1] *Wealth of Nations*, p. 316. [2] *Ibid.*, p. 319.

[3] Svend Ranulf, *Moral Indignation and Middle Class Psychology*, esp. chaps. iii and iv.

passage; industry, thrift, and capital accumulation are virtues and goals of the mercantile classes, and idleness, profligacy, and unproductive spending are attributed to the royal courts and their aristocratic retinues.

The rest of chapter iii of Book II continues with the praise of parsimony and the condemnation of prodigality. The latter is called 'misconduct', clearly a moral judgment.[1] Actually, parsimony is even better than industry, because 'it is the immediate cause of the increase in capital.' The class distinction and the higher evaluation of the 'productive' classes becomes quite clear in the following statement:

> What is annually saved is as regularly consumed as what is annually spent . . . but . . . by a different set of people. That portion of his revenue which a rich man annually spends, is . . . consumed by idle guests and menial servants, who leave nothing behind them in return for their consumption. That portion which he annually saves, as for the sake of the profit it is immediately employed as capital, is consumed . . . by a different set of people, by labourers, manufacturers and artificers, who reproduce with a profit the value of their annual consumption.[2]

Parsimony and saving are good because they lead to capital formation; capital formation is good because it provides an occasion for the practice of these virtues. The use of savings in employing productive labour is a desirable activity, because it does not destroy the results of accumulation but preserves and increases them through the creation of profit. All these elements are part and parcel of the syndrome which we called the 'economic value complex'.

Professor Hla Myint has pointed out that the classical economists had a concept of economic welfare different from the one of the marginalists and the neoclassical schools. They were not so much concerned with the optimum allocation of resources as with 'the struggle of man against nature' in producing material wealth, with the technical problems of physical productivity and capital accumulation. He also discusses in this connection Adam Smith's distinction between productive and unproductive labour and defines the former as 'that labour which produces material necessities or wage goods which enable society to maintain a greater quantity of labour for future production.'[3] Welfare concepts are based on ethical ideals.

1 *Wealth of Nations*, p. 321.
2 *Ibid.*, p. 321.
3 Hla Myint, *Theories of Welfare Economics*, p. 5 and esp. chaps. i and v.

Capital accumulation, saving, parsimony, industry, and profit-making are treated as ethical duties in the *Wealth of Nations*. Within the framework of the Protestant and Puritan ethic, these activities were considered virtues. After they had become, in a secular form, a part of the internalized value complex of the new economic civilization they were explained and justified by utilitarian arguments. Instead of calling them virtues and duties toward God, they were considered necessary for reasons of economic welfare. Their exercise is required for capital accumulation and for the increase of the annual produce. However, the maintenance and the increase in capital and in the annual produce are in themselves normative, ethical goals; and Adam Smith interconnects them with the economic virtues of the Puritan ethics.

He also tries to show that the exercise of these virtues and the attainment of these goals is dictated by self-interest. It propels people to act, as the economic system wants them to act:

> By what a frugal man annually saves . . . he establishes . . . a perpetual fund for the maintenance of an equal number (of productive hands) in all times to come. The perpetual allotment and destination of this fund indeed is . . . guarded . . . by a very powerful principle, the plain and evident interest of every individual.

The prodigal wastes this fund and

> pays the wages of idleness with those funds which the frugality of his forefathers had . . . consecrated to the maintenance of industry. He . . . tends not only to beggar himself, but to impoverish his country . . . every prodigal appears to be a public enemy, every frugal man a public benefactor.[1]

If there is any doubt about the ethical character of these distinctions, they are removed by the open moralizing of the following statements:

> With regard to profusion the principle which prompts to expense, is the passion for present enjoyment; which . . . is in general only momentary and occasional. But the principle which prompts to save, is the desire of bettering our condition, a desire which, though generally calm and dispassionate, comes with us from the womb, and never leaves us till we go to the grave. . . . An augmentation of fortune is the means by which the greater part of men propose and wish to better their condition . . . and the most likely

[1] *Wealth of Nations*, pp. 322, 324.

> way of augmenting their fortune is to save and accumulate . . . the principle of frugality seems not only to predominate, but to predominate very greatly.[1]

All the elements of the economic value complex are combined here; and they are, true to the method of the new science of political economy, represented as facts. Ideals are interpreted as natural human traits and modes of conduct as dictated by natural self-interest. This is the way in which the majority of people supposedly act and behave. Thus any doubts about the moral validity of these ideals are silenced: if one acts according to the economic value complex and its ideals, one acts not only naturally but also in conformity with the majority of one's contemporaries; this should suffice to demonstrate the adequacy of such conduct.

We have devoted so much space to a discussion of Adam Smith's concept of productive labour in order to show the plausibility of our theory: namely, that the choice of labour as the main foundation and determinant of economic value may have something to do with the glorification of labour as a virtuous kind of activity. Book II, chapter iii, makes clear the ethical attitude of Adam Smith toward labour expended in production: he approves of it morally as much as of parsimony, saving, industry, and capital accumulation. It is this type of labour which he has in mind when he talks about labour 'being the first price, the original purchase money that was paid for all things.' Productive labour enters into the commodity, restores the value of the wages which are paid to the labourers, and adds profit to the total value of the commodity.[2] Definitely, it is productive labour which is the basis of value and not the ephemeral, evaporating, non-durable, unproductive kind of labour which merely renders non-enduring services. Adam Smith's entire theory of value refers to goods and not to services. In Book I, chapter v, where he develops this theory, he discusses continuously the value of goods which a person possesses and might exchange for other goods, and he identifies, to some extent, labour bestowed on the production of goods and labour commanded in exchange.[3]

Labour is embodied in goods which last after they have been produced and can, therefore, be exchanged against other goods, enabling the owner to command the labour of other people. Such goods, however, are only the result of productive labour 'which realizes itself in some particular subject or vendible commodity.'

[1] *Wealth of Nations*, pp. 324–25.
[2] *Ibid.*, p. 314.
[3] See below, pp. 60 ff.

His labour theory of value is obviously based on the concept of productive labour; it is this type of labour which determines the exchangeable value of goods. This establishes a link between the the ethical idea of productive labour and the labour theory of value. By assuming that economic value is determined by the amount of productive labour expended in the production of a commodity, the virtues and ideals connected with the idea of productive labour, such as industry, thrift, parsimony, and systematic striving for the accumulation and maintenance of capital, are brought into the theory of value. Thus economic values receive an ethical sanction. Although the ethical element is merely implied in the chapters of the first book of the *Wealth of Nations* which deal directly with value theory, it becomes quite explicit if one realizes their interrelation with Adam Smith's moral preference for productive and his rejection of unproductive labour.

Absolute Value versus Market Prices

The Historical Background

The choice of labour as the determinant of value was also influenced by the endeavour to find an absolute basis for economic values and for the fluctuation of market prices. Medieval thought on the subject is full of concepts of 'true value' and 'just price': immutable quantities conforming to religious and ethical standards. Albertus Magnus identifies true value with just price, which includes the expenses necessary to call forth the required supply.[1] Thomas Aquinas distinguishes between the value or worth belonging to the thing itself and the price in money given for it in exchange: the latter is an accidental thing, differing from the true value.[2] He associates true value with the sacrifice required to produce a thing; it is the labour expended on it rather than the satisfaction derived from it which determines the true and absolute value. The Italian Schoolmen of the sixteenth century, struggling to combine Catholic ethics with the needs of capitalist merchants, included in the just price of a good the expenses necessary to procure it. In the thought of Grotius, dominated by the ideas of nature and reason, the 'common price' is the one determined by labour and the expenses of the sellers.[3]

Pufendorf derived from the law of nature the idea that value is

[1] H. R. Sewall, *The Theory of Value before Adam Smith*, p. 13, esp. n. 1.

[2] *Ibid.*; the Thomistic distinction corresponds to the Aristotelian and scholastic classification of qualities as *essentialia* and *accidentalia*.

[3] Grotius. *De Iure Belli et Pacis*, ii. 12. 314, 'On Contracts' (1623).

the result of natural substance and based on moral considerations. Value exists, irrespective of exchange.[1] He is much concerned with developing a natural and just standard of price and value. Locke clearly distinguished between intrinsic or natural value—which stems from utility, the fitness to supply necessities, and conveniences —and marketable value, which is the relation of things in exchange.[2]

Sir William Petty contrasts intrinsic or natural value with extrinsic or accidental value; the latter is value in exchange. Prices are influenced by intrinsic causes, such as the inner qualities and virtues of the thing—weight, extent, colour (e.g., the clearness of diamonds)—and by extrinsic causes, such as fluctuations of supply and demand.[3] His famous statement about the 'original factors' is well known: 'Labour is the father or active principle of wealth as Lands are the mother.'[4] He was concerned with establishing the natural value of commodities by the quantity of land and labour which entered into their production and reduced both to one common denominator by expressing the value of everything in either alone.[5]

Cantillon joined those who distinguish between the intrinsic value of a thing, which he defines as the measure of the quantity of land and labour which enters into its production, on the one hand, and exchange value on markets, which does not always conform to the intrinsic value.

> The earth is the material, labour is the form of all food and merchandise; and . . . one might be able to find a relation between the value of labour and that of the products of the earth.[6]

The Institutional Background

Is there a psychocultural meaning to this distinction between an absolute, deeper, more stable, real, and substantial kind of economic value and the ephemeral, fluctuating market prices and exchange values? A glance at the actual economic situation of the period may

1 *Of The Law of Nature and Nations*, Book II, chap. iii, p. 115; in Sewall, *op. cit.* pp. 38 ff.

2 John Locke, 'Some Considerations of the Lowering of Interest and Raising the Value of Money' (1691), *Works*, II, pp. 4 ff.

3 *The Economic Writings of Sir William Petty*, 'Political Arithmetic', I, 260; 'Taxes and Contributions', I, 6, chap. x; in Sewall, *op. cit.*, pp. 70 ff.

4 'Taxes and Contributions,' in *The Economic Writings of Sir William Petty*, I, 68, chap. x.

5 'Taxes and Contributions,' in *Economic Writings of Sir William Petty*, I, 43, chap. iv; see Sewall, *op. cit.*, p. 72.

6 *Essai sur le commerce*, chap. x; see Sewall, *op. cit.*, pp. 80, 83.

provide the answer. One can easily imagine that the new phenomenon of the market and its prices caused puzzling and anxiety-generating feelings. Wherever it developed, the market economy had destroyed the traditional way of life. People who, in the previous subsistence economy, could live in relative security, although on a low level of need-satisfaction and comfort, were now at the mercy of price fluctuations. The history of the market system is a history of social upheavals, destruction of the old ways of life, shifts of population, and pauperization, even where such pauperization was a transition to higher standards for the children and grandchildren of those who were smashed by the maelstrom of competition.[1]

In view of these upsetting effects, it does not seem surprising that people sought for an explanation which had to perform two psychocultural functions: to find a stable centre for the market fluctuations and to provide an ethical justification for prices. Thus the continuous search for an absolute, intrinsic value concept in preclassical economic philosophy shows the attempt of individuals to believe that market values have a stable foundation and are ethically justified. The Scholastics made a sharp distinction between absolute, intrinsic, true, and just value, on the one hand, and the actual market price and exchange values, on the other. Thomas Aquinas sees no necessary connection between the two; he, the son of a precapitalist culture, did not need to justify market prices. With capitalism, the psychocultural necessity to interconnect absolute value and market and exchange value became urgent. People felt, probably unconsciously, that they could not live without a belief in a substance behind market prices and without a belief in their justice. A *rapprochement* between the two value concepts took place. The cost which the merchant wanted to charge to his customers entered more and more into just price. Even the natural-law doctrine, which distinguished between natural and exchange value, the first absolute and stable, the latter ephemeral, included the cost element in the natural price. In this development the growing acceptance of the market system and its prices manifested itself.

Adam Smith on Absolute Value and Market Prices

How does the thought of the classical economists fit into this picture? They oscillated between the desire to arrive at an absolute foundation and measure of value, on the one hand, and their realization of the relativity of prices, on the other. They saw that prices are nothing but relative exchange relations between goods; nevertheless, they tried to preserve the concept of absolute value.

[1] K. Polanyi, *The Great Transformation*, esp. pp. 68, 71, 73.

Adam Smith distinguishes explicitly between a real price in labour and a nominal price in money.[1]

Thus the real price is the price measured by the amount of labour which it costs to acquire a good and by the amount of labour (or produce of labour, which are supposedly identical) for which it can be exchanged. This labour value is considered to be an absolute, identifiable, precise magnitude. It is a stable quantity because

> equal quantities of labour, at all times and places, may be said to be of equal value to the labourer. . . . He must always lay down the same portion of his ease, his liberty and his happiness. The price which he pays must always be the same, whatever may be the quantity of goods which he receives in return . . . but it is their value which varies, not that of the labour which purchases them. . . . Labour alone, therefore, never varying in its own value, is alone the ultimate and real standard by which the value of all commodities can at all times and places be estimated and compared. It is their real price; money is their nominal price only.[2]

Labour thus becomes the foundation on which value ultimately rests. It does not change with space or time or individuals. It is clearly and unequivocally an absolute concept of value.

This was discussed in chapter v of the first book of the *Wealth of Nations*. In chapter viii, however, dealing with the wages of labour, a difficulty arises; the spectre of relative prices begins to haunt Adam Smith. He talks about the 'original state of things which precedes both the appropriation of land and the accumulation of stock', in which 'the produce of labour constitutes the natural recompense or wages of labour', and where 'the whole produce of labour belongs to the labourer' (p. 64). He then discusses the following case (translated here into modern terms): the productivity of labour in industries A and B increases tenfold, whereas the productivity in a particular industry X had increased only twofold. Ten times the original product A and B would purchase only twice the original product X. The question arises: Did product X rise or fall in value? The answer will be different according to the yardstick used: if an absolute yardstick is used, namely, labour expended in production, commodity X has become halved in value. If, however, we look at its relative exchange value in relation to commodities A and B, 'it would appear to be five times dearer than before.' Adam Smith decides for the first solution as the *real* one:

> In *reality*, however, it would be twice as cheap. Though it required five times the quantity of the other goods to purchase it,

1 *Wealth of Nations*, Book I, chap. v, pp. 31, 32. 2 *Ibid.*, p. 33.

it would require only half the quantity of labour either to purchase or to produce it. The acquisition, therefore, would be twice as easy as before.[1]

The entire problem of absolute value versus relative prices is clearly reflected in these passages. Absolute values and relative prices (exchange values) do not coincide. What appears to be an increase in relative prices constitutes a fall in the value measured by the absolute standards of labour-time. Why does Adam Smith consider the increase in exchange value as the 'apparition' and the fall in absolute value as the 'reality'? The quest for an absolute standard of value had to be successful, because it satisfied the basic psycho-cultural need for intellectual safety and unity. Exclusive concentration on relative prices would expose the price structure and its changes as an impenetrable and unpredictable maze of haphazard processes. This unbearable conclusion had to be avoided. A quasi-metaphysical 'reality' had to be found behind the ephemeral phenomena of the market; for philosophical, political, and ethical reasons, it was found in labour.

The Multiplicity of Value Theories

In the *Wealth of Nations* Adam Smith offers not one but several theories of value and price. In addition to (*a*) the labour theory of value, he also presents (*b*) a theory of natural price and (*c*) a demand-and-supply theory of actual market prices. In Book I, chapter v, he expounds the labour theory of value as universally applicable and valid. In chapter vi, however, he relegates the validity of this theory to the 'early and rude state of society which precedes both the accumulation of stock and the appropriation of land'[2] and establishes the concept of natural price, which 'resolves itself into . . . three parts of rent, labour and profit.'[3]

The concept of natural price coexists with the concept of labour value in the systems of both Smith and Ricardo. Adam Smith tries to show that the natural price is 'the centre of repose and continuance', the 'central price to which the actual market prices of all commodities are continually gravitating' (p. 58). 'The natural price is the real worth of a commodity measured in terms of what it costs to bring it to the market' (p. 55).

In chapter vii, however, he also presents his theory of market prices. They 'may either be above, or below, or exactly the same with their natural prices.' They are determined by 'effectual' demand, supply, and competition between buyers and sellers. The

1 *Wealth of Nations*, p. 65. 2 *Ibid.*, p. 47. 3 *Ibid.*, p. 50.

deviation of the actual market prices from the natural ones are called 'accidents', although it is admitted that

> particular accidents, sometimes natural causes, and sometimes particular regulations of police, may, in many commodities, keep the market price, for a long time together, a good deal above the natural price.[1]

The natural price is the price established under free competition; want of knowledge, secrets of manufacturers, scarcity of particular soils, monopolies, exclusive privileges, or corporations, etc., keep the actual market price above its natural rate. It can seldom continue long below its natural price. 'Perfect liberty' of competition will push it up to its natural level. All this makes it obvious that the actual market prices are ephemeral, fluctuating phenomena, whereas the economic values, determined by labour and the natural elements of rent, wages, and profits, are 'the centres of repose and continuance', the fixed poles in the vagaries of market phenomena.

This strange structure of concepts requires a deeper probing. Why is Adam Smith's theory of value beset with dichotomies such as real versus nominal price, labour value versus natural price, natural price versus market price? What is the psychocultural meaning of this multiplicity of value theories?

Natural Price versus Labour Value

The multiplicity of value and price theories in the *Wealth of Nations* may indicate an unconscious doubt of the validity of any one of the absolute-value theories, especially of the validity of the labour theory of value. It is as if Adam Smith wants to say:

> If one of my absolute-value theories does not hold in the light of scientific reasoning and factual observation, there is another one which is perhaps more likely to be valid; this other theory, too, leads to an absolute and stable value concept.

Thus the theory of natural price may be considered a diluted substitute for the labour theory of value, both leading to absolute-value concepts.

Adam Smith did not present these theories without a logical framework which made them mutually compatible. As observed before, he relegates, in Book I, chapter vi, the labour theory of value to the early and rude state of society before appropriation and accumulation had taken place. After that stage the natural price,

[1] *Ibid.*, Book I, chap. vii, p. 59.

composed of wages, rent, and profits, determines value. However, the statement that 'labour is the real measure of the exchangeable value of all commodities' in Book I, chapter v, of the *Wealth of Nations* is of such certainty that the later banishment of that theory to a nebulous historical past comes as a surprise.

The reference to that 'early and rude state', however, is somewhat more than an exile for the labour theory of value. The philosophy which Adam Smith absorbed from his Scottish predecessors and contemporaries cherished what has been called a 'rationalistic primitivism'.[1] The belief in the universality of reason and nature led to the conclusion that it must have been known to the earliest, least sophisticated men; more so, these early ancestors of ours, unspoiled by civilization, must have had a better insight into nature than did the men of later periods.[2]

This, however, indicates that Adam Smith did not want to demote the labour theory of value by projecting it into the past; on the contrary, it shows that he considered the determination of economic values by labour as one of the universally valid primordial laws of nature. However, in order to maintain at least the semblance of a logical structure, he had to restrict it to a past historical period and apply the natural-price theory to the present economy; otherwise, the contradiction between the labour theory and the theory of natural price would be too blatant.

The distinction between labour value and natural price, between early and advanced society, reflects the difference between a precapitalist type of society and the capitalist profit-and-wage system. The two stages are characterized, respectively, by the absence and the presence of appropriation of land and of accumulation of stock. This dichotomy corresponds to the theological conception of a 'prelapsarian' state, a paradisiac period before the 'fall' and a 'postlapsarian' state of 'original sin' afterward. In the distinction between the early and rude state and the advanced society, these theological concepts are used in a secularized form and applied to economic conditions. The 'fall' is represented by the emerging of private ownership of capital and land. 'Prelapsarian' means, then, the absence of private ownership of capital and land; 'postlapsarian', its presence.

Private ownership of land and stock changes the character of the economic system and thereby the basis of value. Adam Smith

[1] G. Bryson, *Man and Society: The Scottish Inquiry of the Eighteenth Century*, p. 14.

[2] *Ibid.* To project wish dreams and ideals which conflict with reality and/or with other ideals into the future (empire of heaven, classless society) or into the distant past (paradise, state of nature, golden age) is a common intellectual procedure.

assumed that there existed at first an ideal primitive state without private ownership of land and stock, in which labour values reigned supreme. The original sin of the introduction of private property prevents these values from materializing in the more advanced state. There the labourer has to share with landlord and master, and rent and profit have to be added to wages, to arrive at the natural price. Adam Smith's sympathies seem to lie with the early and primitive state, in which 'the whole produce of labour belongs to the labourer.'[1]

Could one not read a condemnation of profits in the statement that

> the profits of stock . . . bear no proportion to the quantity, the hardship, or the ingenuity of this supposed labour of inspection and direction. They are regulated altogether by the value of the stock employed . . . and the owner of this capital though he is thus discharged of almost all labour, still expects that his profits should bear a regular proportion to his capital.[2]

Cannot this word 'still' be interpreted as an expression of ethical indignation, after the whole previous chapter (v of Book I) was devoted to a proof that labour and labour alone is the basis of value and reward?

Such moral indignation is undeniable and quite obvious in Smith's outcry against the landlords who, 'as soon as the land of any country has all become private property . . . like all other men, love to reap where they never sowed.'[3] Does not this statement reflect clearly the idyllic picture of Lockian individualism, where the individual works with his body and hands to reap what he sowed and nothing more? If anything, this famous passage makes clear the interconnections between the Puritan work ethic, Locke's philosophy of individual liberty and property, and Adam Smith's theory of economic value. It shows the moral indignation against any type of property and reward which is not the result of labour and individual effort. In the light of this sentence, our interpretation of Adam Smith's veiled condemnation of profit becomes rather plausible.

The need for intellectual security, however, required that these conflicts should be eliminated in thought as much as possible. The natural price, at first somewhat surreptitiously condemned from a moral point of view, must somehow be combined with the labour

[1] *Wealth of Nations*, Book I, chap. viii, p. 47.
[2] *Ibid.*, pp. 48, 49.
[3] *Ibid.*, Book I, chap. vi, p. 49.

theory of value. Therefore, the statement at the end of this discussion:

> The real value of all the different component parts of price . . . is measured by the quantity of labour which they can, each of them, purchase or command. Labour measures the value not only of that part of price which resolves itself into labour, but of that which resolves itself into rent, and of that which resolves itself into profit.[1]

It is revealing that in the first edition this sentence read merely: 'the real value of all the different component parts of price is in this manner measured.' At first, no attempt was made to eliminate the conflict between the labour theory and the natural-price theory of value. The primitive state was dominated by labour values; in the advanced state, with appropriation and accumulation, labour became only one of the three determinants of value; enterpriser and landlord receive payments on different grounds. In the second edition, Smith obviously felt the necessity of bridging this gap somehow by tracing rent and profit back to labour.

In Adam Smith's theory of actual market prices, the market system is finally seen as it is. Prices fluctuate according to supply and demand; that is perhaps the only, definitely the most realistic, insight which classical value theory has provided. Finally, reality comes into its rights; the quasi-metaphysical and ethical interpretations are dropped. That this reality was experienced as unsatisfactory can be seen from the fact that Smith gives the supply-and-demand theory a rather low rating. It is built into the theory of natural price toward which market prices are supposed to gravitate. The individual living under the market system has difficulties in facing economic reality. He has to trace the fluctuating prices back to a fictitious, absolute, stable concept.

Labour values, natural prices, cost-of-production prices, are 'centres of repose and continuance', goals of market developments. We find here, without the use of the term, the concept of the equilibrium price. The desire for a stable and absolute substance behind the fluctuating prices has led to a combination of an absolute-value concept with the idea of a stable equilibrium. The equilibrium price, that is, the natural price, is implicitly presented as something desirable and ethically positive. It is what a thing is really worth, the amount which gives due reward to all productive factors in the form of rent, wages, and profits. It covers all the cost of production, and it can be ultimately traced back to labour. Now

[1] *Wealth of Nations*, p. 50.

it can be assumed that market prices are not forever fluctuating in a haphazard fashion: they gravitate toward an ascertainable centre (cost of production), driven by a force (competition) and this force determines (long-run) prices in an ethically legitimate way (prices and incomes correspond to labour effort). Thus the intellectual and ethical unity of the system is preserved and cultural anxiety warded off.

To summarize: Adam Smith was probably unconsciously torn by a conflict between his ethical beliefs and his desire to accept the system of private property and the exchange economy. Ethically, he believed that economic values and rewards should be proportionate to individual effort, labour, work; this is the cultural heritage he took over from Puritanism and Lockian philosophy. On the other hand, it must have been obvious to him that, in reality, prices and incomes often did not conform to this ethical precept. However, he did not want to reject and condemn this system openly. The result is an intellectual compromise which, although within a logical, meaningful framework, is full of more or less hidden contradictions. On the one hand, Smith tries to unify all his value theories under the aspect of the labour theory: labour is the basis of all exchange value; the components of natural price can be derived from labour; and the actual market prices gravitate toward the natural price. Thus the ethical and metaphysical unity of economic value based on labour seems to be salvaged. On the other hand, there are three incompatible price and value theories: a labour theory (for the early and rude state), a theory of natural prices (for a society with appropriation of land and accumulation of stock), and a supply-and-demand theory of actual market prices. The three price and value theories are conflicting: the first is based on labour, the second shows that rent and profits have little relation to labour, the third abandons all pretence of arriving at a stable, absolute-value concept.

We have here a clear manifestation of intellectual ambivalence caused by conflicting psychocultural tendencies. Already Adam Smith, three-quarters of a century before Karl Marx, oscillates unconsciously between a conservative and a revolutionary attitude toward the system of market prices and private property. The revolutionary elements of the labour theory of value, later elaborated by Marx, are present in embryonic form in the *Wealth of Nations*, as our analysis shows. Nevertheless, the explicit content of the book is predominantly apologetic for the system of free enterprise. The conflict may have been largely unconscious; what in the hands of Marx became an intentional, political weapon was unconsciously predicated in the thought of Adam Smith. He (like Ricardo) repressed the revolutionary part of the system and gave overt, conscious expression mostly to the conservative aspect. Psychocultural analysis, however, is able to uncover the hidden revolutionary aspects which reveal themselves between the lines.

Adam Smith's Ambivalence toward the Free-Market System

In spite of his advocacy of economic liberty and of his approval of the pursuit of self-interest, Adam Smith criticized actions which were obviously dictated by just that self-interest. We noted earlier his veiled criticism of profit because it has no relation to effort and his open condemnation of the landlords because they love to reap where they never sowed.[1] His moral indignation about the masters who

> are always and everywhere in a sort of tacit, but constant and uniform combination, not to raise the wages of labour above their actual rate . . . and to sink it even below this rate,[2]

is not only a rejection of monopolistic practices but also an implied criticism of the pursuit of self-interest which motivates entrepreneurs to form such combinations. In spite of his overtly optimistic approach to a system of economic liberty, he decries the bad effects of high profits and condemns the entrepreneurs:

> Our merchants and master-manufacturers complain much of the bad effects of high wages in raising the price and thereby, lessening the sale of their goods. . . . They say nothing concerning the bad effects of high profits. They are silent with regard to the pernicious effects of their own gains. They complain only of those of other people.[3]

This is inconsistent with the idea of laissez faire and of the natural harmony of interests; Adam Smith admits here that there are pernicious effects of the pursuit of self-interest. He criticizes implicitly those who act selfishly and with disregard of the interests of others. Here, as elsewhere, he also attacks the very group for which his philosophy became the economic bible and whose value attitudes he propounded in his ideal of the prudent man.

The most obvious exception to the natural harmony of interests is found in the passages dealing with distribution and class structure.[4] The interests of the 'three great original and constituent orders of every civilized society' are by no means in natural harmony with one another. The interests of the landlords and of the labourers are 'strictly and inseparably connected with the general interest of the

[1] *Wealth of Nations*, pp. 48–49; see above, p. 40.
[2] *Ibid.*, pp. 66–67 (abridged). [3] *Ibid.*, p. 98. [4] *Ibid.*, pp. 248–50.

society.' But again Adam Smith condemns the entrepreneurs economically and morally:

> The interest of this third order [those who live by profit] has not the same connexion with the general interest of the society as that of the other two. Merchants and master manufacturers . . . exercise their thoughts commonly rather about the interest of their own particular branch of business than about that of society. . . . The interest of the dealers . . . in any particular branch of trade or manufactures is always in some respect different from and even opposite to that of the public. . . . The proposal of any new law or regulation of commerce which comes from this order . . . comes from an order of men . . . who have generally an interest to deceive and even to oppress the public, and who accordingly have, upon many occasions, both deceived and oppressed it.[1]

Such outcries are more than merely a criticism of monopolistic practices, as some later interpreters were inclined to believe. The difficulty in combining the idea of the ultimately beneficial results of egotistic conduct with the obvious fact that the striving for selfish gains is often incompatible with whatever people consider to be the common good is only a special case of the basic problem of a free society. In economics this problem was and is discussed as the question whether economic freedom and free competition lead inevitably to monopoly. This, however, points to the broader problem of individual interest versus the common good. If one views society and the economy exclusively in terms of external institutions, it is difficult to deny that complete freedom and the pursuit of self-interest must lead to exploitation by privilege-seeking minorities. After external restrictions are removed, freedom requires that inner ties and restrictions replace them, in order to avoid anarchy and predominance of special privilege. Adam Smith recognized this implicitly when he related his ideas of the invisible hand and of the benign director and administrator of the universe to the impartial spectator in our breast.[2] Without the inner gyroscope[3] which propels

[1] *Ibid.*, p. 250 (condensed).

[2] 'No man . . . ever trod steadily and uniformly in the paths of prudence . . . whose conduct was not principally directed by a regard to the sentiments of the supposed *impartial spectator*, of the *great inmate of the breast*, the *great judge and arbiter of conduct*. If in the course of the day, we have swerved in any respect, from the rules which he prescribes to us; if we have either exceeded or relaxed in our frugality; if we have either exceeded or relaxed in our industry . . . it is this inmate who in the evening, calls us to an account for all those omissions and violations . . .' (Adam Smith, *The Theory of Moral Sentiments*, p. 385).

[3] D. Riesman, *The Lonely Crowd*, p. 16.

every individual toward ethical behaviour, a free society would break up in anarchy and result in exploitation. Absolute power would then be required to establish order and justice. The absence of external control has to be balanced by inner control. All this was not clear to Adam Smith, nor has it been clear to his followers among economists up to the present day.

However, the seeds of these thoughts were contained in his writings. Economic liberalism had been thinking much too much in terms of external economic institutions. It could see only the problem of freedom from government restrictions. To arrive at the concept of an economic order, Adam Smith had to prove that the individual pursuit of self-interest really leads to the common good; his own statements, however, show that this was not the case.

The idea of the harmony of interests and of the invisible hand indicates clearly that economists felt the necessity for providing an ethical justification for the new value complex. As a psychocultural heritage of the anti-chrematistic ethic, the pursuit of economic self-interest was considered morally reprehensible. Thus it had to be shown that it does lead to the general welfare; that, although it was felt to be immoral for the individual, it is 'moral' from the viewpoint of the whole. The conflict between the aims of the individual and those of society has been, both implicitly and explicitly, a central theme of economic thought since Adam Smith. The idea of the harmony of interests, maximization of total utility, social welfare, total satisfaction, the concept of equilibrium, etc., have been used to eliminate it intellectually. Such intellectual constructs perform the function of doing away with the conflict between two value systems, which would otherwise make life unbearable. They may be attempts, largely unconscious, to justify economic egotism by asserting that it is at least socially beneficial. Why was it felt that such a justification was necessary? Because the socially co-operative ethic which condemned the pursuit of mere self-interest as ethically reprehensible was, to some extent, still alive in the eighteenth and nineteenth centuries.

The idea of the harmony of economic interests can be interpreted as the result of an inner conflict between two types of ethical directives, both of which have become an unconscious, internalized part of the character structure of middle-class Western individuals. It shows the remnants of the non-capitalist ethic in so far as it attempts an ethical justification of the pursuit of economic self-interest. Within the ethical framework of the economic value complex, the pursuit of gain does not need any social justification; it is a method of proving one's worthiness and success and an end in itself from the viewpoint of a purely individualistic value system. If economics were merely a 'science', and if, as many economists maintain, the striving for economic self-interest were a natural human trait, any ethical justification would be superfluous. The emphasis on its beneficial social effect is a remnant of the pre-capitalist ethic. However, the result of this ratiocination is the excellent conscience of the businessman, who pursues his economic self-interest without any inhibitions; he can now be sure that he, *nolens volens*, promotes the common good. If one considers adaptation to environmental conditions as the end of organic life and thought as one of the instruments of adaptation, one can interpret this whole process as a link in the chain of the adaptive processes of our culture. The businessman has to act as the socioeconomic institutions require him to act. Given the way the human mind works, a certain unity of normative directives is necessary; otherwise the individual is torn apart by conscious and unconscious conflicts and is exposed to anomic lack of direction. The intellectual syndrome of the harmony of interest permits modern man to escape this predicament and to act as he has to act, with a good and undivided conscience.

All this led to an overt dichotomy within the system of economic liberalism and optimism of the *Wealth of Nations*. It betrays Adam Smith's inner conflict and his inner doubt about the validity of his theory and about the ethical justice and beneficiality of the system he advocates. The optimistic and affirmative evaluation is counterbalanced by criticism. The latter is directed not only against the mercantilistic economy but also, in a covert form, against the system of economic liberty which he advocated. At least, the seeds of criticism and an inkling of the inner inconsistencies and conflicts of this system are present in his thought. Thus it is not too far fetched to assume that this conflict is implicitly present in his theory of value, as we have shown above. His criticism of the conduct of the master-manufacturers and merchants is also reflected in the multiplicity of his value theories and in his partial rejection of types of incomes and values which are not based on labour, work, and effort.

Part III

The Ricardian Theory of Value

Chapter V

THE BACKGROUND OF RICARDO'S THEORY OF VALUE

RICARDO was the great logician among the classical economists. Nobody tried harder than he to create a consistent theory of economic value. And yet his entire system of thought is beset with inner conflicts and dichotomies. The very intensity of his efforts to unify the theory of value may be a symptom of inner doubt in the justice and beneficiality of the economic system of which he became the foremost interpreter of his time.

In his theory of value (this is the only part of his system with which we are concerned here) Ricardo struggled with the same problems as did Adam Smith.[1]

Ricardo tried to arrive at an absolute concept of economic value and to prove that absolute and, to a large extent, relative value is determined by the quantity of labour bestowed (embodied, expended, used) on the production of a commodity (briefly called 'labour bestowed' in the following). His last paper can be regarded as a summary of his ideas on value. There he states unequivocally what he considers as such an absolute criterion of value:

> I may be asked what I mean by the word value, and by what criterion I would judge whether a commodity had or had not changed its value. I answer I know no other criterion of a thing dear or cheap but by the sacrifices of labour made to obtain it.

[1] If objections should be raised against a re-examination of a seemingly obsolete idea, such as the Ricardian labour theory of value, we are indeed in a fortunate position to meet them. The newly discovered paper on 'Absolute Value and Exchangeable Value', which he wrote shortly before his death in September, 1823, has just been published by Dr. Sraffa (see *The Works and Correspondence of David Ricardo*, ed. P. Sraffa, IV, pp. 357–412). This edition will be quoted here as *Works* with number of the volume and page following. Quotations from the *Principles* of Ricardo without further notation are from the 3rd edition ('Everyman's Library'). The three editions of the *Principles* are cited as ed. 1, 2, 3. This newly discovered essay may lead to a renaissance of Ricardian studies and does justify a re-examination of his value theory quite apart from the fact that the application of the psychocultural method to this theory represents an approach not yet tried.

> Everything is originally purchased by labour—nothing that has value can be produced without it. . . . That the greater or less quantity of labour worked up in commodities can be the only cause of their alteration in value is completely made out as soon as we are agreed that all commodities are the produce of labour and would have no value but for the labour expended upon them.[1]

Labour bestowed performs a number of functions in the Ricardian theory: (1) it is the foundation, source and substance of value; (2) it is the cause of changes in absolute and relative values; (3) it, or a commodity representing it, is the closest approximation to an invariable standard or measure of value.

The meaning of, and the interrelations between, these various concepts cannot be understood without some insight into the conscious and unconscious motives of Ricardo's theory. Labour bestowed (1) serves, at the same time, as an ethical and a socio-economic justification of prices; (2) it interrelates economic value and technology; (3) it establishes a similarity between the methods of physics and of economics. These various aspects of value have to be discussed before we can proceed with an analysis of the Ricardian theory.

The Influence of Physics, Mechanics, and Technology

There is a definite interconnection between three trends of Western civilization: the natural sciences, especially their beginnings in the form of mechanics; the science of society, especially in the form of classical economics; and the methods of production, in the form of manufacturing, which characterized capitalism in the seventeenth and eighteenth centuries.[2] The natural sciences of the seventeenth century are guided almost exclusively by the methods of manufacturing of that period. From Galileo to Newton and for a long time afterward, they consisted of a mathematical formulation of mechanics.

This tendency in science had nothing to do with practical manufacturing problems. Manufacturing of that period did not need the help of science. The great advances of the industrial revolution came after the middle of the eighteenth century. It is science that was influenced by the experiences of production rather than vice versa. Research was based predominantly upon the observations provided by the processes of manufacturing. The basic concepts of mechanics,

[1] *Works*, IV., p. 397.

[2] F. Borkenau, *Der Übergang vom Furdalen zum Burgerlichen Weltbild.* The following pages are a summary of some of Borkenau's ideas.

as developed by Galileo and his contemporaries, are often the exact formulas of the relations which developed in the manual processes of manufacturing between human labour and its object. Mechanics, the science of the manufacturing period, is the scientific elaboration of the production process of manufacturing.

The basic problems of mechanics are related to the general problems of human labour. Both are concerned with such questions as: Which force is necessary to accomplish a certain amount of labour and production? Which task does a certain force perform? In manufacturing, human labour was considered only as general, quality-less labour, and all results of labour as quality-less matter. The development from the medieval type of work to the new methods of manufacturing consisted in replacing qualitatively distinct, often artistically refined, labour by simple mechanical labour which was split up into movements to accomplish precision and speed. This destroyed quality and skill; labour became mere labour quantity. This process increased the amount of production and reduced its cost; furthermore, it made costs and profits calculable. Only pure quantities are completely commensurable and comparable; the comparability of amounts of labour requires the reduction of the quality of labour to general, purely quantitively measurable labour. Mechanics is the exact science of comparison of quantities of labour. In this way manufacturing became the socioeconomic matrix of modern mechanics.

To summarize: the character of reasoning in the early natural sciences shows similarities with the techniques of early manufacturing. Both sciences and manufacturing techniques can be interpreted as emanations of basic attitudes of the times, mutually moulding and influencing one another. These basic attitudes consist of: (1) abstraction from quality; (2) interpretation of the world in quantitative terms, to picture natural and social relationships as consisting of relations between qualitatively homogeneous magnitudes, reducible to a common quantitative denominator; (3) a trend toward calculability; natural and social phenomena have to be made calculable in order to be comprehensible; measuring becomes the most important instrument of acquiring scientific knowledge; (4) a tendency to represent natural and social phenomena in analogy to mechanical processes; the concepts of force and matter are applied to extra-mechanical events; (5) atomization of the universe and of the social world is a necessary concomitant of the quantified and mechanical world outlook. The sciences search for basic units and entities which are not divisible in themselves. Their interrelations, according to the laws of mechanics, are the object of scientific analysis.

All these elements can be found in classical economics, especially in the Ricardian system. Adam Smith had already indicated that the actual market prices are surface phenomena, gravitating around an underlying system of real values. His distinction of the 'real' as against the 'nominal' price betrays this style of thinking. Ricardo also distinguishes the actual or market price from the primary and natural price.[1] Adam Smith consistently identifies goods and labour.

> What is bought with money or with goods is purchased by labour. They contain the value of a certain quantity of labour which we exchange for what is supposed at the time to be an equal quantity of labour.[2]

This statement implies the belief that the reality behind the 'screen of goods' is labour, that the exchange relations between commodities are nothing but reflections of the interrelations between labour quantities. Exchange relations between goods and money are merely nominal; the real exchange relations exist between labour quantities. This conforms to the tendency of the natural sciences to mistrust sensory experiences. Matter is not what it appears to be, an agglomeration of an innumerable variety of colours, surfaces with different tactile effects, sounds, etc., but consists, 'in reality', of atoms, molecules, etc. The choice of 'labour bestowed' as a standard of value may also have been influenced by technology. Production can be regarded as a process in which labour is set to work on materials and produces commodities. According to the labour theory of value, the value of a good is determined by a factor involved in the production process. This corresponds to the idea of mechanics, where forces are supposed to act on matter and put it into motion.

Ethical Problems

Ricardo's theory of value was thus influenced by trends in science and by the tendency to unify the world outlook in interpreting the creation of economic value in analogy to mechanical and technological processes. However, the same ethical idea which motivated Adam Smith is also present in his system. Ricardo wanted to prove that labour bestowed in production determines exchange values, because the idea that economic rewards should be commensurate with work effort formed a part of the internalized value system of his period. He shared with Smith and with his time the ideal of the hardworking, frugal economic man.

His Jewish background may have contributed and reinforced this attitude. The Protestant and Puritan work ethic has important

[1] *Principles*, chap. iv, p. 48. [2] *Wealth of Nations*, Book I, chap. v, p. 30.

roots in the Old Testament.[1] The Jews were to some extent forerunners and carriers of capitalism and of the 'capitalist spirit'.[2] The idea that effort and reward are interrelated may also have been a part of Ricardo's upbringing. We know that in his childhood he was subject to a rigorous discipline.[3] The idea that only the industrious will be rewarded and that he will be rewarded in conformity with his effort may have been instilled into Ricardo by his parents and relatives.[4]

Some hints as to his ethical attitude toward labour and work can be found in the *Principles*. In his peroration on the Poor Laws he shows the same moral dislike for idleness and for imprudence and the same high evaluation of industry, of independence, of prudence and forethought, as Adam Smith did:

> They [the Poor Laws] have rendered restraint superfluous, and have invited imprudence, by offering it a portion of the wages of prudence and industry. The nature of the evil points out the remedy. By gradually contracting the sphere of the Poor Laws; by impressing on the poor the value of independence, by teaching them that they must look not to systematic or casual charity, but to their own exertions for support, that prudence and forethought are neither unnecessary nor unprofitable virtues, we shall by degree approach a sounder and more healthful state.[5]

And:

> The principle of gravitation is not more certain than the tendency of such laws to change wealth and power into misery and weakness; to call away the exertions of labour from every object, except that of providing mere subsistence.[6]

It is obvious from these passages that Ricardo places a moral premium on industry, exertion, labour, and work. Although he does so ostensibly for utilitarian and economic reasons, the ethical overtones are clearly discernible. An interesting passage in edition 2 of the *Principles* gives some insight into Ricardo's moral attitudes in respect to economic conduct. He criticizes people, especially the Poles and the Irish, for their

> habits of indolence which make them prefer present ease and

[1] See Max Weber, *Gesammelte Schriften zur Religions Soziologie*, Vol. III; and S. Nelson, *The Idea of Usury*.

[2] W. Sombart, *Die Juden und das Wirtschaftsleben*.

[3] J. Hollander, *David Ricardo: A Centenary Estimate*, p. 30.

[4] Maria Edgeworth in A. J. C. Hare (ed.), *Life and Letters of Maria Edgeworth*, II, p. 380.

[5] *Principles*, chap. v, p. 62.

[6] *Ibid.*, p. 63.

> inactivity, though without security against want, to a moderate degree of exertion, with plenty of food and necessaries. . . . The remedy . . . is to stimulate exertion, to create new wants and to implant new tastes. . . . The facility with which the wants of the Irish are supplied, permits that people to pass a great part of their time in idleness.[1]

We have here all the earmarks of the economic value complex: the work ethic, according to which labour and work become ends in themselves; need-satisfaction is interpreted as a means of stimulating exertion for the sake of capital accumulation: 'for those countries must accumulate a much larger amount of capital.' Of course, Ricardo criticizes idleness because it prevents 'security against want'; and he advocates more capital accumulation for the same reasons. The emphasis, however, lies on how to get people to exert themselves and how to get them to accumulate more capital.

Ricardo's thinking, however, is beset with a moral conflict between his high evaluation of work as expressed in the labour theory of value and the idea that enjoyment is the end of economic activity. The two value orientations are reflected in his distinction between value and riches. He attacks J. B. Say in chapter xx of the *Principles* for using the terms 'value' and 'riches' synonymously:

> Thus far Mr. Say . . . but in his account of value and riches he has confounded two things which ought always to be kept separate and which are called by Adam Smith value in use and value in exchange. If by an improved machine I can, with the same quantity of labour, make two pair of stockings instead of one, I in no way impair the utility of the one pair of stockings, though I diminish their value.[2]

According to Ricardo, riches consist of

> necessaries, conveniences and amusements of human life. . . . Value, then, essentially differs from riches, for value depends not on abundance, but on the difficulty of or facility of production.[3]

When labour becomes more productive through the invention of machinery, by a better division of labour, etc., the amount of riches will be greatly increased, but the value of the single commodities, now produced in greater abundance and measured by labour bestowed, will fall. Whatever commodity or yardstick is used as a standard of value,

[1] *Works*, I, p. 100. [2] *Principles*, chap. xx, ed. 3, p. 186; *Works*, I, p. 279, n. 2.
[3] *Principles*, chap. xx, p. 182.

still it would not be a standard of riches, because riches do not depend on value. A man is rich or poor according to the abundance of necessaries and luxuries which he can command; and whether the exchangeable value of these for money, for corn, or for labour be high or low, they will equally contribute to the enjoyment of their possessor.[1]

The distinction between wealth and riches is more than a logical one; it hides a conflict between opposing value systems. Economic value based on labour bestowed represented the Puritan economic value complex, with its emphasis on productive labour and accumulation of capital as ends in themselves. Riches represent the utilitarian, hedonistic value attitude which makes the satisfaction of needs and utility the basic factors in human conduct. The conflict between these two approaches is very obvious in Ricardo's discussion. Value and riches vary inversely, as has already been discovered in connection with the paradox of value. This recognition of the conflict between value and riches is the intellectual reflection of a conflict which began to permeate economic civilization with growing intensity in the nineteenth century. With the changing character of the economy from a system with little capital equipment to a highly capitalized economy, the old value system which prescribed prudence, frugality, parsimony, and hard work as ultimate virtues began to disintegrate. The emphasis shifted to consumption and need-satisfaction. Although this development is reflected in economic thought in the theories of the marginalist and neoclassical schools, it is foreshadowed in chapter xx of Ricardo's *Principles.* When consumption becomes more important, the old virtues become questionable. To an ethical system which considers labour and work as ends, it matters most whether harder work and effort receive a higher reward than less effort. This is the essence of the labour theory of value. To a value system which emphasizes enjoyment and consumption it matters whether prices are related to subjective utilities and whether incomes allow adequate need-satisfaction.

Chapter xx of the *Principles* shows very clearly the conflict between the two orientations. What has a high value from the viewpoint of the labour ethic has a low value from the point of view of the utilitarian, hedonistic value system. Production may double or treble the riches of the country, without adding anything to economic value. If the same quantity of labour produces 2,000 instead of 1,000 pairs of stockings, this doubtedly means an increase in riches, but not in value measured by labour bestowed. In all cases of

[1] *Principles*, p. 184.

technological improvements by which the productivity of labour will be increased, 'society will, notwithstanding its augmented riches and its augmented means of enjoyment, have less amount of value.'[1] One gains the impression that, to some extent, Ricardo deplores the decrease in value which accompanies the augmentation of riches. This undertone stems from the conflict of ultimate aims. Ricardo solves this conflict by a compromise. In his value theory he chooses labour bestowed in production as the determinant of value, thereby emphasizing the interrelation between effort and reward according to the work ethic. In Chapter xx of the *Principles* he gives his due to the utilitarian goal of enjoyment and riches.. The emphasis, however, lies on the work ethic because of the central role of the labour theory of value in his thought.

The Socioeconomic Conflict

In Book I, chapter vi of the *Wealth of Nations* Adam Smith confined the application of the pure labour theory of value to the early and rude stage of society, before accumulation of stock and appropriation of land had taken place. In the advanced economy, value centred around the natural price, composed of wages, profits, and rent, is the 'centre of repose and continuance'. Although Adam Smith tried to reduce these three components of value to labour, his basic idea was that values and prices in the later stages of society differ from the pure labour values. Ricardo, in order to make his labour theory universally applicable, had to disprove these contentions. He had to prove that labour bestowed on the production of a commodity determines value in the later as well as in the earlier stages; that profits and rent have no or little influence on value and prices. Ricardo's main concern was with Adam Smith's opinion that private ownership of capital and land have changed the law of value and thus made the 'labour-bestowed' theory of value inapplicable.

Ricardo rejected Smith's multiplicity of value theories and his distinction between the early and rude state and the later stages of society, because of their anxiety-generating implications. The anxiety stems from the indictment of the market system, which may follow from the recognition that labour values do not determine prices after the accumulation of stock and the appropriation of land have taken place. In this case the correspondence between reward and effort would be destroyed. This would imply that prices would lack ethical justification. This conclusion had to be avoided at all costs.

[1] *Principles*, chap. xx, pp. 182–83.

Ricardo's concern in this matter was clearly expressed in chapter i, Section III, in editions 1 and 2 of the *Principles*:

> . . . Though Adam Smith fully recognized the principle that the proportion between the quantities of labour necessary for acquiring different objects, is the only circumstance which can afford any rule for our exchanging them for one another, yet he limits its application to 'that early and rude state of society, which precedes both the accumulation of stock and the appropriation of land': as if, when profits and rent were to be paid, they would have some influence on the relative value of commodities, independent of the mere quantity of labour that was necessary to their production.[1]

The early and rude state is characterized by pure labour values, by the identity of labour bestowed in production and labour commanded in exchange (see below, pp. 60 ff.) and by the identity of absolute and relative values. It represents the paradisiac state of affairs before the 'fall', in which harmony reigns. The 'original sin' of capital accumulation and appropriation of land destroyed this harmony, and created these dichotomies. Ricardo's problem consisted of dealing with them in such a way as to eliminate the dichotomies, or to minimize them, and to develop a unified theory applicable to both stages. His (unconscious) motive was to show that the same moral and intellectual beliefs which lead to the assumption of labour bestowed as the source and measure of value are also valid in a system of private property and in an exchange economy. The strained artificiality of his constructs and definitions, however, may indicate that his striving for justification may have been impelled by some hidden hostility against the system and by doubts about its moral justice.

[1] *Works*, I, pp. 22–23, n. 3.

CHAPTER VI

LABOUR BESTOWED VERSUS LABOUR COMMANDED

The Conflict

THE distinction between labour bestowed and labour commanded reflects the conflict between the early and the later state of the economy. Labour bestowed on the production of a commodity is a universally applicable concept wherever goods are produced 'in the sweat of man's brow'. It does not require an exchange economy. Labour commanded in exchange cannot be used as a yardstick of value unless exchange relations are established. In order to unify the theory of value, Ricardo had to use a concept of labour which is applicable in both situations. Therefore, he had to use labour bestowed as a determinant of value.

In chapter i, Section I, of the *Principles* (pp. 5–7), Ricardo formulates his main thesis that the quantities of labour expended in the production of commodities regulate their exchangeable values and that this value varies directly with the quantity of such labour. He then proceeds to criticize Adam Smith for 'using another standard measure of value than labour bestowed on their production' and for estimating value 'in proportion as they will exchange for more or less of this standardized measure.'[1]

Ricardo discusses value in exchange and relative prices.[2] Nevertheless, he rejected Adam Smith's approach of measuring the value of a commodity in terms of the quantity of other goods for which it can be exchanged, and he ended by arriving at an absolute-value concept in labour bestowed in production. To some extent, Adam Smith treated labour bestowed in production of a commodity and labour commanded by the commodity in exchange as equal. Both Smith and Ricardo hold that these two types of labour were identical in the early and rude state of society. For the 'postlapsarian' state, however, Ricardo makes a clear distinction between the two and does not consider them identical magnitudes.

[1] *Principles,* chap. i, p. 7.

[2] *Ibid.*, p. 6.

Ricardo's Interpretation

Ricardo based his distinction between labour bestowed and labour commanded on a misinterpretation of Adam Smith. He redefined the latter's concept of 'labour commanded'. In his general analysis of value in the *Wealth of Nations*, Book I, chapter v, Adam Smith had in mind a society of independent producers without any wage labour, without the existence of the two classes of capitalists and labourers. He had in mind, at least implicitly, the early and rude state. In such a state the whole product belongs to the one who produces it by his labour. Therefore, the labour bestowed on commodity A is equal to the labour bestowed on commodities B and C, which are given in exchange for commodity A. Thus labour bestowed on commodity A and labour commanded in exchange by commodity A are equal. By exchanging a given commodity for a quantity of goods, the producer merely saves himself the trouble of producing these goods himself. According to the 'pure' labour theory of value, commodities 'containing' a certain quantity of labour exchange for other commodities which 'contain' an equal quantity of labour.

Thus, when Adam Smith talks about 'labour commanded in exchange', he does not mean the amount of labour services which can be hired with the amount of money for which the commodity can be sold, because his 'model' of the pure labour theory of value does not assume the existence of hired wage labour. However, this is what Ricardo means by 'labour commanded'. For Ricardo, labour commanded means the amount of labour services which can be hired by a certain quantity of goods. This transformation of Adam Smith's concept of labour commanded into something quite different takes place in the following passage:

> Sometimes he speaks of corn, at other times of labour, as a standard measure; not the quantity of labour bestowed on the production of any object, but the quantity which it can command in the market: as if these two were equivalent expressions, and as if, because a man's labour had become doubly efficient, and he could therefore produce twice the quantity of a commodity, he would necessarily receive twice the former quantity in exchange for it. If this indeed were true, if the reward of the labourer were always in in proportion to what he produced, the quantity of labour bestowed on a commodity, and the quantity of labour which that commodity would purchase, would be equal and either might accurately measure the variations of other things; but they are not equal; the first is under many circumstances an invariable standard,

> indicating correctly the variations of other things; the latter is subject to as many fluctuations as the commodities compared with it.[1]

The use of the term 'labourer' is decisive. By using it, Ricardo changes the assumptions of Adam Smith from an economy of independent producers to the assumption of a society in which capitalists and wage labourers exist. Here the work is done by labourers who do not own capital and provide only labour services, that is, bestow labour on goods. Thus the process of production and exchange becomes more complicated. The employer exchanges goods which have been produced by labourers. The amount of labour bestowed on the goods he commands in exchange is, according to the labour theory of value, identical with the amount of labour bestowed on the goods which he gave in exchange. The amount of goods which the wage labourer receives as a wage, however, is not identical with the amount of goods he produced (on which he bestowed his labour). 'Labour commanded' could mean the amount of labour contained in the goods which the capitalist receives for the product or the amount of labour services rendered by a wage labourer which can be purchased with a certain quantity of commodities (of corn, food, and necessaries, i.e., of wage goods). Ricardo uses the term 'labour commanded' in the latter sense. The same definition is repeated later:

> Is not the value of labour equally variable, being not only affected, as all other things are, by the proportion between supply and demand . . . but also by the varying price of food and other necessaries, on which the wages of labour are expended?[2]

Here 'labour' does not mean labour bestowed on the production of a commodity. It means the commodity labour which a certain parcel of wage goods, a certain 'quantity of food and other necessaries', can command in exchange. Instead of being the foundation of the exchange value of goods in general, labour becomes a fluctuating quantity of labour services measured in terms of wage goods.

One of the reasons for Ricardo's emphasis on labour as a commodity may be the development of the wage system as an essential feature of the market economy. Wage labour already existed in Adam Smith's times, but it was of much less importance than in Ricardo's time, because, meanwhile, the factory system had emerged. Whereas for Smith the British economy was still mainly composed of independent individual proprietors, for Ricardo factories with dependent labour forces had become widespread. More

[1] *Principles*, chap. i, Sec. I, p. 7.

[2] *Ibid.*, p. 8.

capital meant a greater divergence of prices and wages, a larger share for the capitalists. Thus the identity of 'labour bestowed' and 'labour commanded', or of effort and reward, was impossible to maintain, even in the vague formulation of Adam Smith. This was another reason why Ricardo had to retreat to the concept of 'labour bestowed' as the only basis for an absolute-value concept.

Ricardo points out that the amount of labour bestowed on the production of food may rise without the wages of labour, in terms of food, diminishing, to prove that 'labour bestowed' and 'labour commanded' are not equal. Or the productivity of labour may increase and thereby, according to the labour theory of value, reduce the price of the product; but the reward of the labourer, measured in real terms, will not necessarily rise. The effects of competition and the increase in population will, in the long run, lower the real wages to more or less the same level as before.

Thus the essence of Ricardo's argument with Adam Smith is that 'labour bestowed' and 'labour commanded' are not equal because (*a*) 'labour commanded' is the amount of labour services bought at a certain real wage; (*b*) this real wage does not, in the long run, necessarily vary with changes in the productivity of labour; an increase in labour productivity does not necessarily cause an increase in real wages.

A Psychocultural Explanation

To interpret the meaning of the distinction between 'labour bestowed' and 'labour commanded', one has to realize that this dichotomy, like the distinction between the pre- and the postlapsarian state, reflects doubts about the ethical justification of the market and price system. As pointed out before, 'labour bestowed' can be a source of value, even without the existence of an exchange economy. 'Labour commanded' presupposes exchange. 'Labour bestowed' is an absolute standard of value. If, as Ricardo points out in criticizing Adam Smith, the quantity of 'labour commanded in exchange' is not the same as the quantity of 'labour bestowed', he indicates, implicitly and unconsciously, that the actual market price does not conform to the absolute standard of value. With this he lays the foundation for the later Marxian criticism. A commodity may be produced by the labour of two men. If exchanged on the market, the goods received in exchange for it may embody more than the labour of two men. Or the commodities received as a wage by one man-hour may have less value than the commodities produced by one man-hour. The concept of surplus value is already implied in the first section of Ricardo's *Principles*. He is convinced that 'labour bestowed' should determine economic values, prices, and wages. That means that commodities should exchange in relation to the amounts of labour bestowed (embodied, expanded, used) in their production. From this it follows that one man producing a commodity should, if he sells this commodity, receive commodities on which equal amounts of labour have been expended as he himself has invested in the production of the first commodity. But it follows, furthermore, that the worker who works for an employer should also receive a reward which corresponds to the productivity of labour; his real wage should rise with increasing productivity of labour.

It was obvious to Ricardo that these consequences—'logical' from the viewpoint of his theory—did not coincide with reality. He was troubled by the fact that changes in wages were not related to changes in the productivity of labour. There seemed to be an interrelation between the changes in the productivity of labour and the prices of goods. With increasing productivity, prices fell, and thus the amount of commodities exchanged for some product with stable price may have increased. The producer—in classical terminology, the 'capitalist'—received more goods in exchange for the product he sold because the prices of other goods declined as a consequence of the increased productivity. Not so the labourer; his reward and wage may not change in proportion to his productivity. Although he might produce more in one hour than he did before, the labourer might not receive more commodities in exchange because his wage might not increase in proportion to the increase in productivity. This threatened to invalidate the labour theory of value, because it destroyed the equality of labour quantities in the commodities exchanged, at least for the commodity labour. Labour did not exchange in conformity with the basic principle of the labour theory of value, which required equality of the commodities exchanged, the equality being measured in terms of 'labour bestowed'. The commodities received by the labourer as a reward for his labour embodied a smaller amount of labour time than did the commodities he produced. It is again, in Marxian terminology, the problem of surplus value which puzzled Ricardo and his contemporaries.

The conflict between the ethical ideal that remuneration should be commensurate with effort, on the one hand, and the different reality of the price system, on the other, is hidden behind the theoretical discussion on labour bestowed and labour commanded. Adam Smith, in trying to postulate the equality between 'labour bestowed' and 'labour commanded', attempts to deny this conflict.

Ricardo's approach shows clearly his ambivalent attitude toward the exchange economy. He does not accept Adam Smith's method of denying the conflict. He plainly points out the difference between labour bestowed and labour commanded, which is incompatible with the pure labour theory of value. He sharply criticizes Adam Smith's attempt to pretend that the modern exchange economy shows more or less the same equality of the two types of labour as did the early and rude state. He insists, with almost painful intensity, on recognizing the changes brought about by the division of classes and the existence of wage labour. This procedure represents an aggressive attitude toward the exchange economy, the hostile branch of his ambivalence.

However, the hostile approach is tempered by a line of thought in which the opposite tendency manifests itself. Ricardo states the conflict only in order to eliminate it. He rejects Smith's vagueness about the relation between the two types of labour and points out that they are not equal. But he restores the unity of the system by applying the same law of value to the 'prelapsarian' and to the 'postlapsarian' states. In both, according to Ricardo, it is labour bestowed which determines value. Thus he finds intellectual outlets for both tendencies of his ambivalence. The hostility is expressed in rejecting Adam Smith's implicit assumption about the equality of the two types of labour. Through this rejection, he reopens the gap between the precapitalist and the capitalist economy which Adam Smith had tried to close. But, practically in the same breath, he closes the gap again by proclaiming labour bestowed as the universal basis of value in the advanced as well as in the early and rude state. Through this device he justifies unconsciously the capitalist economy by showing that, in spite of the existence of capitalist property, reward and effort are in conformity with each other. Thus his attack against Adam Smith prepares the way for attaining the same goal as that of Adam Smith.

The Subsistence Theory of Wages

After reinterpreting Smith and contrasting the absolute-value concept based on labour bestowed with the relative and fluctuating value of labour as a commodity, Ricardo closes the breach by subordinating even the commodity labour to the universal principle that value is determined by labour bestowed. This is done through the subsistence theory of wages. It applies the 'labour-bestowed' idea to the commodity wage labour. Like any other commodity, labour services have to be produced by 'labour bestowed'. Labour belongs to the category of commodities which 'may be multiplied' and can be produced by 'labour'. The labour bestowed on the production of the commodity labour is identical with the labour bestowed on the production of wage goods, of food, and necessaries for the subsistence of the labourer. This theory had already been developed by Adam Smith.[1] Ricardo elaborated it in chapter v of the *Principles*:

> The natural price of labour, therefore, depends on the price of food and necessaries and conveniences required for the support of the labourer and his family.[2]

The standard and measure of this natural price is the amount of labour bestowed on the production of these commodities. This is quite clearly the opinion of Ricardo, expressed implicitly and explicitly in many passages:

> In like manner, if labour fell very considerably in value, relatively to all other things, and if I found that its fall was in consequence of an abundant supply, encouraged by the great facility with which corn and the other necessaries of the labourer were produced, it would, I apprehend, be correct for me to say that corn and necessaries had fallen in value in consequence of less quantity of labour being necessary to support them, and that this facility of providing for the support of the labourer had been followed by a fall in the value of labour.[3]

This states quite clearly that the value of labour follows the value of the necessaries of subsistence and that their value is determined by the quantity of labour bestowed on their production. Thus the unity of the labour theory of value is preserved; 'labour bestowed' is the only determinant of value, applicable also to labour as a commodity.

This theory shows the production- and technology-mindedness of the classical economists; labour services are interpreted as output, produced by the input of food and necessaries; labour bestowed on these wage goods produces the commodity labour and determines its value. For Ricardo, 'labour bestowed' is a mechanical cause, a force which produces commodities and gives them value. The unity of the whole system would be endangered if this concept could not be applied to all things exchanged on the market; therefore, a way had to be found to apply it to labour services also. By interpreting, in a mechanistic way, labour services as being 'caused' by the commodities consumed by the labourer and his family, labour bestowed

1 *Wealth of Nations*, Book I, chap. viii, p. 68.

2 *Principles*, chap. v, p. 52.

3 *Ibid.*, chap. i, p. 10.

is preserved as the universal determinant of value. This interpretation reflects the general tendency of political economy to reify social interrelationships. Labour services are nothing but a link in the chain of production; they produce exchangeable commodities, but they are, in turn, 'produced' by exchangeable commodities. The labourer consumes commodities in order to be able to produce commodities. People's purpose in life is production for the market. The economic value complex is reflected in this theory—work and production are ultimate ends. Thus the mechanistic and the ethical outlook are welded into a unified world picture.

Chapter VII

THE ELIMINATION OF CAPITAL AS A DETERMINANT OF VALUE

IN order to preserve the unity of his system and for the same reasons for which he rejected 'labour commanded' as a basis of value, Ricardo had to prove that the existence of capital has little or no influence on values and prices. Here again he was confronted with the problem of closing the gap between the pre-capitalist and the capitalist economy. Here we shall find manifestations of the same ambivalence which we have already noticed in his treatment of the labour-bestowed versus labour-commanded question.

Briefly, the argument of Section III in chapter i runs like this: (*a*) Exchange values (relative prices) of commodities are not determined merely by direct labour but also by the labour bestowed on capital goods used in the production of these commodities. (*b*) The existence of two classes, of capitalists and labourers, the one owning the implements of production, the other furnishing the labour, has no influence on exchange values; nor does the distribution of the final product between the two groups in terms of profits and wages bring about any change in relative prices. Improvements in productivity will reduce the exchange value of goods in the production of which less labour is used, whether the labour savings take place in direct production or in the production of the capital goods used in such an industry. (*c*) A rise in wages does not influence exchange values if the capitals used in the production of the respective commodities are of equal durability (if the same proportion of fixed and circulating capital is used and if the fixed capitals are of the same durability).[1]

All this serves to confirm the theory that it is labour bestowed in production which determines exchange values (relative prices) and their changes. In order to arrive at this conclusion, Ricardo resorts to a number of definitions and assumptions which are unsurpassed in their subtlety and by which he has set an example for the

[1] *Principles*, chap. i, Sec. III, pp. 15, 18.

style of thinking which, to this day, has been followed by economic analysis.

Capital Is Accumulated Labour

Ricardo starts with denying implicitly the difference between capital and labour, by dissolving capital into labour. Capital becomes 'accumulated labour'.[1] This enables him to formulate the thesis that the value of the final product is regulated not solely by the time and labour necessary for its direct production but also by the time and labour necessary for producing the capital. Through this ingenious formulation he reduces capital to labour time, at least in so far as it exercises an influence on value.

This is another instance in which he follows the procedure of the natural sciences to reduce qualitative differences to a homogeneous, quantifiable substance. The obvious physical, qualitative differences between capital and labour are eliminated by transforming capital into accumulated labour.

Another aspect of this formulation which has also become a pattern for later economic analysis is that it represents circular reasoning. It follows from Ricardo's labour theory of value that anything which influences value has to be connected with labour bestowed. Therefore, capital could not exercise any influence on value unless it could be reduced to labour bestowed. However, in order to prove the labour-bestowed theory of value, one has to demonstrate that capital does not influence value. If this is done by calling it labour, one has not proved anything; the entire line of reasoning is purely tautological. This type of tautological reasoning, however, has the psychological function of convincing the author himself and of silencing his own unconscious doubts about the validity of his theory. Such reasoning, deduced from postulates, consists of purely analytical judgments. It is not legitimate to regard it as proof and as representing synthetic judgments providing new knowledge.

With the help of the definition of capital as accumulated labour, Ricardo solves the problem of the differences in exchange values of goods produced with the same amount of direct labour but with different amounts of capital, without having to admit any influence of capital on value. It enables him to conclude that the

> exchangeable value of commodities produced would be in proportion to the labour bestowed on their production; not on their immediate production only, but on all those implements or machines

[1] *Ibid.*, chap. i, Sec. IV, p. 21.

required to give effect to the particular labour to which they were applied.[1]

Commodities which use capital goods produced by more labour than others will have a higher relative value: the opposite holds true for commodities produced with capital goods of higher durability. In the latter case the argument is that

of the durable implement only a small portion of its value would be transferred to the commodity, a much greater portion of the value of the less durable implement would be realized in the commodity which it contributed to produce.[2]

Thus, again, labour bestowed emerges triumphantly as the determinant of exchange-value differentials, although this result is accomplished only by a rather peculiar definition of capital. It seems quite legitimate to conclude that this definition was chosen in order to arrive at the result and that the result is postulated for extraneous reasons.

Values and prices, however, are influenced not by capital as such but by the desire of the owners of capital to make profits. In order to eliminate the influence of capital on value, Ricardo had to prove that profits do not influence values and prices. He accomplishes this, at first, by a peculiar definition of profits and wages.

Wages and Profits Vary Inversely

In Section III of chapter i, Ricardo defines wages and profits as shares of the total product. He assumes that every capitalist receives the same percentage share of his total product and has to pay out the same percentage in the form of wages. The size of the share of capital and labour will be determined by the supply of capital and wage goods, respectively; it will affect all industries equally. Obviously, Ricardo implied that, in the long-run, any differentials in the rates of profit and the share of labour will be equalized by shifts of capital and labour from the less profitable to the more profitable industries.[3]

[1] *Principles*, chap. i, Sec. III, p. 14. Notice how capital is here treated deprecatingly, not only by interpreting it as accumulated labour, but also by demoting it to an 'assistant' of labour, in the phrase 'required to give effect to the particular labour.' Cf. also the use of the term 'unassisted labour' in ed. 1, *Works*, I, p. xliii and p. 63.

[2] *Ibid.*, chap. i, Sec. III, p. 13. This argument is interesting because it betrays again the substantial and mechanical nature of the Ricardian thinking. Value is transferred like a substance and energy, quasi-physically from the factors of production to the finished product. See the same line of thought in Karl Marx *Capital*, I ('Modern Library' ed.), pp. 208 ff.

[3] *Ibid.*, chap. i, Sec. III, p. 14.

According to these definitions, a rise in wages means an increase in the share of the total product received by the labourers. A fall in profits means a decrease in the share of the total product received by the capitalists. Therefore, wages and profits vary inversely.[1] Again, this is a tautological conclusion following from the definition of wages and profits as shares of the total product. Therefore, a change in wages or profits, a change in the division of the total product between the two classes, capitalists and labourers, or a rise or fall in their relative shares in the form of profits and wages does not influence the relative values of commodities. These are determined by the proportion of labour bestowed directly on their production and on the production of capital goods used.[2] Profits and wages may rise or fall,

> yet, this division could not affect the relative value of these commodities, since whether the profits of capital were greater or less . . . or whether the wages of labour were high or low, they would operate equally on both employments

(in the two occupations, the killing of beavers and of deer which he used in his example).[3]

In this manner Ricardo excludes any influence of profits and wages on exchangeable values; they are exclusively determined by the direct and indirect labour bestowed on their production.

The Effect of a Rise in Wages, with Capital of Equal Composition and Durability

However, Ricardo was well aware of the fact that profits can cause differences in relative values, which cannot be traced back to different amounts of labour bestowed in production. In order to restrict the incidence of such a possibility, Ricardo makes two different assumptions, which underlie his reasoning in Sections III and IV, respectively:

> In the former Section [III] we have supposed the implements and weapons necessary to kill the deer and the salmon to be equally durable, and to be the result of the same quantity of labour, and we have seen that the variations in the relative value of deer and salmon depended solely on the varying quantities of labour necessary to obtain them [p. 18].

In Section IV he abandons this assumption (see below, pp. 74 ff.).

[1] *Ibid.*, chap. i, Sec. IV, p. 21.

[2] *Ibid.*, chap. i, Sec. III, pp. 14, 17, 21.

[3] *Ibid.*, p. 14.

In Section III this assumption of equal composition of capital[1] is defined as capital used in two different occupations, such as hunting and fishing, being of 'equal value and of equal durability . . . both being the produce of the same quantity of labour.'[2]

On the basis of this assumption, Ricardo states again that a change in wages does not affect relative values or prices of commodities. Their comparative prices can be changed only by a change in the quantity of labour bestowed directly on their production or indirectly on the production of capital. A rise in wages will not cause a rise in the relative price of the commodity whose labourer-producers received a wage increase:

> The proportion which might be paid for wages is of the utmost importance in the question of profits; for it must at once be seen that profits would be high or low exactly in proportion as wages were low and high; but it could not in the least affect the relative value of fish and game, as wages would be high or low at the same time in both occupations.[3]

This argument is merely an application of his previous line of thought to the case of equal durability of capital. In this case changes in wages and profits, defined as shares of the total product and affecting all industries equally, will not change relative values. In edition 2, Section III concluded with the unequivocal statement in which Ricardo's motive for his argument is revealed:

> It appears then by this section, that notwithstanding the accumulation of capital, commodities would not necessarily vary in relative value from a rise in wages, unless it was accomplished by increased facility or difficulty in the production of one or more of them.[4]

The stress in this statement lies on the words 'not necessarily'. Ricardo means to say that, under the assumption of equal composition and durabilities of capitals which underlies Section III, relative values will not be influenced by a rise in wages.

Why does Ricardo put so much emphasis on the effects of a rise

[1] Marx uses this term to mean 'the proportion in which it [capital] is divided into constant . . . and variable capital,' or 'into means of production and . . . labour-power' (*op. cit.*, Vol. I, chap. xxxv, p. 671).

[2] *Principles*, chap. i, Sec. III, p. 15.

[3] *Ibid.*, p. 16.

[4] *Works*, I, p. 56, n. 1. The statement quoted above has been eliminated in ed. 3. This does not indicate a change of mind on the part of Ricardo. The conclusion was already drawn in the previous paragraph of Sec. III, with which this section ends in ed. 3.

in wages?[1] Ricardo's argument is directed against Adam Smith and others who have maintained that a rise in wages will increase prices. Ricardo could not admit this for various reasons. For one, wages represent labour commanded in exchange; they consist of a quantity of goods which 'command' a certain quantity of labour in exchange. If a change in wages should cause a change in relative values, it would mean that labour commanded has an influence on value. Ricardo, having decided on labour bestowed as the basis of value, could not admit this. Therefore, he had to prove that a change in wages does not cause a change in relative prices.

Furthermore, the fact that wages are paid at all implies the existence of a capitalist economy, with two classes sharing the total product, a separation which did not exist in the early, rude state of society. If a rise in wages affected values, the laws of value would be different in the two stages, because the wage system did not exist in the precapitalist society. Again it is the unity of the law of value which forces Ricardo to deny any effect of rising wages on prices.

The statement quoted last provides the key to Ricardo's motives for his definition of wages and profits as shares of the total product equal in all industries, for assuming their inverse variation, and for concluding that their changes have no influence on relative prices. He wanted to show, and says so himself, that private ownership of capital and the wage system did not change the law of value, that labour bestowed determines exchange values in all stages of society. Again he wants to close the gap between the precapitalist and the capitalist economy for intellectual and ethical reasons.

This throws some light on the psychocultural meaning of Ricardo's model-building. The exclusion of a rise in wages (or fall in profits) as a determinant of relative prices in Section III was made possible not only by their definition as shares of the total product but also by the assumption of equal composition and durability of capital. This assumption serves to limit the sphere within which anything else but labour bestowed exercises an influence on relative values and prices. Ricardo's conclusion is that if capital were of equal durability and were used in the same proportion to labour in all industries, the variations in relative value would be caused solely by the varying quantities of labour necessary to obtain them. Thus his assumption made it possible to extend the sphere of applicability of the pure labour-bestowed theory of value.

[1] This will become clearer in our analysis of chap. i, Sec. IV (see below, pp. 74 ff.).

Unequal Durability of Capital Admitted

In Section IV this assumption of equal proportions of the two types of capital and of its equal durability and value is abandoned. Now it is admitted that circulating capital may 'be returned to its employer in very unequal times' and that fixed and circulating capitals may be used in different proportions in different industries and trades.

Under these circumstances the answer to the question about what causes a change in relative values is different from the one given in Section III. The examination of this situation leads Ricardo to admit, as a second cause of such changes, 'the rise in the wages of labour' or 'a rise in the value of labour'.

> But although commodities produced under similar circumstances would not vary with respect to each other from any cause but an addition and diminution of the quantity of labour necessary to produce one or the other of them, yet, compared with others not produced with the same proportionate quantity of fixed capital, they would vary from the other cause also which I have mentioned before, namely a rise in the value of labour, although neither more nor less labour were employed in the production of either of them.[1]

In this case, the same quantity of labour expended in direct and indirect production would not lead to the same exchange values. The enterpriser who uses more fixed capital (e.g., machinery) will have to include in his total revenue (price *times* quantity sold), the profits (interest) of the capital invested in the machine for the time from the initial investment to the moment the product of the machine is marketed. His prices will therefore have to be higher than the ones of an enterpriser who uses no (or less) fixed equipment:

> On account of the different durability of their capitals, or, which is the same thing, on account of the time which must elapse before one set of commodities can be brought to market, they will be valuable, not exactly in proportion to the quantity of labour bestowed on them—they will not be as two to one, but something more . . . to compensate for the greater length of time which must elapse before the most valuable can be brought to market.[2]

Ricardo uses an example of three employers, each of whom employs 100 men during the first year; two employ labour to construct machines, one employs labour to grow corn. In the second year the two machine producers will use these machines to produce cloth

[1] *Principles*, chap. i, Sec. IV, p. 20.

[2] *Ibid.*, pp. 20, 21.

and cotton goods, respectively, employing their machines together with 100 men; the farmer will again employ 100 men in the cultivation of corn:

> During the second year they will all have employed the same quantity of labour, but the goods and machines together of the clothier and also of the cotton manufacturer, will be the result of the labour of two hundred men employed for a year . . . whereas the corn will be produced by the labour of one hundred men for one year, consequently if the corn be of the value of £500, the machine and cloth of the clothier together ought to be of the value of £1,000. . . . But they will be more than twice the value of the corn, for the profit on the clothier's . . . capital for the first year has been added to their capitals . . . while that of the farmer has been expended and enjoyed.[1]

Ricardo's own conclusion is:

> Here, then, are capitalists employing precisely the same quantity of labour annually on the production of their commodities, and yet the goods they produce differ in value on account of the different quantities of fixed capital, or accumulated labour, employed by each respectively.[2]

It would be logical now to conclude that the theory which considers labour bestowed as the sole determinant of value has to be abandoned. If the proportions in which each enterprise uses fixed and circulating capital are different, there is another cause which influences values.

Nothing, however, is further from the mind of Ricardo. Although he cannot entirely eliminate the influence of capital and profits on price, he tries to minimize it and to tie it in as closely as possible with the labour-bestowed theory of value; and he shows that the influence of capital on prices works in the opposite direction from that which Adam Smith and his followers had assumed. All this he accomplishes by the following arguments:

(*a*) Again he invokes the formula that fixed capital is really 'accumulated labour'. In the passage just quoted (on p. 74, from the *Principles*, p. 21, second paragraph), a new answer is given to the question of what causes differences in exchangeable values. The existence of fixed capital is one of the reasons why commodities have different exchange values. Obviously, this admission destroys the unity of the labour-bestowed theory of value and seems to confirm Adam Smith's opinion that the law of value has been changed by

[1] *Ibid.*, p. 20.

[2] *Ibid.*, p. 21.

the accumulation of capital—a result which is distasteful to Ricardo, who tries to refute this opinion. Therefore, it seems significant that the magic transformation formula, 'fixed capital or accumulated labour', is invoked in the same sentence in which the exception to the labour-bestowed theory is stated. It is as if Ricardo wants to ward off, anxiously and right away, any conclusions dangerous to his theory. Ricardo seems to say:

> Although I have to admit here that labour bestowed is not the only determinant of value, the cause of this exception is, after all, again labour, in the accumulated form of capital.

The sentence 'and yet the goods they produce differ in value on account of the different quantities of fixed capital or accumulated labour, employed by each respectively' is an expression of ambivalence. What is admitted is retracted almost in the same breath. The 'and yet' is perhaps the most concentrated expression of this ambivalence: the goods are produced by the same quantities of labour, 'and yet' they differ in value; 'and yet' they differ in value only 'on account of the different quantities of . . . accumulated labour.' It would be hard to express two conflicting thoughts more concisely in the same sentence.

(*b*) Ricardo admits that the use of capital (or accumulated labour) can cause differences in the exchange values of goods produced with equal quantities of direct and indirect labour. But he uses a different term when he discusses the role of profits in causing alterations in exchange values. He calls that 'other cause' of alterations in relative values which represents to him an odious exception from the labour-bestowed theory of value, alternatively 'alteration in the wages of labour' (p. 17), 'rise in wages' (*ibid.*), 'rise in the value of labour' (pp. 20, 21), 'rise of labour' (p. 21), and 'rise or fall of labour' (pp. 22, 23). The use of these terms can again be interpreted as a defence mechanism against too openly admitting the influence of capital and profits on changes in value and prices. He reverts here to the definition of wages and profits as shares and to his assumption of their inverse variations. This enables him to avoid talking directly of profits and their effects on prices. Thus he can call a fall in profits a rise in wages or in labour or in the value of labour. When, in Section IV, he is finally brought to admit an influence of capital and profits on changes in relative values, he prefers to admit it in terms of wages or of labour, instead of profits.

This terminology tends to tone down the importance of the admission. It seems as if Ricardo is saying:

> Yes, I have to admit that capital and profits cause changes in prices; but it is not really profits that are the prime cause; it is the rise in wages; no, it is not even the rise in wages, but the rise in the value of labour or the rise in labour.

Actually, the frequent use of the phrase 'rise in the value of labour' or 'rise or fall of labour', instead of 'rise in wages', confirms this interpretation. It means that Ricardo wanted to avoid mentioning either wages or profits, both institutions of the capitalist economy which were absent in the precapitalist economy. By talking merely of a rise of 'labour' or of the value of 'labour', he creates the impression that it is, after all, again labour which influences prices in another form. Although this is not labour bestowed but wages, that is, labour commanded by wage goods, this terminology has the same psychological meaning as the use of the term 'accumulated labour' for capital. It is an instrument of unconscious or half-conscious self-deception, a subtle form of convincing one's self and others that every determinant of value is somehow connected with labour and that, therefore, the labour theory of value is still valid.

(*c*) To minimize the importance of this admission, Ricardo contradicts Adam Smith in respect to the effect of a rise in wages. He points out that rising wages do not increase, but reduce, prices, at least of those commodities

> which are produced by very valuable machinery, or in very valuable buildings, or which require a great length of time before they can be brought to market' (p. 22).

Ricardo called this opinion 'Adam Smith's original error respecting value.'[1] Ricardo himself had originally believed that rising corn prices would, by causing wages to rise, lead to a general price increase. However, he found himself compelled to abandon this theory because 'the supposed general rise of prices obscured the simple relation of the rise of wages to the fall of profits.'[2]

In the *Principles* he argues as follows: a rise in the value of labour (a rise in wages) means a fall in profits, a conclusion which follows from his definition of wages and profits as shares.[3] If the rate of profits falls, the amount to be added to the value of the final product will fall. This amount is added to compensate the capitalist for profits which accrued but were not realized during the period in which the fixed capital was produced. If wages rise and profits fall, the exchange values of goods produced with much fixed capital will fall

1 *Works*, I, p. xxxv.

2 *Ibid.*, I, p. xxxiii.

3 *Principles*, chap. i, Sec. IV, pp. 21–22.

in comparison with those produced with little fixed capital (p. 22). Thus Adam Smith is proved wrong, at least in respect to the highly capitalized types of production.

Ricardo was forced to admit that, of two commodities produced with the same amount of labour, the one on which more fixed capital was used would have a higher exchange value. Thus he had to admit unwillingly that profits (the inverse of wages) do sometimes lead to higher exchange values. Then he proceeds to show that wages (the inverse of profits and the other important institution of the capitalist economy) will, if they rise, cause a reduction in exchange values of goods produced with much fixed capital. Again, we see the peculiar dialectic way in which Ricardo's mind works. Consciously or unconsciously, he tries again to take back what he has first admitted. Both wages and profits are institutions of the market and exchange economy; they are characteristics of the advanced state of society. It is obvious that the admission of their role in value determination does not fit into the Ricardian system. His basic objection to such a role is that, if wages and profits—institutions of the capitalist economy but absent in the precapitalist economy—do influence values, the labour-bestowed theory would apply to the early and rude state and not to the advanced society and that the unity of the law of value would be destroyed. Ricardo argues that accrued profits increase values but that rising wages reduce them. In this way the two institutions of the new economy cancel each other out, at least in their effects on goods produced with different proportions of fixed capital.

One of his unconscious motives may have been simply to contradict Adam Smith. He tries to prove that the existence of the wage system works sometimes in the opposite direction from that which Adam Smith and his followers assumed: it does not raise prices, but it will lower them. It is as if Ricardo wants to say: 'I resent your contentions about the influence of wage labour on prices, but I cannot help admitting that such an influence exists: however, you are wrong at least in respect to the direction of that influence.'

(*d*) In spite of all these arguments there remains the sting of the admission that the use of capital and the accrual of profits distort pure labour exchange values. Therefore, Ricardo expresses the opinion that

> this cause of the variation of commodities is comparatively slight in its effects . . . could not exceed 6 or 7 per cent; for profits could not, probably under any circumstances admit of a greater general and permanent depression than to that amount. . . . An alteration

> in the permanent rate of profits, to any great amount, is the effect of causes which do not operate but in the course of years, whereas alterations in the quantity of labour necessary to produce commodities are of daily occurrence.[1]

In reality, both causes have been effective in the short and in the long run, unless one wants to interpret the term 'permanent rate of profits' as some never actualized equilibrium rate with little factual meaning. However, what makes these passages interesting to us is that they are obviously a link in the chain of arguments which try to preserve labour bestowed as the final cause of price determination.

The tendency to minimize the influence of capital and profits on exchange value and its changes can be found in all Ricardo's literary production. Already the statement in edition 3 that exchangeable value depends 'almost exclusively' upon the quantity of labour realized in a commodity[2] had intended to minimize the influence of capital on prices.

> The other passages introduced in edition 3 to the same effect were as follows: 'it would be . . . incorrect to attach much importance to it,' below p. 36; 'another, though minor variation,' p. 42; 'comparatively slight in its effects,' p. 36 and again p. 45.[3]

All this betrays the same psychological tendency to develop verbal defence mechanisms against the anxiety-generating idea that the unity of the system will be difficult to maintain and that labour bestowed may, after all, not be the only, and not even the main, cause of value and its changes.

(*e*) The last crowning link of this chain is the courageous resolution to

> consider all the great variations which take place in the relative value of commodities to be produced by the greater or less quantity of labour which may be required from time to time to produce them . . . although it would be wrong to omit consideration of the effect produced by a rise or fall in labour.[4]

Although the rate of profit (interest) for fixed capital varying inversely with the wages of labour does have some influence on variations in relative values, Ricardo heroically decides to disregard this, together with all the other causes of relative price changes; only changes in labour bestowed on production are recognized. The labour theory of value is saved; the unity of the system and the

1 *Principles*, p. 22.
2 Replacing the 'solely' of eds. 1 and 2 (*Works*, I, xxxix).
3 *Ibid.*
4 *Ibid.*, pp. 22, 23.

integrity of its ethical basis—labour as the foundation of value—is preserved.

Economists steeped in modern economic analysis will interpret this last statement of Ricardo as one of those hypothetical assumptions so frequently used in economic model-building. I have pointed out elsewhere that such 'abstractions' have a psychological meaning.[1] One abstracts from what one rejects and represses, from parts of reality which are, mostly for unconscious reasons, inconvenient to acknowledge. Repression and denial of reality are psychological phenomena, well known to psychiatry. In the intellectual sphere they make themselves felt whenever the unity either of the world outlook or of the ethical system is threatened. To avoid such anxiety-generating realizations, the ego refuses, unconsciously, to recognize the conflict-generating aspects of reality. In the thought of the classical economists, the labour theory of value has become an instrument of unification and of ethical apology for the emerging economic system. All elements of reality which endangered the validity of this theory had to be eliminated, argued away, diluted, and demoted in importance. The preceding analysis uncovers a very clear trend in this direction in the writings of Ricardo.

Thus the entire tortuous argumentation of chapter i, Sections III and IV, can be briefly summarized as follows: In respect to existing differentials in exchange values: Section III: (*a*) the existence of capital is one of the causes of such differentials, but capital, after all, is nothing but accumulated labour. (*b*) The distribution of the final product among capitalists and labourers in the form of wages and profits does not influence relative values.

In respect to changes in relative values: Section III: if equal composition and durability of capital are assumed, the rise and fall of wages and, therefore, the fall and rise of profits do not change relative values. Section IV: (*a*) if unequal composition and durability of capital are assumed, rising wages (or falling profits) will change relative values. However, this influence works differently than Adam Smith assumed: it will reduce the exchange values of goods produced with large fixed capital; (*b*) this influence is of minor importance and can be disregarded by economic theory.

Some of these arguments are repeated in Ricardo's discussion of the measure of value, to which we now turn.

[1] 'Psychological Aspects of Economic Thought.'

Chapter VIII

THE MEASURE OF VALUE

Cause and Measure of Value

RICARDO discusses the problem of value from two aspects. On the one hand, he inquires into the foundation of exchange values, into the cause for their differences and changes; in this context he poses the question of the 'why' of value. On the other hand, he deals with the problem of the standard measure of value; here he raises the question of how to measure value, of how values can be ascertained and compared. The first involves a 'substantial' and 'causal' line of reasoning. To Ricardo, labour bestowed is, at the same time, a substance of value and a force or energy which creates value and is the cause of its changes. The second approach—the search for a standard measure of value—is logically different; measuring value is not the same thing as looking for the substance and cause of value. In his thought, however, the two approaches are intermixed; he uses both to establish labour bestowed as the main determinant of value.

Right on the first page of the *Principles*, Ricardo rejects utility as the 'measure of exchangeable value'. And on this same first page he criticizes Adam Smith for choosing the wrong 'standard' of value. The opening words of this paragraph show clearly that Ricardo almost completely identified the concept of cause, source, foundation of value, on the one hand, and the concept of standard and measure of value, on the other:

> Adam Smith who so accurately defined the original source of exchangeable value . . . has himself erected another standard measure of value, and speaks of things being more or less valuable in proportion as they will exchange for more or less of this standard measure.'[1]

Here Ricardo talks in one breath about source and standard measure. All throughout the chapter on value, he discusses both concepts together.

[1] *Principles*, chap. i, Sec. I, p. 7; see *Works*, I, xli.

In editions 1 and 2, he had already raised the problem of an invariable standard at the end of chapter i, Section I:

> If any one commodity could be found which now and at all times required precisely the same quantity of labour to produce it, that commodity would be of an unvarying value, and would be eminently useful as a standard by which the variations of other things might be measured . . . Of such a commodity we have no knowledge.[1]

Nevertheless, he maintains that it is useful to 'ascertain what the essential qualities of a standard are, that we may know the causes of the variation in the relative value of commodities.' The standard is supposed to uncover the cause of the variations in value; measuring and causal explanations are identified.

In edition 3 this passage was dropped, but it was replaced by a discussion which shows the same approach to the concept of an invariable standard.[2] There, in his polemic against Adam Smith, he again ties together the problem of cause and of the measure of value: 'Two commodities vary in relative value, and we wish to know in which the variation has really taken place.'[3]

Here the question is definitely as to what causes the change in value. The question is formulated in such a way that the cause is expected to be something 'within' the commodity. A commodity has changed in value if something has happened to it and not to another commodity. If a commodity A exchanges for the same quantities of other commodities as before, whereas commodity B exchanges for different quantities of the same commodities than before, we may conclude that commodity B has changed its value and not the commodities used as a basis for the comparison. If we then find out that the quantity of labour necessary to produce commodity B has changed, whereas no change in labour productivity has taken place in respect to the other commodities, 'we are sure that the variation is in the single commodity: we then discover the cause of its variation.'[4] According to Ricardo, the main function of a measure is to indicate the cause of the variation in value. A standard which would indicate a change in value without anything actually having happened to this commodity would not be an appropriate standard measure. The standard measure has to point to the cause; otherwise it would not serve the purposes of a standard measure of value; and the cause must be something 'within the commodity'!

The same idea is expressed in chapter i, Section III:

[1] *Works*, I, 17, n. 3.

[2] *Principles*, pp. 7 ff.

[3] *Ibid.*, p. 9.

[4] *Ibid.*, p. 10.

> If there were any other commodity which was invariable in its value, we should be able to ascertain by comparing the value of fish and game with this commodity, how much of the variation was to be attributed to a cause which affected the value of fish, and how much to a cause which affected the value of game. Suppose money to be that commodity.[1]

Here again the function of the measure is to show the cause, and the cause is assumed to be found within the sphere of production of the particular commodity. In all this we can detect an endeavour to arrive at an absolute-value concept which can serve, at the same time, as a substance, cause, and yardstick for the measuring of fluctuating exchange values.

The basic ideas of Ricardo in respect to the interrelations of 'cause' and 'measure' of value are very well brought out in his polemic against Torrens in his last paper on 'Absolute and Exchangeable Value'. There Ricardo stresses the distinction between

> . . . two things which ought to be kept quite distinct—if a piece of cloth will exchange for less money than formerly he [Torrens] would say that cloth had fallen in value but he would also say that money had risen in value because it would exchange for more cloth.
>
> This language may be correct as he uses it to express only exchangeable value but in Political Economy we want something more, we desire to know whether it be owing to some new facility in manufacturing cloth that its diminished power in commanding money is owing, or whether it be owing to some new difficulty in producing money. To me it appears a contradiction to say a thing has increased in natural value while it continues to be produced under precisely the same circumstances as before.[2]

And in his answer to Torrens' argument that money 'has risen in value as compared with cloth' Ricardo answers:

> It [money] is undoubtedly of a higher relative value than cloth but how it can be said to have risen in value because another commodity has fallen in value does not appear clear to me nor can it be warranted but by an abuse of language.

This passage shows Ricardo's inability to abandon the idea of an absolute cause of value and to shift entirely to a relativistic concept of exchange value. In a system of relative prices we can see nothing but relative changes. Every change in price is a change only in relation to another commodity. In the absence of an invariable standard

[1] *Principles*, p. 16.

[2] *Works*, IV, 374–75.

we can only say that the value of a commodity has fallen or risen in relation to some other commodity. Obviously, then, the relative change in value of one commodity finds its inverse correlation in the opposite movement of the other commodity. Thus, if A falls in value in relation to B, B must rise in value in relation to A. Both statements are only different ways of expressing the same event. In one case, B is the independent variable (the measure, the standard); in the other case it is A. Ricardo, however, cannot accept this language Why? Because, to him, value and changes in value are not something entirely relative. In spite of frequent statements that he is talking about exchangeable value, he has always in the back of his mind the idea of an absolute substance, cause, and invariable measure of value (all three concepts more or less interrelated and identical). Money, just one commodity among others, cannot rise in value merely because another commodity has fallen in value. A rise in the value of money can be caused only by a change which takes place in the production of money, and, what is more, it can be caused only by an increase in labour bestowed on its production ('owing to some new difficulty in producing money'). A 'force' has to work on money or the commodity in question; a change in the value-generating substance or energy has to take place, in order to increase its value. A mere change in exchange relations with another commodity is not enough. The substantial, causal, and absolute element in Ricardo's thinking is nowhere so clear as in this passage.

The interpretation of the foundation and cause of value as a substance or energy is also implied when Ricardo refers rather approvingly to the following assertion:

> The average strength of 1,000 or 10,000 men it is said is nearly the same at all times. A commodity produced in a given time by the labour of 100 men is double the value of a commodity produced by the labour of 50 men in the same time.[1]

It is easy to see again, in these statements, Ricardo's technological approach to the problem of economic value. In the actual technological production process, labour sets things in motion. Labour applied to raw materials produces commodities which have exchange value. Ricardo considers production as the value-generating process. This conforms to the technological bent of Ricardo's century and the importance that was attributed to production. Not the utility of the commodity for the individual is the basis of economic value; producing a commodity and giving it value are one and the

[1] In the draft of 'Absolute Value and Exchangeable Value,' *Works*, IV, p. 381: the same idea is expressed on pp. 392 and 401–2.

same thing. The two are identified in a stage of industrialism in which the problems of production, of the 'hardness of the materials',[1] were of primary importance. In that sense the creation of value is divorced from the exchange process. Value created by labour bestowed in the production process thus acquires the characteristics of an absolute-value concept.

We may pause for a moment to compare Ricardo's approach with what neoclassical theory would have to say in the matter. When cloth falls in price, we would try to discover whether this is due to a changed market situation in the market for cloth or whether it is due to a change in the purchasing power of money. The neoclassical economist would, like Ricardo, ask in what 'sphere' the cause of this price change has been operating, in the sphere of money or in the sphere of cloth. The same question would be raised if the exchange relation between two commodities changed. Neoclassical theory is also interested in determining 'causes'. However, this interest in causes does not prevent it from talking about a fall in the price of cloth and, at the same time, about a rise in the purchasing power of money.

The differences between this and Ricardo's approach is that neoclassical theory does not identify the cause and the measurement of price changes. Neoclassical theory considers price changes as the effects of changes in supply and demand. The measurement of these effects, however, is completely separated from the causal explanation. Price changes are measured in terms of money, that is, in wholly relative terms, and not in terms of a fictitious, invariable standard.[2]

The conflict between a relativistic and an absolute approach to values and prices can also be discerned in chapter xxx of Ricardo's *Principles*. There he rejects emphatically the notion that prices are 'ultimately' regulated by 'the proportion between supply and demand'.[3] He relegates their influence to the short run. He quotes Lauderdale, who states that the value of goods, if they could be measured in terms of a substance with a fixed value, would vary in accordance with the changes in supply and demand and that, in the absence of such an invariable yardstick, they vary with the

[1] David Riesman, *The Lonely Crowd*, p. 115.

[2] It is quite in line with the remnants of the substantive thinking in the Ricardian system that the concept of a 'numéraire' did not occur to him. One may speculate how far this substantive approach to the problem of a standard measure of value was influenced by the fact that money was to Ricardo primarily gold and that paper money did not yet play such an important role as it did toward the end of the nineteenth century, when Walras used the concept of a 'numéraire'.

[3] *Principles*, p. 260.

changes in their own supply and demand and with the changes in the supply-and-demand situation of the goods used as a standard measure.[1] This is a realistic appraisal of market processes. Ricardo, however, restricts its validity to monopolized commodities;

> but the prices of commodities which are subject to competition, and whose quantities may be increased in any moderate degree, will ultimately depend, not on the state of demand and supply, but on the increased or diminished cost of production.[2]

The supply-and-demand theory did not satisfy Ricardo's and his contemporaries' unconscious desire for intellectual security. Lauderdale makes it quite clear that there is nothing fixed and stable behind the fluctuations of exchange values; everything is subject to the haphazard vagaries of supply and demand. This was incompatible with Ricardo's labour theory, which established a stable and intrinsic yardstick for value. The supply-and-demand theory would force him to relinquish this defence against his unconscious anxiety and frustrate his quest for intellectual security; therefore, he had to reject the supply-and-demand theory of prices and exchange values.

There is no difference between neoclassical and classical theory as far as the final long-run result is concerned. Both would agree that the long-run competitive, equilibrium price will be identical with the (lowest possible) cost of production (the minimum average total unit cost of all firms, under purely competitive conditions). The difference is that neoclassical theory envisages this as a result of changes in quantities supplied and demanded. Ricardo, however, does not want to admit this. It is labour 'expended' on the production of goods, and 'it is the cost of production which must ultimately regulate the price of commodities and not . . . the proportion between supply and demand.' There must be an objective force, a basic, stable, ultimate substance behind prices. He obviously rejects the thought that cost of production is nothing stable and is also exposed to the vagaries of supply and demand. They are determined mainly by labour bestowed in production, 'under many circumstances an invariable standard.'

The Invariable Measure in Physics and in Classical Economics

It is of interest to notice that the problem of an invariable standard arose also in physics in respect to the definition and measurement of motion. John Locke had already recognized the relativity of the

[1] *Principles*, p. 261; quoted from the Earl of Lauderdale, *An Inquiry into the Nature and Origin of Public Wealth.*

[2] *Ibid.*, p. 262.

concept of motion and position.[1] Newton was aware of the relativity of motion when he formulated the principle that 'the motions of bodies included in a given space are the same among themselves whether the space is at rest or moves uniformly forward in a straight line.'[2] Thus the scientists of the seventeenth century already knew that, in order to define motion, one has to refer to a yardstick, an object in relation to which a body is in motion and that, without such an object, the fact of motion or of velocity of motion cannot be ascertained. The problem that arose was: Is motion something purely relative, ever changing with changes in the object of comparison, or is there such a thing as absolute motion? Newton believed that 'in the remote regions of the fixed stars or perhaps far beyond them, there may be some body absolutely at rest.' He sought for an absolute, invariable yardstick of motion and velocity, just as Ricardo did in respect to variations in prices and values. Newton finally concluded that space itself may serve as such a yardstick and that space is a 'physical reality, stationary and immovable.' He justified this assumption by the theological argument of the divine omnipresence of God in nature.[3]

Post-Newtonian physicists abandoned this theological deduction, but they retained the idea of an absolute measure of motion and found it in a substance, namely, ether. Thus

> a universe permeated with an invisible medium in which the stars wandered and through which light travelled like vibrations in a bowl of jelly was the end product of Newtonian physics. It provided a mechanical model for all known phenomena of nature, and it provided the fixed frame of reference, the absolute and immovable space, which Newtonian cosmology required.[4]

At the end of the nineteenth century, experiments proved the assumption about ether to be false. In the relativity theory of Einstein, the concepts of absolute space, time, and motion were finally abandoned.

Even this short historical account shows astonishing parallels with the problems of classical economics and the Ricardian search for the 'chimera of an invariable standard of value.'[5] Ricardo tries to interpret the economic system in accordance with the pattern established by mechanical physics. Commodities and their value are treated as matter, and changes in value as matter in motion. Like

[1] *Essay on Human Understanding*; see quotation in L. Barnett, *The Universe and Dr. Einstein*, p. 30.

[2] Barnett, *op. cit.*, pp. 31–32. [3] *Ibid.*, p. 33. [4] *Ibid.*, p. 34.

[5] *Works*, I, xl, quoted from E. Cannan, *A Review of Economic Theory*, p. 174.

Newton and Locke, Ricardo knew that changes in prices are of a relative character and that their magnitude depends on the yardstick used in their measurement. However, like the old physicists, he strives for an invariable standard. Newton resorts ultimately to a theological justification for his assumption of an absolute space. A parallel to this may be found in Adam Smith's deistic approach and in his concept of the invisible hand. Although Adam Smith does not penetrate so deeply as Ricardo into the problems of substance, cause, and standard of value, he laid the foundation for the labour theory of value, and he traced his concept of natural price back to labour (see above, pp. 38 ff.). Natural price, in turn, is tied in with equilibrium and harmony, in so far as everyone who pursues his self-interest will receive a natural and just reward for his efforts. These activities will lead, guided by an invisible hand, to the benefit of the whole. Thus the absoluteness of labour as a yardstick of value has a deistic tinge in the system of the *Wealth of Nations*, as the absoluteness of motion has in the Newtonian system of thought. The Ricardian phase of the history of this problem conforms rather to the 'ether' stage of physics. A substance, ether, is the absolute, invariable standard for the measurement of motion; in Ricardo's thought, it is another 'substantial' concept: labour bestowed in production.

It is important to notice again the dichotomy of concepts which betrays, in physics as well as in political economy, an inner conflict and inner doubts. The conflict is between recognizing the relativity of motion and price changes, on the one hand, and the desire to assume that there is an absolute standard, on the other hand. This desire stems, as repeatedly emphasized, from the need for intellectual security. Scientific analysis and observation discovered the relativity of the phenomena of motion and price fluctuations. However, the human mind cannot entirely accept this discovery, because it exposes man to the anxieties generated by the idea of an ultimately incomprehensible universe without a 'centre of repose and continuance.' Thus physics and economics resort to the use of metaphysical or quasi-metaphysical concepts which permit the assumption of an invariable yardstick, of motion and of economic value.

The Invariable Standard and the Elimination of Capital as a Determinant of Value

Although Ricardo interrelates cause and measure of value, he does not use the same 'substance' for both. Labour bestowed is the main cause of value. It cannot, however, serve as a measure of value. This function can be performed only by a commodity.

However, the commodity which he would have chosen as a standard of value, had it existed, would be one which 'now and at all times required precisely the same quantity of labour to produce it,' which means that, after all, it is labour bestowed which serves as a standard. One cannot say that Ricardo had to choose a commodity instead of labour bestowed as a measure of value, because commodities are real, whereas labour bestowed is a theoretical concept. A commodity which always requires the same quantity of labour for its production is also purely hypothetical. 'Of such a commodity we have no knowledge.'[1] The reason for this distinction between labour as the 'cause' of value and the commodity serving as a standard measure of value is Ricardo's technological and scientific approach to the value problem. Economic value is created during the production process. It is the effect of this process. The postulates of natural science require a distinction between cause and effect. The quantity of value cannot be measured by its cause (labour bestowed); this would obliterate the distinction. On the other hand, cause and effect have to be interrelated and proportional. Therefore, the measure must be of such a nature as to indicate the cause; that means it has to measure only changes in value caused by changes in labour bestowed. Therefore, the measuring commodity has always to be produced by the same quantity of labour.[2]

Wherever Ricardo talks about the 'invariable' measure, he points out that such a measure would show changes in value only if and when the quantity of labour bestowed in production has changed. It is invariable only if it registers nothing but changes in value 'caused' by changes in labour bestowed. The 'measure' of value thus confirms the labour theory, at least in respect to variations in value. It is another case of interpreting *idem per idem*.

In chapter i, Section III, Ricardo concluded that 'if there were any other commodity which was invariable in its value' and if we 'suppose money to be that commodity,' we could trace a rise in exchange value to the fact that 'more labour might be required to obtain' the commodity, whose exchange value has risen.[3]

In the last paragraph of Section III, the way is already prepared for the establishment of an invariable standard finally developed in Section VI.[4]

[1] *Works*, I, p. 17, n. 3; for a similar statement see 'Absolute Value and Exchangeable Value,' *Works*, IV, p. 402.

[2] See *Principles*, chap. i, Sec. III, p. 12: '. . . if a tenth, a fifth, or a fourth [of labour bestowed] has been added or taken away, an effect proportional to the cause will be produced on the relative value of the commodity.'

[3] *Ibid.*, p. 16.

[4] This last paragraph of Sec. III, ed. 3, appeared also in eds. 1 and 2; see

As has been indicated, Ricardo had to eliminate or minimize the influence of capital and profits on value and prices in order to preserve his labour theory of value. For this purpose he uses the concept of an invariable standard. He repeats the tortuous argument by which he eliminates capital as a price determinant in his discussion of the measure of value. The line of thought of chapter i, Section VI ('On an Invariable Measure of Value'), parallels exactly the arguments of Sections III, IV, and V. The same ideas are presented in his last paper on 'Absolute and Exchangeable Value.'[1] In Section III the thought is expressed that a standard is invariable if it is produced with 'the same proportion of fixed and circulating capital, and fixed capital of the same durability' as the commodity whose changes in value are measured by it. Such a standard, if applied to such commodities, would show

> that the utmost limit to which they could permanently rise . . . was proportioned to the additional quantity of labour required for their production; and that unless more labour were required for their production they could not rise in any degree whatever.'[2]

One could say facetiously that Ricardo defined an invariable standard as a measure which will prove his theory of value to be correct.

This line of thought is further elaborated in Section VI, newly inserted in edition 3. There the main problem is to find something which 'should itself be subject to none of the fluctuations to which other commodities are exposed.' This is a logical requirement for an absolute standard of value. However, Ricardo interprets this to mean that it should 'not be subject to require more or less labour for its production.' By setting up this specific requirement, Ricardo begs the question. If a measure is to serve its purpose, one cannot construe it in such a way as to anticipate the results of the process of measurement. First, one has to apply the measure, and then one can state what the results of measuring are. Ricardo proceeds in exactly the opposite way. One could object that it is quite legitimate to try to anticipate the results of measuring. However, one falsifies the process of measuring, if one starts with guessing these results and then constructs the yardstick and the measure in such a way as to make sure that the expected results will follow. This is exactly what Ricardo does.

He proceeds to argue that even if a medium, for instance money,

Works, I, p. 56. Therefore, the new Sec. VI, added in ed. 3, does not really contain an entirely new line of thought. Cf. the thorough historical discussion of Ricardo's treatment of the 'invariable standard' by Sraffa in *Works*, I, xl–xlii.

[1] See below, pp. 93 ff. [2] *Principles*, p. 17.

conformed to this requirement,[1] it would not be a 'perfect standard . . . because it would be subject to relative variations from a rise or fall of wages'—this on account of (*a*) the different proportions of fixed to circulating capital, (*b*) the different degree of durability of the fixed capital, and (*c*) the different time length necessary to bring to the market the measuring and the measured commodities (*Principles*, p. 27). For instance, gold would be 'a perfect measure only for all things produced under the same circumstances, precisely as itself, but not for others.' After then affirming that there is no appropriate measure of value, Ricardo, in respect to the measure, pulls the same trick as that concerning the cause of value; he minimizes the importance of variations in profits and wages:

> Neither gold, then, nor any other commodity, can ever be a perfect measure of value for all things: but I have already remarked that the effect on the relative price of things, from a variation in profits, is comparatively slight; that by far the most important effects are produced by the varying quantities of labour required for production; and, therefore if we suppose this important cause of variation removed from the production of gold, we shall probably possess as near an approximation to a standard measure of value as can be theoretically conceived.[2]

The inconvenient 'other cause', the rise or fall of wages (and profits), is thus removed.

Another method of accomplishing the same result is based on the idea that any commodity can serve as a standard measure for other commodities produced under the same circumstances. Ricardo wants to use gold as a standard measure. Therefore, he suggests:

> May not gold be considered as a commodity produced with such proportions of the two kinds of capital as approach nearest to the average quantity employed in the production of most commodities?[3]

This assumption enables Ricardo to use gold as a 'standard so nearly approaching to an invariable one' and thus to measure the alterations in value of commodities, 'without embarrassing myself on every occasion with the consideration of the possible alterations in the value of the medium.'[4]

By constructing such a standard, Ricardo manages to exclude the

[1] Of not being subject to fluctuations in value because it always requires the same amount of labour for its production; this is the only requirement mentioned in eds. 1–2, *Works*, I, xliii, 17, n. 3, 43, n. 5, 63.

[2] *Principles*, chap. i, Sec. VI, p. 28. [3] *Ibid.*, p. 29. [4] *Ibid.*, p. 29.

influence of changes in the rate of profit on the value of the measured commodities. When the rate of profit falls, the value of the standard measure (of gold) will also fall.[1] In this case the fall in the rate of profits will have 'no effect' on the value of the measured commodities, because the standard by which this change in value is measured has also fallen in value. The change in the rate of profits, whether it rises or falls, will equally affect the standard measure and the measured commodities, the measuring rod and the measured. Therefore, no change in the value of the measured commodities will be registered by the yardstick of measurement. In the measuring commodity itself no change in value through the change in the rate of profits can be noticed. It is itself the yardstick; there is no other measure by which its own change in value could be measured. Hence the measuring commodity, thus defined, will register only changes in the value of the measured commodities caused by a change in the quantity of labour bestowed. We can now easily understand why Ricardo could not abandon the dichotomy of cause and measure of value. If he had unified his system to the extent of using labour bestowed in production as cause and measure of value, he would have had to admit (as he has obliquely done) that value and prices do not always change in accordance with this standard. The use of fixed capital and the time needed for roundabout methods of production distort values in comparison with pure 'labour-bestowed' values. What he would gain in unity, on the one hand, he would lose, on the other hand, by having to admit exceptions to the law of value. By distinguishing between cause and measure, he makes possible the choice of a measure which establishes that labour bestowed is the cause of changes in value. Thus the dichotomy is necessary to establish a higher degree of unity, which, at the same time, preserves the ethical, technological, and scientific bases of his system.

In order to arrive at this result, so obviously desirable from his point of view, Ricardo had to go through three stages of assumptions, in each of them eliminating certain disturbing facts. The first step consisted in assuming that the standard is always produced with the same quantity of labour: labour bestowed on it is assumed to be constant. Second, the effect of variations in profits on relative prices is assumed to be 'comparatively slight.' Third, gold is assumed to be produced with the 'average' quantity and proportion of fixed and variable capital. One could call this piling-up of assumptions of increasing abstractness the method of 'gradual alienation' from reality, in contrast to the method of 'gradual approximation.' In

[1] See *Principles*, chap. i, Sec. IV.

order to arrive at the desired explanation of value, one obstacle after another is minimized or removed by assumption.

A fourth abstracting assumption is contained in the use of the term 'average' in relation to the composition of capital. Ricardo wants to exclude the influence of capital and profits as price determinants; this he could accomplish only by a measure produced with the same composition of capital as the measured commodities. To assume, however, that the average composition is the same composition implies another fiction.[1] The mathematical average is an abstract figure with no counterpart in reality. Its very essence consists in being something which integrates mathematically a great many actual numbers without being identical with any one of them. Ricardo, however, has to resort to the assumption that the average is equal to the majority of actual cases; he has to identify the average with a statistical 'cluster' or mode, in order to arrive at the desired results.

Ricardo's Last Paper

In his paper on 'Absolute Value and Exchangeable Value' the emphasis shifted from the question of the foundation and cause of value to the problem of the measure. Whereas the *Principles* shows a greater explicit emphasis on exchange values, the last paper openly strives for an absolute-value concept, which was rather covertly treated in the *Principles*.[2] We shall briefly discuss those points of the last paper which are related to our previous interpretation of Ricardo's theory of value.

After repeating the requirements of a measure of value, namely, that it should have value and that it should be invariable, Ricardo rejects the standards suggested by Malthus, Torrens, James Mill, and McCulloch. Malthus' standard, the pay for a day's labour, is rejected for the same reasons as Adam Smith's labour commanded in exchange is rejected in the *Principles*—because its value is not invariable.

Then Ricardo proceeds to discuss three cases in which only labour bestowed would determine relative values: (*a*) 'If all commodities were produced with labour alone and brought to market immediately after having one day's labour bestowed on them' (p. 363). In this case the influence of capital on relative values is eliminated directly through assuming its non-existence. Labour bestowed and labour commanded would be equal. (*b*) 'If *all* commodities

[1] In his last paper, Ricardo uses the terms 'medium' and 'mean' in the same context (*Works*, IV, pp. 372, 405).

[2] *Works*, I, xlvi. All following quotations without additional notation are from *Works*, IV, pp. 357–412.

required a year's time before they were in a state to be brought to the market, and required the continued labour of men to produce them during that time' (p. 364). (*c*) 'If all commodities required 2 years' time before they could be brought to market' (p. 364). In these two cases Ricardo interprets capital as a function of the time it takes to produce goods and to make them ready for sale. Capital is thus reduced to a function of time in the same way as, in physics, motion becomes a function of space and time.

Ricardo neutralizes the influence of capital on value by assuming the use of equal 'capitals' in all lines of production. With production periods of equal length, changes in profits (and in wages) would affect all goods alike; therefore, a change in the rate of profits would *not* change relative values. 'Consequently any commodity which continues always to require the same quantity of labour to produce it will be a perfect measure of value' (p. 367).

This is Ricardo's old line of thought, already expressed in edition 1 of the *Principles*. Actually, labour bestowed becomes here not only the substance and cause, but also the measure of value; it is only thinly hidden by the 'veil of Maya' composed of commodities and their prices. Any change in labour bestowed will cause changes in relative values, which can be measured by the invariable quantity of labour bestowed on the measuring commodity.

Again, Ricardo admits, but minimizes at the same time, the 'other cause' of changes in value. 'Though this is by far the greatest cause, it is not strictly the only one' (p. 367). The other cause is again called 'variations in the value of labour' and is belittled by the statement that it is comparatively of rare occurrence, 'but cannot be omitted in this important enquiry' (p. 368).[1]

[1] It is of psychological interest that in his draft of the paper Ricardo repeated, with only slight variations, the paragraph in which he made this admission (see pp. 367–68). According to Sraffa, the second version 'was evidently intended as an alternative to the preceding one' (*ibid.*, p. 368, n. 1). This may have been the conscious intention of Ricardo. However, the draft contained many insertions and deletions noted by Sraffa; it is therefore surprising that Ricardo did not delete one of the two paragraphs duplicating each other.

In his study on Leonardo da Vinci, Freud points to a passage in the former's diaries referring to his expenses at the funeral of his father, in which the hour of the father's death is mentioned twice. Freud calls such a repetition a 'perseveration' and interprets it as the symptom of an unsuccessful repression of an emotion. Leonardo had an ambivalent attitude toward his father, loving and emulating him as well as hating him unconsciously. The repetition of the hour of his death expresses the conflicting feelings of Leonardo (see S. Freud, *Leonardo da Vinci*, pp. 95 ff.).

It may be that Ricardo's repetition has a similar emotional background. In the repeated paragraph Ricardo had to admit an exception to his theory, an admission which was obnoxious to him. The exception meant that, after all, profits

Finally, the difficulty which was eliminated by the previously discussed assumptions is tackled. Commodities are produced in production periods of different length, for which the capitalist has to make advances to the labourer (pp. 368–70). The distinction between the *Principles* and this last paper by Ricardo is that, in the latter, differences in the composition and durability of capital are reduced to differences in production time, thereby homogenizing these differences and reducing them to a common quantitative denominator. A commodity chosen as measure

> 'is not a commodity produced by labour alone, nor a commodity whose value consists of profits alone, but one which may fairly be considered as the medium between these two extremes, and as agreeing more nearly with the circumstances under which the greater number of commodities are produced . . .' [p. 372].

Again, the same device is used as in chapter i; after the differences in the time length of the production periods are admitted, they are eliminated immediately by assuming that the greater number of commodities are produced more or less in the same time; again the commodity used as measure and yardstick of value is assumed to be produced during the same time as the greater number of commodities: the average—the medium between extremes—is identified with the cluster or mode—the majority of cases; again all this leads to the conclusion that the measure will show changes in value mainly in proportion to the increased or diminished difficulty of production, that is, in proportion to changes in the quantity of labour bestowed; in this case ' . . . price and value would be synonymous' (p. 373).

However, Ricardo is enough of a logician to realize that even the use of his average, mean, or medium standard measure will not entirely exclude the influence of capital and profits on relative values or prices. 'If the measure was perfect it ought not to vary at all' (p. 373) from a rise in labour, i.e., a fall in the rate of profits; a perfect measure is one which registers only changes in value proportionate to changes in labour bestowed, that is, one which con-

do have an influence on prices. This implies that rewards do not conform to effort in a capitalist economy and that it is not possible to explain prices simply by the labour-bestowed principle. All this reflects an ambivalent attitude of Ricardo toward his theory and toward the capitalist system which may have found expression in this and in other 'perseverations'. Anybody who has followed our argument will be unable to overlook Ricardo's 'perseverance' on the intricacies of his value theory. The same ideas are rehashed, redigested, repeated over and over again, as if to silence the author's own doubts. Thus 'perseveration' not only is found in the above paragraphs but is a characteristic of all Ricardo's writings.

firm's Ricardo's theory. Yet his measure is not perfect; therefore, it will show changes in value 'caused' by changes in wages and profits.

If he had chosen a measure with extreme composition of capital: 10 per cent profit and 90 per cent labour; or 40 per cent profit and 60 per cent labour, the variations in value from a change in wages and profits would be small in the first case and much larger in the second case.

> These are the two extremes, and it is evident that by choosing a mean the variation in commodities on account of a rise or fall in wages would be much less than if we took either of the extremes (p. 373).

Here Ricardo states quite explicitly that the measure is chosen because it minimizes the influence on values of any other cause than changes in productivity of labour. His line of reasoning runs from the postulate of faith that labour bestowed determines value and its changes, to the choice of a measure which will prove this assumption.

Ricardo's summary in the draft of his last paper (on pp. 379–97) contains a final formulation of all his ideas on the subject. It is psychologically interesting to notice how Ricardo, although he seems to intend merely a summary, struggles again and again with the same problem, as if to convince himself and as if, by repeating and refining his quasi-magic formulas, he tried to hold down his own inner doubts about their validity. Points 4–6 discuss the requirements of a 'measure'. The analogies are taken from the natural sciences. Ricardo regards value as something analogous to length, like a physical characteristic of a thing, like a natural quality measurable in the same way as length, for example, with the help of a natural criterion. (It is assumed that nature provides criteria for invariability.) However, 'in the measure of value we have no such criterion' (p. 380). We have plenty of measures to measure the relative value of commodities at the same time, but none to measure changes in value over time (point 6, p. 381). If we cannot have an absolutely uniform measure, how can we find the best approximation (point 7)? We do have labour as a standard, because the average strength of 100 or 10,000 men is nearly the same all the time (point 8). Again, Ricardo thinks of the cause of value in physical terms. Strength of man is a datum of nature comparable to the force of mechanics. 'Having discovered this standard we are in possession of a uniform measure of value as well as a uniform measure of length' (point 9, p. 382). Value is then translated into length or weight by coordinating 1,000 yards of cloth or 100 ounces of gold to the labour of 80 men, who produced them. Yards and ounces are 'natural' measures. By relating them to a certain 'quantity of labour' (in terms of men), the impression of a natural, invariable yardstick of value is created. The 'yards' and 'ounces' are identified with labour bestowed (labour of 80 men). Gold and cloth can serve as a measure because they are nothing but an embodiment of labour. This standard would measure 'absolute value directly in proportion to the quantity of labour bestowed upon' commodities. Here the interrelation between labour bestowed as a cause and measure and as an absolute-value concept is clearly expressed.

But there is one difficulty: the difference in the time length of the production period. Absolute value determined by labour bestowed cannot be measured by a commodity serving as standard measure unless its production period is of the same length as the one of the measured commodity. 'A commodity that requires the labour of 100 men for one year is not precisely double the value of a commodity that requires the labour of 100 men for 6 months . . .' (p. 382). 'A commodity produced in two years is worth more than twice a commodity produced with an equal quantity of labour in one year . . .' (p. 383), because the capitalist has to receive a 'fair remuneration of profits' (p. 384) for the longer period for which he advances capital. Three commodities on which the same actual quantity of labour has been bestowed would thus have different values according to the length of the period during which labour is employed in their production and according to the length of the period which passes before they are brought to market and sold.[1]

In order to eliminate these differences and to confine changes in value to those 'caused' by changes in labour bestowed, Ricardo suggests that a commodity be used as measure which is produced and brought to market in a year, and that

> the commodity to be measured must be valued annually, and must not be valued by the quantity of labour actually employed on the commodity, but by the quantity which its value could employ if devoted to the production of the commodity which is the measure' [pp. 385–86].

This new formulation of the measure of value contains the following assumptions:

(*a*) If the production period of the measuring commodity is one year, it cannot measure the value of the measured commodity at the end of a shorter or longer period, but only at the end of the same period, namely, one year.

[1] The two are not necessarily identical, for example, in the case of wine stored for ageing.

(*b*) The value of the measured commodity after one year is not determined by the quantity of labour bestowed on it during this year but by the quantity of labour bestowed on the measuring commodity during one year.

Ricardo uses as an example three cases (p. 385):

Commodity 1: a commodity with a production period of one year is produced with £100 worth of labour during the first year and and sold at the end of this year for £100 plus 10 per cent profit =£110. During the second year, the same process is repeated, and the total value at the end of 2 years is £220.

Commodity 2: a commodity has a production period of two years. During the first year, £100 are invested, which, plus 10 per cent profits, are worth £110 at the end of the first year. This amount cannot be realized at the end of the first year and remains invested; at the end of the second year the entire value of the commodity is £110 plus 10 per cent =£121 plus another £100 invested during the second year at 10 per cent: total value=£231.

Commodity 3: a commodity is produced in one year with an investment of £200; at the end of the year it is worth £200 plus 10 per cent profit=£220. The commodity may be wine which is kept in the cellar for another year: at the end of the second year, its value is £220 plus 10 per cent profit=£242. Thus there are three commodities produced with the same quantities of labour but of different value because of the different length of the production periods.

At the end of the first year, commodity 3 is worth £220, and each of commodities 1 and 2 is worth £110. Ricardo says that their values are in conformity with the labour bestowed on them during that year (£200 worth of labour on commodity 3, and £100 worth of labour on commodities 1 and 2, respectively, plus 10 per cent profit).

During the second year the measuring procedure should be as follows in respect to commodity 2: the amount actually invested (which, for Ricardo, is either labour or capital) is £110 plus £100, a total of £210. This, at 10 per cent profit, results in a value of £231. This is the meaning of his principle: 'The commodity must be valued annually' not for two years, but for each year separately, because the production period of the measuring commodity is one year. And it must be valued by the quantity of labour which its value could employ if devoted to the production of the measure. That is £210, because the measure is produced and brought to the market in one year and the amount invested during this one year (the second year) is £210.

At this point the intricacy of Ricardo's thinking has reached its apex. Folklore believes that people have an unconscious premonition of their own deaths. It seems that Ricardo may have had an unconscious feeling like that when he wrote this last paper and that he gathered his last strength to defeat, once and for all, the enemy of his system: capital and profits as a factor disturbing the smooth elegance and consistency of his labour-bestowed theory of value. He points out and admits this disturbing influence; but again he reinterprets it and reduces it to fit into his theory with the help of a standard measure which will eliminate the obstacle. The basic idea is again the same as in the *Principles* (especially chap. i, Sec. VI): to reduce the multiplicity of conditions of production caused by the disturbing variety of types of capital, first by interpreting them as differences in length of time necessary to produce the goods and to bring them to market; second, by equalizing the conditions of production of the measuring and the measured commodity. As formulated a second time:

> ... The commodity valued must be reduced to circumstances precisely similar (with respect to time of production) to those of the commodity in which the valuation is made. ... Though it is not strictly right to say that these two commodities are valuable in proportion to the quantity of labour actually bestowed on them, would it not be correct to say that the value of wine after two years was in proportion to the labour which might have been employed on wine or on some other commodity if it had been brought to the market after the first year of its production ... [pp. 386–87].

Thus if commodity A is brought to the market after two years and its value is measured by commodity B, brought to the market after one year, the two commodities would have the same value after the first year. If the capital plus profits of commodity B were reinvested for another year, they would have the same value after the second year as commodity A. In reality, cloth and wine produced with the same amount of capital (or labour) will, when finally sold, have different prices. Ricardo, however, equalizes them by measuring their value annually for each year separately; thus the values will be equal at the end of each year. The difference in values and prices is caused by the different time periods of production. Ricardo eliminates this difference by equalizing the time periods through the method of annual measuring.

Throughout this entire discussion, he also completely identifies capital and labour, not only by calling the former 'accumulated labour', but also by measuring both in terms of money. The same sum of £100 invested each year means that the same quantity of labour is employed each year. This is based on the assumption that wages are given data, constant over time. However, it obliterates completely the difference between fixed and circulating capital and the different durabilities of capital, so important in the *Principles* (see chap. i, Secs. III, IV, V, VI). The terms 'fixed' and 'circulating capital' are not used at all in this last paper. There they are reduced to differences in the length of the production period.

This procedure enables Ricardo to translate durable capital into labour with the greatest of ease:

> . . . An oak which is the growth of 100 years in like manner has perhaps from first to last only one day's labour bestowed upon it, but its value depends on the accumulations of capital by the compound profits on the one day's labour and the quantity of labour which such accumulated capital would from year to year have employed . . . [p. 388].

This reasoning is persuasive in so far as the 'capital' sunk into this tree or into any other fixed capital good must bear the interest that it would have earned in any other investment; otherwise, the investor would not have any incentive to invest and to tie it up in this particular fixture. Ricardo understands this very well, and this idea is implied in the entire argument (pp. 383–90). His peculiarity, however, is that he does not talk about 'capital invested' but about 'one day's labour bestowed' and that he explains the accumulation of value and profits from year to year by a fictitious 'quantity of labour' which such accumulated capital would have employed from year to year. Profits are explained by the potential employment of labour, and thus the obnoxious disturbing factors—capital and profits—are again reduced to labour. We have here the root of a Marxian thought, namely, that it is labour which creates profits. This in spite of the frequent allusions to profits as a necessary incentive to enterprise—again a clear manifestation of Ricardian ambivalence.

Finally, the argument ends with the same conclusions as in the *Principles*:

> As it is desirable that we should have the measure of value which it is acknowledged cannot be accurate for all objects, to which shall we give the preference? . . . But if as is most certain a much greater proportion of the commodities which are the objects of exchange amongst men are produced under circumstances similar to those under which gold and cloth are produced, and are the result of labour and capital applied for a *year*, then gold or cloth is the most proper measure of value (while they require precisely the same quantity of labour and capital to produce them) and to that

measure should we always refer when we are speaking of the rise or fall in the absolute value of all other things [pp. 389–90].

We have analysed this method before: by establishing the fiction of a 'majority' composition of capital and a 'majority' length of a production period, and by choosing as a measure a commodity produced under these 'majority' conditions, Ricardo eliminates any cause of changes in value except changes in labour bestowed. This value whose change is caused solely by labour bestowed is an absolute-value concept. It saves the ethical, technological, and mechanical foundations and the logical unity of the theory. Labour bestowed emerges as the secure anchoring point of economic value.[1]

[1] We do not want to extend this discussion beyond the point necessary to make our interpretation plausible. However, in the remaining pages of the draft, Ricardo clearly and explicitly defends the concept of absolute value against all attacks. He had already used the concept in the *Principles*, ed. 1 (*Works*, I, xlvi, pp. 21, 63) and in ed. 3, where he called it 'real value' (*ibid.*, I, xlvi, pp. 42–43), as well as in his letters (*ibid.*, I, xlvi, n. 3). In the draft of his last paper it appears on p. 382: 'Commodities would then have an absolute value directly in proportion to the quantity of labour bestowed upon them.' On p. 394 he takes up the discussion with Col. Torrens (see p. 375 and above, pp. 83 ff.), and distinguishes between relative value and 'real' value, i.e., absolute value. He definitely states that 'real' value may alter, although relative values may stay the same (p. 394). The same distinction is made in the sentence: 'But if I asked him whether their value, leaving out the word exchangeable, had altered he would be puzzled for an answer' (p. 395). Here, Ricardo criticizes Torrens again for considering value as a purely relativistic concept and for not providing any measure which would detect only absolute-value changes.

In sheets *a* and *b*, as well as in the fragmentary final drafts of this last paper (*Works*, IV, pp. 360, 396 ff.), absolute value is frequently mentioned. 'It is a great desideratum in Political Economy to have a perfect measure of absolute value' (the 'absolute' is inserted, *Works*, IV, p. 396, n. 1). 'By exchangeable value is meant the power which a commodity has of commanding any given quantity of another commodity without any reference whatever to its absolute value' (p. 398). 'In the same manner, if we had a perfect measure of values, itself being neither liable to increase or diminish in value, we should by its means be able to ascertain the real as well as the proportional [identified with 'exchangeable' on p. 398] variations in other things' (p. 400). Thus there cannot be the slightest doubt that Ricardo wanted to establish an absolute-value concept.

Chapter IX

RICARDO ON RENT

THE aim of the Ricardian theory of rent is clearly announced in the first paragraph of his chapter on rent:

> It remains, however, to be considered, whether the appropriation of land and the consequent creation of rent, will occasion any variation in the relative value of commodities independently of the quantity of labour necessary to production.[1]

The way in which Ricardo formulates his problem already indicates his main concern: to save the labour theory of value from the possibility of being invalidated by the fact that land has been appropriated and that rent had to be paid. Again, he is out to disprove Adam Smith's theory of natural price, which acknowledges rent as a component of price. Ricardo's answer was obviously in the negative; it had to be in the negative to save labour as the only determinant of value.[2] The conclusion is drawn a few pages later:

> If the high price of corn were the effect, and not the cause of rent, price would be proportionally influenced as rents were high or low, and rent would be a component part of price. But that corn which is produced by the greatest quantity of labour is the regulator of the price of corn; and rent does not and cannot enter in the least degree as a component part of its price. Adam Smith, therefore, cannot be correct in supposing that the original rule which regulated the exchangeable value of commodities, namely, the comparative quantity of labour by which they were produced, can be at all altered by the appropriation of land and the payment of rent. Raw material enters into the composition of most commodities, but the value of that raw material, as well as corn, is regulated by the productiveness of the portion of capital last employed on the

[1] *Principles*, chap. ii, pp. 33 ff. See also his statement about 'getting rid of rent' in the letter to McCulloch, June 13, 1820, No. XV, p. 72, *Works*, I, viii, p. 194 and I, xxiii.

[2] G. Myrdal, *The Political Element in the Development of Economic Theory*, p. 63.

land and paying no rent; and therefore rent is not a component part of the price of commodities.[1]

Quod erat demonstrandum. The preceding quotation contains the essence of Ricardo's theory of rent as far as it concerns us here; it is too well known to bear repetition. It will be sufficient to stress the method by which Ricardo eliminates rent as a determinant of price.

(*a*) The way Ricardo defines rent already indicates the result of his argument. If 'rent is that portion of the produce of the earth which is paid to the landlord for the use of the original and indestructible powers of the soil,'[2] it is a payment for fertility only. As there are lands of different fertility, differential rents must arise, except for the owners of the marginal, least fertile lands. In reality, there is no such thing as rent as defined by Ricardo. The actual payment for the use of land will almost always include a payment for capital improvements; and in economic life and in the minds of people these various elements of rent are never distinguished or separated. For those who thus have to pay rent for the use of land, including its improvements, etc., rent is a cost item, and they will try to recover it in the prices of their products. This applies also to the tenant of marginal lands, who does not pay any rent in the Ricardian sense but who has among his costs an item popularly called 'rent.'

(*b*) At first, Ricardo mentions capital and labour to be employed,[3] but he conveniently omits capital later on: '. . . for rent invariably proceeds from the employment of an additional quantity of labour with a proportionally less return.' And 'the exchangeable value of commodities . . . is always regulated . . . by the greater quantity of labour necessarily bestowed on their production by those who have no such [peculiarly favourable] facilities'; and, finally:

> the reason, then, why raw produce rises in comparative value is because more labour is employed in the production of the last portion obtained, and not because a rent is paid to the landlord. The value of corn is regulated by the quantity of labour bestowed on its production on that quality of land, or with that portion of capital, which pays no rent.[4]

The frequent repetition of the term 'labour' creates the impression

[1] *Principles*, pp. 40–41. [2] *Ibid.*, p. 33.

[3] '. . . For rent is always the difference between the produce obtained by the employment of two equal quantities of capital and labour' (*Principles*, p. 36).

[4] *Ibid.*, p. 38.

that it is the increased amount of labour bestowed which causes the price of corn to rise, conveniently omitting the influence of capital.

(*c*) If one accepts Ricardo's definition, this theory of rent cannot be denied to have validity. Modern economic analysis has merely enlarged the concept of rent to include any excess over and above the minimum-of-supply price of any factor units.[1] The main difference, however, between the Ricardian and the modern concept of rent is the formulation. Modern theory explains it in terms of supply and demand. Rent arises because expanding demand will, in the long run, call forth an increase in supply, which, in return, makes necessary the cultivation of inferior lands; this creates rent for the more fertile lands. The 'cause' of this rent is the large demand in proportion to the scarcity of fertile lands. Ricardo, however, formulates the same set of facts in terms of the productivity of labour; it is the quantity of labour used in cultivation which determines the price of the product; marginal lands require more labour, and, therefore, the product has a higher value.[2]

Thus it is the quantity of labour used to produce the marginal corn on the least fertile land which determines the price of corn, and labour emerges again with flying colours as the only determinant of value.

[1] Joan Robinson, *The Economics of Imperfect Competition*, p. 102.

[2] This difference in formulation opens up interesting psychocultural vistas. The difference between the 'subjective' and the 'objective' value theory becomes quite clear. The neoclassical school approaches market phenomena from the point of view of demand; that is, from the point of view of individual utility; Ricardo does so from the point of view of production interpreted as a physical, mechanistic process. Ricardo looks for a 'moving force' which 'causes' prices, and he finds it in labour. Therefore, in his theory of rent, he selects labour from the many variables involved and considers it as the 'cause' of prices. This procedure is, from a purely logical point of view, as legitimate as considering demand as the 'moving force' or *prima causa*. It cannot be denied that more labour is used on marginal than on intra-marginal lands and that, therefore, prices are driven up. The fact that greater demand makes the charging of higher price possible is not in conflict with Ricardo's statement. It merely does not interest him, because he wants, consciously or unconsciously, to preserve the labour theory of value. Purely from the point of view of causal analysis, there is no logical reason to consider even consumers' demand or individual utility as a 'last' or 'prime' cause; one could trace it back to cultural standards, habits, income distribution, advertising, etc. Modern economic analysis is not interested in the 'causes' of utility; utility is taken as 'given' and as the ultimate cause of value. The choice of the starting-point in a chain of causation thus proves to be a judgment of value which reflects the attitude of the time.

Part IV

Male and Female Symbolism in the Thought of Ricardo, Malthus, Engels, and Marx

Chapter X

RICARDIAN DYNAMICS

A DISCUSSION of Ricardian dynamic theory and his treatment of questions of economic development is made difficult by the fact that his theory of rent is part of his static theory of value and, at the same time, the basis of his dynamics. As far as the theory of rent arrives at the conclusion that it is again labour bestowed on marginal land which determines the price of agricultural products, it fits into Ricardo's system and eliminates land and rent as determinants of value. As far as his theory of rent is based on the law of diminishing returns, it forms the basis of his theory of economic development. Therefore, we have discussed the value aspects of his theory of rent in Part III, which deals with value theory, and have separated it from the discussion of its dynamic aspects. A further difficulty arises from our interpretation of Ricardian and Malthusian long-run dynamics. We have found striking interrelations between the treatment of the earth, the mother and the female in mythology and symbolic language, on the one hand, and in nineteenth-century economic thought, on the other. This requires an excursion into mythology and symbolic language. Furthermore, Ricardo's ideas about dynamics tie in closely with those of Malthus. And both can be better understood if contrasted with the discussion of similar problems by Engels and Marx. Therefore, this part will start with an exposition of Ricardo's dynamic theories of wages and profits and then branch out into some discussion of male and female symbolism, in order to revert again to the thought of Ricardo and Malthus and compare it with ideas of Engels and Marx.

The Law of Diminishing Returns

Halévy has stated that 'there is a diametrical opposition in Ricardo between the fundamental principles of economic statics and dynamics.'[1] With this statement he has put his finger on another

[1] E. Halévy, *The Growth of Philosophical Radicalism*, p. 329.

one of Ricardo's dichotomies. His dynamic approach shows clearly his pessimism in respect to the final results of capitalist development.[1] That Ricardo was ambivalent toward the market system, as we have already discovered in the analysis of his static theory of value, is confirmed when we analyse his ideas about long-run developments. Halévy points out the difference between the optimism of Ricardian statics and the pessimism of his dynamic laws of population, wages, and profits. We have shown that even in his static value theory an aggressive pessimism is hidden under the surface of his explicit optimistic reasoning.[2] The conflict pointed out by Halévy is just another instance of Ricardian dialectical ambivalence which can be detected throughout his entire system.

Ricardo presented his dynamic theory in chapters ii, v, and vi of the *Principles*.[3] In his theory of rent as expounded in chapter ii, his main purpose was to show that the appropriation of land does not invalidate his general law of value. In this respect the theory of rent fits into his relatively 'optimistic' static theory. The pessimistic aspect of his theory of rent is represented by the law of diminishing returns. It implies that rent arises 'because land is not unlimited in quantity, and uniform in quality, and because, in the progress of population, land of an inferior quality, or less advantageously situated, is called into cultivation.'[4] It is the Malthusian idea of the niggardliness of nature which underlies Ricardo's theory of rent:

> The labour of nature is paid, not because she does much, but because she does little. In proportion as she becomes niggardly in her gifts she exacts a greater price for her work.[5]

This idea is related to the biblical approach to work. 'Man would do more by the sweat of his brow and nature perform less' as long as there is a limited supply of natural resources and 'successive qualities were brought into use.'

Rent is a consequence of the difficulty of providing food for an increasing population, and it increases directly 'as the disposable land decreases in its productive powers.' It arises 'in consequence of the diminished returns obtained by those who employ fresh labour and stock on the less fertile land.'[6]

1 *The Growth of Philosophical Radicalism*, pp. 319 and 329 ff.

2 His value theory is optimistic in so far as it arrives at an ethical justification of prices and values based on the commensurability of reward and effort. In his views on the beneficial effects of free trade, Ricardo is even more optimistic.

3 Quoted again in the following from the 'Everyman's' (3rd) ed.

4 *Principles*, chap. ii, p. 35.

5 *Ibid.*, p. 39, n. 1.

6 *Ibid.*, pp. 38, 39, 40.

The Theory of Wages

The pessimistic conclusions from this law in respect to long-run development are drawn in chapters v and vi. In chapter v, Ricardo begins with the distinction between the natural and the market price of labour. The natural price—a long-run concept—is more real, more permanent, and more just than the market price and represents the underlying reality, measurable in homogeneous quantities of labour bestowed; the market price is an ephemeral surface phenomenon. The idea that there is a natural price of labour is based on the subsistence theory of wages.[1] It is 'that price which is necessary to enable the labourers . . . to subsist and to perpetuate their race without either increase or diminution.'[2] According to the supply-and-demand situation on the labour market, the actual market price may be either higher or lower than the natural price. Ricardo is pessimistic in respect to the long-run natural price of labour:

> When the market price of labour is below its natural price, the condition of the labourers is most wretched: then poverty deprives them of those comforts which custom renders absolute necessaries. It is only after their privations have reduced their number, or the demand for labour has increased that the market price of labour will rise to its natural price, and that the labourer will have the moderate comforts which the natural rate of wages will afford.[3]

Even the natural rate of wages procures for the labourers only moderate comforts. The market rate of wages will rise with capital accumulation and with every improvement in society. But the natural wage will rise only if 'the natural price of those necessaries on which the wages of labour are expended' rises.[4] This implies that, in the long run, the real wages of labour, the amount of goods and services the worker can purchase with his wages, will not rise at all. The natural wage will rise only if wage goods become more expensive; this will merely enable the worker to purchase the same amount of subsistence as before.

Capital accumulation will raise the wages of labour only if there is an abundance of fertile lands. When population increases and land of worse quality is put into cultivation, surplus production, capital accumulation, and, thereby, the demand for labour will diminish because of the law of diminishing returns. The population begins to press against the means of subsistence.

[1] See above, pp. 65 ff.
[2] *Principles*, chap. v, p. 52.
[3] *Ibid.*, p. 53.
Ibid., p. 54.

In this case, even more rapid accumulation of capital is no remedy. Because of the law of diminishing returns, all classes would become equally poor.[1] Thus the only remedy is that

> in all countries the labouring classes should have a taste for comforts and enjoyments, and that they should be stimulated by all legal means in their exertions to procure them.[2]

However, 'in the natural advance of society the wages of labour will have a tendency to fall, as far as they are regulated by supply and demand.'[3] The law of diminishing returns brings about this result. The population and, with it, 'the supply of labourers will continue at the same rate whilst the demand for them will increase at a slower rate.'[4] The final result will be that capital becomes 'stationary when wages also would become stationary and be only sufficient to keep up the members of the actual population.' This sad situation is made worse by the fact that, although money wages will rise because of rising prices of necessities and wage goods, real wages will fall because the money wages 'would not rise sufficiently to enable the labourer to purchase as many comforts and necessaries as he did before.'[5] To add insult to injury:

> notwithstanding . . . that the labourer would be really worse paid, yet this increase in his [money] wages would necessarily diminish the profits of the manufacturer,'[6]

because wages and profits vary inversely. The only class which benefits from this situation is the landlords. Rents will rise, not only in terms of money, but also in real terms. The landlord will receive a larger share of the total product of his land, that is, of corn; and corn will, because of the law of rent, have risen in exchange value; therefore, his higher corn rent will exchange for a greater quantity of other goods.

In the example which Ricardo uses to illustrate these developments he makes a number of assumptions: (*a*) he assumes that three quarters of corn are the minimum of subsistence of a labourer; (*b*) that only the price of corn increases, whereas the prices of other wage goods remain constant; and (*c*) that wages will rise exactly in proportion to the rise in the price of corn.[7]

Under these assumptions the money wage would rise, but the real wage, 'the enjoyments', would remain constant. Later, he assumes that the prices of other wage goods like corn will rise only

[1] *Principles*, p. 56. [2] *Ibid.*, p. 57. [3] *Ibid.*
[4] *Ibid.* [5] *Ibid.* [6] *Ibid.*, p. 58.
[7] *Ibid.*, pp. 58–59.

in proportion as raw produce, i.e., corn, enters into their composition. In this case the real wages would actually decline. It is obvious that all these assumptions are so chosen as to bear out Ricardo's pessimistic outlook for the long run. He is pessimistic to the extent that he believes that sooner or later capital accumulation will come to a stop and wages will become stationary on a level of bare subsistence.

The Theory of Profits

Ricardo's predictions as to the long-run trend of profits (*Principles*, chap. vi) moves along the same lines as his theory of wages. This chapter contains a static theory and a theory of long-run economic development. The static theory of profits harks back to the assumption of chapter i of the *Principles*, that profits vary inversely with wages. The basic distinction between real, natural, constant, necessary prices and profits, on the one hand, and accidental variations, on the other, is repeated.[1]

Ricardo develops here the idea of the equilibrating function of profits which was taken over by neoclassical theory. Profits have the function of driving the accidental market prices toward the natural or necessary price. This natural and necessary price is a long-run equilibrium price. It is determined by the quantity of labour bestowed on the production of the commodity. The accidental price is determined by the short-run supply-and-demand situation. Thus the long-run price assumes here the character of something morally justifiable, because it corresponds to labour effort. As we shall see in our analysis of the Marshallian system, the idea of the long-run equilibrium price has never entirely lost this ethical tinge.

Profits also receive a beneficial colouring. They are the instrument by which the natural and necessary price level is brought about. They help in establishing a desirable situation, which, in turn, makes profits functional and legitimate. High prices cause high profits and

> attract capital to that trade; and as soon as the requisite funds are supplied, and the quantity of the commodity is duly increased, its price will fall, and the profits of the trade will conform to the general level. . . . It is through the inequality of profits that capital is moved from one employment to another.[2]

The general level is the one characterized by natural and necessary prices. In Marshallian language it is the long-run, normal equilibrium level, with normal prices and normal profits. Although

[1] *Ibid.*, chap. vi, pp. 67, n. 1, and 70.

[2] *Ibid.*, p. 70.

Ricardo does not use the term 'equilibrium' in this context,[1] the basic idea of long-run equilibrium is definitely present in his analysis.

This static equilibrium theory of profits is 'optimistic' in so far as profits are supposed to be instrumental in establishing long-run, ethically desirable, natural prices. As in his wage theory (chap. v), this is in contrast with his dynamic theory. The long-run results are unfavourable.

Ricardo discusses, first, the profits of the farmer, then those of the manufacturer. Profits of the farmer will fall in the long run. They will fall because of the rise in wages caused by the increasing difficulties of production when lands of lesser fertility are taken into cultivation. By definition, rising wages mean falling profits. It is true that the price of the farmer's product (corn) will rise. But he will not benefit from this rise by a rise in his profits. The price of corn rises only because of the increased difficulty in its production. More labour and more capital have to be used to 'obtain a given additional quantity of produce', and 'such a rise will always be equalled in value by the additional rent or additional labour employed.'[2] The higher rent, however, is not paid by the farmer but always falls on the consumer. The remainder of the total product has to be divided into wages and profits. If wages rise because the minimum of subsistence of the labourer now costs more and he could not survive on less, profits must fall.

> Thus in every case, agricultural as well as manufacturing profits are lowered by a rise in the price of raw produce, if it be accompanied by a rise of wages.[3]

In the case of the manufacturer, the price—the value of his final product—will rise only if raw produce enters into it. In this case the rise in the price does not increase his profits; the higher rent or the increase in capital and labour necessary to produce the same quantity will absorb the price increase:

> If the farmer gets no additional value for the corn which remains to him after paying rent, if the manufacturer gets no additional value for the goods which he manufactures, and if both are obliged to pay a greater value in wages, can any point be more clearly established than that profits must fall with a rise of wages?[4]

We have discussed the Ricardian treatment of the effects of a 'rise

[1] He uses it in his chapter on foreign trade (chap. vii, p. 87), in relation to international exchange of goods and currencies.

[2] *Principles*, p. 67. [3] *Ibid.* [4] *Ibid.*, pp. 67–68.

in wages' and pointed out that in this discussion he tries to exclude and minimize the value-determining role of capital and profits.[1]

In chapter i he uses the assumption of the inverse variation of wages and profits and his definition of both as shares, as a device to preserve the unity of his labour-bestowed theory of value. In that context this definition and assumption enable Ricardo to arrive at an 'optimistic' result because they help to maintain the basic idea of his value theory: that reward and effort, i.e., labour bestowed in production and prices, are correlated. This is an ethically optimistic conclusion.

The same definition and assumption lead to a pessimistic result in his dynamic theory. In chapter vi he assumes again that wages and profits are shares and that they vary inversely. However, by combining these ideas with his theory of rent and population, he arrives at a pessimistic result. The growing difficulty of cultivation caused by the law of diminishing returns will drive up rents and wages and thereby reduce profits. Thus the inverse relationship between wages and profits which, in chapter i, led to an optimistic conclusion now leads to its opposite:

> The natural tendency of profits then is to fall; for, in the progress of society and wealth, the additional quantity of food required is obtained by the sacrifice of more and more labour.[2]

This passage again betrays the Ricardian ambivalence and represents a typical compromise between conflicting tendencies. The unity of the theory is preserved; it is the increasing amount of labour necessary for food production on lands of lesser fertility which causes the decline in profits. Labour emerges again as the universal determinant of value. In the long run, however, profits will have the same natural tendency to fall as real wages. The natural economic laws, if not interfered with, lead to unfavourable results. The positive aspects of Ricardo's static value theory are contradicted by the negative aspects of his economic dynamics.

Ricardo definitely considered the long-run tendency toward a fall in profits as a negative result. He states that it will put an end to accumulation as soon as the entire net product (after rent) is swallowed by wages.[3] In this case:

> No capital can yield any profit whatever, and no additional labour can be demanded, and consequently, population will have reached its highest point. Long, indeed, before this period, the very

[1] See above, pp. 71 ff.
[2] *Principles*, p. 71.
[3] *Ibid.*

> low rate of profit will have arrested all accumulation, and almost the whole produce of the country, after paying the labourers, will be the property of the owners of land and the receivers of tithes and taxes.[1]

That Ricardo considered this an unfavourable result cannot be in doubt, considering his antagonism toward the economic interests of the landowners. In this 'stationary state', there would be 'no motive for accumulation' for the entrepreneurs, because

> their profits are so low as not to afford them an adequate compensation for their trouble, and the risk which they must necessarily encounter.[2]

These laws regulating long-run profits are represented by Ricardo as valid

> in all countries, and at all times; profits depend on the quantity of labour requisite to provide necessaries for the labourer on that land or with that capital which yields no rent.'[3]

This statement contains in condensed form the essence of Ricardo's theory of value, static as well as dynamic. It is again the quantity of labour bestowed which is decisive, in this case, in determining profits. Rent does not influence value because it is the labour used on marginal, no-rent land which determines profits. Profits are determined by labour bestowed on wage goods, because this labour determines wages and profits vary inversely with them. Profits must fall in the long run because the law of diminishing returns will cause money wages to rise. Wages, however, cannot rise in real terms, because, according to the law of population and the subsistence theory of wages, they will be pushed back to the subsistence level in the long run.

Economic Liberalism and Pessimism of Ricardo and Malthus

The conflict between the optimism of Ricardo's static theory and the pessimism of his long-run dynamics throws some light on his ambivalence in his advocacy of laissez-faire. On the one hand, he believes that the free forces of the market will, in the long run, realize the true labour values and the ethical principle that reward corresponds to effort. If, on the other hand, these forces lead ultimately to

[1] *Principles.*
[2] *Ibid.*, p. 73. Ricardo here develops a twofold justification for profits: as wages of management and as a premium for risk. The first fits into his labour-bestowed theory of value; the second represents an alien element within this value theory.
[3] *Ibid.*, p. 76.

unfavourable results, the basis for the belief in laissez-faire is destroyed. Therefore, Ricardian pessimism is in contradiction to his policy recommendations.

This ambivalence is clearly reflected in chapter v. After his gloomy predictions in respect to the long-run development of wages, Ricardo makes a sudden, complete turnabout from pessimism to an 'optimistic' conclusion:

> These, then, are the laws by which wages are regulated, and by which the happiness of far the greatest part of every community is governed. Like all other contracts, wages should be left to the fair and free competition of the market, and should never be controlled by the interference of the legislature.[1]

One could hardly find a better example of a non sequitur. After Ricardo has explained how, in the long run, real wages will decline until they are just sufficient to keep the existing population alive and how the worker can, in the long run, never improve his lot, he begins to talk about happiness and about the fairness of free competition, although, according to his own analysis, it brings about those dire results. We are confronted here with an example of a subconscious ridicule of the competitive market by Ricardo. It is hardly surprising that some socialists considered Ricardo as their intellectual progenitor.

There is, however, another aspect of this line of Ricardian reasoning. One gains the impression that Ricardo recommends free competition and non-interference in spite of their dire results. To some extent he seems to consider economic freedom as an end in itself, regardless of its possible results. There is an element of quietism in Malthus', as well as Ricardo's, ideas on this matter. Obviously, Ricardian dynamics is greatly influenced by Malthus. The law of of diminishing returns forms the basis of Ricardian dynamics as well as of the Malthusian population theory. The latter's ideas about population have been developed as arguments against Godwin, an idealistic liberal who believed in the goodness of man and who attributed all evil to social instutitions and government. Godwin's attack was directed especially against private property and the inequality of wealth. Malthus' answer was that, even without these institutions, nature would bring about misery. He refutes Godwin's attacks against the institutions of private property and its distribution. These institutions and the attitudes which they require lead to preventive checks or moral restraints which serve to bridge the gap between the population trends and the supply of the means of

[1] *Ibid.*, p. 61.

subsistence. The Malthusian system is thus a mixture between pessimistic and optimistic, between hostile and apologetic, tendencies toward the existing economic system. It is pessimistic concerning the production of food. This represents a certain lack of confidence in the potentialities of technological progress. The pessimistic formulation of an objective natural law of population may also have been motivated by a hostile attitude toward the system which brings about such results. Malthus represents certain detrimental and negative aspects of this system as inevitable and as ordained by nature. Poverty and subsistence wages are considered as inevitable results of the laws of population and of the niggardliness of nature. From these ideas, Socialists derived the iron law of wages. They were against gradualism and reform on the basis of Malthusian arguments. If poverty and misery are inevitable, then all piecemeal social reform is senseless, and radical change is the only remedy. Thus revolutionary aggression and quietism are a pair of interrelated opposites based on the same interpretation of reality. They may, therefore, be interconnected in the unconscious mind.[1]

Quietism of the Malthusian type is, to some extent, discernible in Ricardo. It is one of the bases of laissez-faire philosophy. In this case the reason for 'do-nothingness' is the conviction that it is futile anyway to try to change the ineluctable laws of economic evolution. This attitude goes back to theology; man should not interfere with the designs of God; he is powerless to change his fate; pious acceptance of his destiny is all that is left to him. In the statement quoted earlier from chapter v of the *Principles*[2] this spirit is clearly evident. In spite of the pessimistic long-run predictions, wages should be determined on free markets and without government interference. Perhaps this attitude should not even be called pessimistic. Ricardo paints an austere picture of the majesty of economic laws, which man cannot change and should not interfere with. The entire argument serves to reinforce an attitude of laissez-faire and as an apology for the existing system. Again we find the expression of ambivalent tendencies: hidden criticism and aggression and, at the same time, an apologetic acceptance of existing institutions.

[1] The Socialists were quietists toward the existing economic system and activists about what they considered an ideal society; whereas Malthus shows a consistent quietistic attitude, with a certain degree of activistic orientation in respect to moral restraints. Unconsciously, his pessimistic quietism may have the same aggressive meaning as it obviously had in the thought of the Socialists.

[2] See above, p. 115. 'Like all other contracts wages should be left to the fair and free competition of the market' (*Principles*, p. 61).

Chapter XI

THE UNIVERSALITY OF SYMBOLISM

Symbolic Language

IT may seem superfluous to search for further factors which may have moulded Ricardo's thinking after we have uncovered some of its socioeconomic and intellectual roots. However, human existence is multidimensional. The antinomies of human existence manifest themselves in several spheres. We have found interrelated antimonies in the socioeconomic and philosophical spheres of Ricardian thinking. If we now proceed to examine similar dichotomies in the biopsychological sphere, we do not propose to consider them as the 'prime cause' of his thought but as another manifestation of basic conflicts.

It is one of the difficulties of the holistic and integrative method that it has to take its instruments of analysis from many frames of reference. This creates the impression that the entire system from which concepts are borrowed is taken over and thus accepted in its entirety. In the following discussion, only some of the findings of psychoanalysis will be used. Social scientists still show a great deal of resistance to the use of psychoanalysis in their respective fields. They are especially suspicious of the tendency of some psychoanalysts to 'reduce' everything to psychobiological factors. We cannot stress emphatically enough that we are not advocating any reductionism. A functional interrelation exists between the socioeconomic, intellectual, and cultural situation and the biopsychological factors; and the way in which unconscious symbolism is applied to socioeconomic facts throws a light on the cultural problems and conflicts of the period. It is not only because of certain biopsychological constellations that some economists rejected the female element and denied and minimized the role of land in the economic system, as we shall presently see. It is also because certain factors of production, certain social attitudes, and certain groups were rejected by the prevailing ideology that the anti-feminine mechanisms of the unconscious mind were mobilized. In other words, socioeconomic attitudes and ideologies are not merely variables dependent on unconscious biopsychological tendencies, but such tendencies become activated by socioeconomic and cultural conditions. This will now be demonstrated in detail.

The use of symbols is perhaps the most characteristic and the most distinguishing attribute of the human mind.[1] Symbolism can be used consciously. Symbolic language, however, may also be a manifestation of the unconscious mind. It is the latter meaning of symbolic expression with which we are concerned. The symbols of this language are symptoms of something which lies underneath, of which we have no knowledge except for its traces in symbolic expression. It is the 'language in which inner experiences, feelings and thoughts are expressed as if they were sensory experiences, events in the outer world.'[2] Symbolic language is found in dreams, myths, fairy tales, ritual, poetry, and fiction. However, no forms of cultural expression are completely free of such symbolic elements. All conscious thought has an unconscious matrix and contains traces of symbolism. We find symbolic expression also in conscious systems of thought, such as theology, philosophy, and even science. This justifies the attempt to uncover such elements in social and economic thought. In our civilization the traditional forms of symbolic language, such as religion, mythology, folklore, etc., are of relatively minor importance. However, symbolic language reflects universal human attitudes; they need expression even if the overt mores of the existing culture are not conducive to this type of expression.

The 'forgotten language' of unconscious symbolism is wellnigh universal.[3] The reason for this lies in certain universal characteristics of human nature. Human beings have all the same

> bodily and mental equipment. The universal symbol, one which is shared by all men, is rooted in the properties of our body, our senses, and our mind which are common to all men.

Universal symbolism is a 'natural phenomenon because certain physical phenomena suggest by their very nature certain emotional and mental experiences.'[4] Symbolic language is the language of the unconscious, which does not know the limitations of time and space. Its universality is the result of the relatively archaic and unchange-

[1] For the following, see E. Fromm, *The Forgotten Language.*

[2] *Ibid.*, p. 7.

[3] 'The myths of the Babylonians, Indians, Egyptians, Hebrews, Greeks are written in the same language as those of the Ashantis or the Trukese. The dreams of someone living today in New York or Paris are the same as the dreams reported from people living some thousand years ago in Athens or in Jerusalem' (*ibid.*, p. 7).

[4] *Ibid.*, pp. 17, 18.

able nature of certain aspects of the unconscious. The 'mass psyche' or the 'collective unconscious' of each individual has stored up the entire heritage of mankind.[1]

Some of the contents of the unconscious represents a part of our nature which we have in common with people of other cultures and periods. Therefore, it is legitimate to use examples from ancient mythology, ritual, and folklore to elucidate the unconscious meaning of relatively modern thought. The unconscious elements in the thought of Ricardo and Malthus are, in part, determined by inner experiences similar to those of 'primitives'. This situation is difficult to accept for modern man, who believes in progress and in his superiority over past civilizations. However, it is one of the accomplishments of psychodynamic psychology to have shown that we are closer to preliterate man than we like to believe. Thus, in spite of the different theories of psychologists about the reasons for the universality of symbolism, it is sufficient to acknowledge it as a recognized fact.[2]

1 P. Mullahy, *Oedipus: Myth and Complex*, pp. 65 ff., 145 ff. Both Freud and Jung have used this concept. Freud believed that individual behaviour is often inexplicable in terms of the individual's own experiences but 'can only be understood phylogenetically, in relation to the experiences of earlier generations. . . . The archaic heritage of mankind includes not only dispositions, but also ideational contents, memory traces of experiences of former generations' (S. Freud, *Moses and Monotheism*, pp. 156–57). He also maintained that 'each individual repeats in some abbreviated fashion during childhood, the whole course of the development of the human race' (S. Freud, *A General Introduction to Psychoanalysis*, p. 177). The results of this development are stored up in what Freud calls the 'mass psyche', in which the residues of experiences dating back several thousand years can be found. Thus psychic dispositions can be inherited, and individuals may receive a legacy of primordial feelings (S. Freud, *Totem and Taboo*, in *The Basic Writings of S. Freud*, pp. 928, 938).

C. G. Jung distinguishes between a personal and a collective unconscious (J. Jacobi, *The Psychology of Jung*, and Mullahy, *op. cit.*, pp. 145 ff.). The latter contains traces of the development of mankind 'unconscious, primordial universally human images, ideational representatives of past thoughts of mankind,' corresponding to Freud's mass psyche. It consists of archetypes, 'primordial images, mythical themes, universal categories of intuition and apprehension' (Mullahy, *op. cit.*, p. 148). They represent the universal way in which mankind has always interpreted its relation to the earth, to nature, to the universe. 'Father, mother, and child, male and female . . . are primitive facts which have so impressed themselves on racial thought that they constantly reappear as symbols in the thought of today' (R. S. Woodworth, *Contemporary Schools of Psychology*, p. 177, quoted from Mullahy, *op. cit.*, p. 149).

2 Anthropological literature contains many statements which are based upon the assumption of this universality of symbolic expression. In anthropology this phenomenon has been explained either by the assumption of universal stages of development or by the theory that cultural traits have spread through cultural contacts, importation, and diffusion (R. H. Lowie, *The History of Ethnological*

Earth, Land, Mother, Female

Symbolic language is concerned with basic human situations. Foremost among them are the relations between the child and the parents and between the sexes. The antithesis of male and female played an important part. Furthermore, these relations are connected with important social and cultural institutions. In all manifestations of symbolic language we find a frequent identification of the earth, the woman, and the mother and a wealth of sexual symbolism in connection with agriculture and economic production.

The symbolic interconnection between the earth and the human female has been caused by the biological situation and its psychological correlates. The earth has always been, even in pre-agricultural cultures, a source of nourishment. Even in the most primitive economies the gathering of wild plants has been a source of food.[1] In the life of every human individual the mother is the first source of food. This leads to the identification of everything that procures nourishment with the motherly and the female. The more gardening and agriculture became the source of food, the more this identification assumed importance. Sowing, planting, and ploughing bear resemblance to the biological processes of cohabitation and impregnation, and the processes connected with fertility are very much alike in agriculture and in the human realm. There are other quite obvious parallels between earth and woman. The lengthy gestation period is perhaps one of the most obvious. The earth takes considerable time to produce plants and crops; so does the mammalian

Theory, esp. chaps. v, vi, x, xi. Although these theories have been applied mainly to cultural and social institutions, the close interrelation between socioeconomic institutions, religion, ritual, and magic makes them applicable to mythological and symbolic language as well. The theories of the evolutionists in anthropology would easily explain the universality of symbolism in different cultures and periods, during the same stages of development. If the diffusionists are right, one would have to prove that certain symbols have spread from one culture and period to the other. However, even the diffusionists make certain assumptions which are not too far from the idea of universality of certain culture traits, institutions, and their symbols. Thus some diffusionists find 'a formal resemblance, neither inherent in the nature of the phenomena compared nor due to geographical causes' and 'the chance association of a whole series of elements in two regions' (*ibid.*, p. 158, quoting Graeber). In order to explain the similarity of cultural traits, institutions, and symbols, even the diffusionists and the more cautious anthropologists have to resort to such assumptions as 'the uninventiveness of the human mind'; and even they have developed theories 'which purport to define the course of culture throughout the globe and throughout human existence' (*ibid.*, pp. 158–59). All this indicates that the idea of the universality of symbolic expression is a fact based on the findings of anthropology.

[1] M. J. Herskovits, *Economic Anthropology*, chap. iv.

mother. Both are subject to cyclical variations; the seasons of the earth have a counterpart in the female menstrual cycle.

All these associations can be found in the mythology, folklore, and religion of all times and cultures. In most cultures the earth has been identified with the woman.[1] Numerous examples can be found throughout the literature on anthropology, mythology, magic, religion, etc.

A. Dieterich, in a monograph devoted entirely to the identification of earth and mother, concludes that

> many peoples who could not have communicated directly with each other, regarded the earth as the mother of men, wherefrom they come and to which they return in order to be reborn.[2]

These beliefs originated in folk religion and survived in mystical cults of historical periods. In the cosmogonies and theogonies of these cults the symbol of mother-earth occupied an important position. The female Greek goddesses, the Eumenides,[3] blessed earth and marriage and promoted the fertility of both the soil and the human female. In Greek mythology, as in many others, the soil and the seed corn were identified with the woman and with the semen. Human birth and the growing of plants and crops were regarded as one and the same phenomenon. It was believed that the rain, the water from heaven, impregnates the earth and makes fruits grow, as the semen impregnates the ovum. In Euripides' *Chrysippos* the ether, standing for Uranos, heaven, is said to copulate with the earth, which, after having received the fertilizing rain, gives birth to man but also to plants and animals; therefore, the earth is the mother of all.[4] According to ancient custom in Attica, marriages were dedicated to heaven and earth, the couples prayed to the earth for fertility and children. Sowing and harvesting of crops were interconnected with procreation and birth of men. Phallic symbols were thrown into the depth of the earth in order to stimulate the growth of fruits and the birth of human beings. Many Attic writers used the same word for sowing, ploughing, and impregnating.[5]

In ancient Athens a custom existed by which a member of an old clan, whose ancestor was supposed to have been the first who tied a bull to a plough, had to repeat the action as a sacramental rite in which the earth was fertilized symbolically by the plough in the form of a phallus.[6]

1 R. Briffault, *The Mothers: A Study of the Origins of Sentiments*, III, p. 56 ff.

2 A. Dieterich, *Mutter Erde*, pp. 31, 32.

3 See J. J. Bachofen, *Das Mutterrecht*; Fromm, *op. cit.*, p. 214.

4 Dieterich, *op. cit.*, pp. 38–42. 5 *Ibid.*, pp. 45–7. 6 *Ibid.*, p. 50.

In Plato's *Menexenes* the earth is compared to a woman because, like woman who has nourishment for the child, the Attic earth has produced food for the human species in the form of wheat and barley. Plato says that the earth has not imitated women in respect to pregnancy and birth but that the women have emulated the earth. This is not a queer idea of Plato's, but it represents Attic folklore, which was still alive in the fourth century B.C.[1] The cult of the earth and mother, very much alive in old religion and folklore, was retained in the mystery cults like the one of Eleusis. The main object of worship was mother-earth under the name of Demeter. The initiation of the neophytes consisted in a secret rite in which, through a sacramental act, they become children of this mother. The rite was interpreted as a rebirth by the great mother.[2]

These quotations could be multiplied by examples from Greek and from many other cultures. They indicate the close interrelation which existed in the human mind not only between life, earth, and mother but also between sexual activities and agriculture.

There are many instances in which the fertility of the earth was stimulated by ritual copulation taking place in the fields.[3] Symbols of penis and vulva often appear in magic rites for the promotion of fertility. The act of copulation in the fields is supposed to make the earth fertile and germinating.

> Harvests were celebrated with pictorial and plastic reproductions of the male and female genitals, with exposure and denudation of women, with the utterance of obscene sexual expressions, etc.[4]

Frequently the plough is used as a magic instrument of fertilization; it is assumed to impregnate the earth. In some rituals the plough is pulled by naked virgins. The Zuni pour water on the plough and on the ploughing person and combine in this fashion fertilization and rain-making magic. Copulation on the field was also practised among the old Germans.[5] The idea behind these magic practices is to force the earth to become fertile not only in producing crops but also in increasing human fertility; it was believed that these rites would promote both. This is not considered merely an analogy but is based on a belief in the identity of both processes. Seed and fruit of the earth, impregnation and birth of human beings, are considered as two aspects of the same situation. Copulation on the field causes the earth to germinate, and seed corns

[1] Dieterich, *op. cit.*, p. 53.
[2] *Ibid.*, pp. 55–56.
[3] *Ibid.*, p. 57, n. 2; Briffault, *op. cit.*, I, pp. 123, 197 ff.
[4] Dieterich, *op. cit.*, p. 94.
[5] *Ibid.*, p. 97.

thrown into a grave cause the rebirth of the dead. The womb of mother-earth is wherever the plough makes a furrow, wherever a human being is born.[1] In folk religion, rites, myth, and lore, an identity of rain and human semen, plough and male sex organ, the hollow and the female womb, the furrow and the female genitalia, is assumed.[2]

According to psychoanalysis, the unconscious mind invests many activities with a sexual meaning.[3] Ploughing and the making of fire are used as symbols for the act of cohabitation in dreams as well as in myth and folklore. The similarity in the external physical activities may have fostered such associations. In ploughing and planting, movements penetrating the earth and the injection of the fertilizing seed present perfect analogies to the acts of cohabitation and impregnation. In all languages one finds expressions for sexual activity and organs borrowed from the sphere of agriculture.[4] The bull, representing male power, appears frequently in primitive religion as pulling the plough and fertilizing the earth at the same time. According to Diodorus, the sacred Egyptian bulls Apis and Mnevis had helped the discoverer of corn in sowing seed and procuring the benefits of agriculture.[5] In Greek and Latin, as well as in oriental languages, the expression for ploughing is also used for cohabitation; in Greek the words for 'garden', 'meadow', and 'field' are used as nicknames for the female genitalia; in the Song of Songs it is symbolized by the 'vineyard'.

An interrelation between the female menstrual cycle and the earth was often established in primitive cultures through the intermediary of the moon, which was considered a female symbol.[6] The moon was supposed to cause menstruation. At the same time, it was regarded as the producer of vegetation, as the patron(ess) of agriculture. The moon was considered to be the controller of moisture and water, which played an important role in the procurement of food. At the same time, the moon was especially worshipped by women and regarded as their protective deity.[7]

The identification of heaven with the father and of earth with the

1 *Ibid.*, pp. 98–100.

2 *Ibid.*, p. 101.

3 O. Rank and H. Sachs, *Die Bedeutung der Psychoanalyse für die Geisteswissenschaften* (English translation, *The Significance of Psychoanalysis for the Mental Sciences*, by C. H. Payne).

4 *Ibid.*; O. Rank, *Psychoanalytische Beiträge zur Mythenforschung*, pp. 28 ff.

5 Briffault, *op. cit.*, I, p. 194, with many other similar examples.

6 *Ibid.*, I, p. 194; II, p. 572 ff.

7 *Ibid.*, Vol. II, chap. xx. For the importance of water in primitive economies see Herskovits, *op. cit.*, p. 68.

mother is generally found in many mythologies. 'At the beginning of time father-heaven was lying closely pressed against mother-earth.'[1] The belief that the heaven is the father and the earth the mother of the world can be found not only in Babylonian, Egyptian, and Greek mythology but also throughout Oceania, in China, in old India, in Semitic and Nordic mythology.[2] Freud has pointed out

> the frequency with which landscapes are used in dreams to symbolize the female sexual organs; that one can learn from mythologists how large a part has been played in the ideas and cults of ancient times by 'mother-earth'; how the whole conception of agriculture was determined by this symbolism.[3]

Bachofen, who is the intellectual ancestor of the doctrine that matriarchy is an older form of society than patriarchy, has piled up an impressive number of examples of the identification of earth and mother, of the representation of earth by the female, of the interrelations of plants, vegetation, and matriarchy, and of the moon and earth as earthly, female, motherly symbols.[4]

[1] Frobenius, *Das Zeitalter des Sonnengottes*, Vol. I, quoted from Otto Rank, *Das Inzestmotiv in Dichtung und Sage*, p. 279.

[2] Rank, *Incestmotiv*, pp. 279 ff.

[3] S. Freud, *A General Introduction to Psychoanalysis*, p. 145.

[4] Bachofen, *op. cit.*

Chapter XII

APOLOGISTS AND ANTAGONISTS

Land as the Source of Evil in Ricardo's and Malthus' Thought

THE reader may have asked himself with growing puzzlement what all this has to do with economics. However, Sir William Petty had used symbolic language in calling labour the father or active principle of wealth, as lands are the mother.[1] Land and its fertility have played an important part in economics. The Physiocrats considered land to be the only productive factor and the work of the farmer as the only productive economic activity. The *produit net* was considered to be the result of agriculture. Adam Smith, greatly influenced by the Physiocrats in spite of his polemic against them, had a high regard for agriculture as the most profitable and productive type of investment. He explains rent in terms of the special value-creating powers of the soil; Ricardo takes him to task for this opinion:

> Nothing is more common than to hear of the advantages which the land possesses over every other source of useful produce, on account of the surplus which it yields in the form of rent. Yet when land is most abundant, when most productive, and most fertile, it yields no rent.[2]

The fertility of land and of women and their interrelationship stood in the centre of Malthusian thought. Ricardo and Malthus both attribute a peculiar role to land. For them it is the source of all economic ills, the evil principle in their universe of discourse. Malthus believed that population growth outruns the production of food with the inevitability of a natural law. This implies an unfavourable comparison of the fertility of the earth with the fertility of the human female. Whereas the primitive mind assumes a certain harmony between both, Malthus sees a conflict. However, his ideas

1 '*Taxes and Contributions,*' chap. xi, in *The Economic Writings of Sir William Petty*, ed. C. H. Hull, I, p. 68.

2 Ricardo, *Principles*, chap. ii, p. 39.

are in conformity with primitive symbolism in so far as he sees in both the hand of Nature, which

> has scattered the seeds of life abroad with the most profuse and liberal hand; but has been comparatively sparing in the room and the nourishment necessary to rear them.[1]

This conflict is the 'Leitmotif' of Malthus' work:

> It may be safely pronounced, therefore, that population, when unchecked, goes on doubling itself every twenty-five years or increases in a geometrical ratio.

The rate at which the population of the earth could increase is slowed down by the law of diminishing returns:

> When acre has been added to acre till all the fertile land is occupied . . . a fund, which, from the nature of all soils, instead of increasing, must be gradually diminishing . . . in proportion as cultivation extended, the additions that could yearly be made to the former average produce must be gradually and regularly diminishing.[2]

Thus nature works to the detriment of mankind along two lines: by retarding the increase in food production through declining productivity of the earth, on the one hand, and by causing female fecundity to increase population beyond the means of subsistence, on the other. In both cases it is 'female' nature which causes this unfavourable situation. The earth, the soil, the land—all primeval female symbols—are niggardly in producing food. And the blame for the excess of population over the supply of food is clearly put on the women:

> The fecundity of the human species is a distinct consideration from the passion between the sexes, as it evidently depends more upon the power of women in bearing children, than upon the strength and weakness of this passion.[3]

Here the unfortunate quality of fecundity is definitely characterized as an attribute of the female, as distinguished from the sexual passion. The male, who, after all, participates in the latter, is in this way exonerated from the blame of causing overpopulation. Female fecundity is

> a law however exactly similar in its great features to all the other laws of nature. It is strong and general, and apparently would not

[1] Malthus, *Essay on Population* ('Everyman's' ed.), I, p. 6.
[2] *Ibid.*, pp. 8, 9.
[3] *Ibid.*, II, p. 157.

admit of any very considerable diminution. The evils arising from it are incidental to those necessary qualities of strength and generality.[1]

We find here the concepts of nature, its laws, female fecundity, and the evils caused by it, all together, combined in one paragraph, indicating the close, albeit unconscious interconnections between them in the mind of Malthus.

In a similar fashion Ricardo considers the 'female' land as the ultimate factor which causes all the unfortunate results expounded in his long-run dynamic theory of economic development. Ricardo's pessimistic forecasts rest on three assumptions: (1) the law of diminishing returns, (2) the principle of population, and (3) the subsistence theory of wages. The law of diminishing returns causes (*a*) the decrease in capital accumulation because of the decline of the net product, thereby (*b*) the decline in demand for labour, and (*c*) the increase in the price of agricultural products and raw materials (corn). The principle of population causes wages to return in the long run to the subsistence level. The subsistence theory of wages makes them dependent on the price of corn; this price rises because of the law of diminishing returns; thus the circle is closed. These three assumptions form an ingenious web, which, with the inevitability of fate, must lead to the pessimistic conclusions of Ricardo in respect to the long-run trend of wages and profits (see above, pp. 109 ff.).

All three of these assumptions have to do with the scarcity of fertile lands. The law of diminishing returns is only the exact formulation of the effects of nature's inadequacy in providing subsistence in proportion to the increase in population. The subsistence theory of wages, i.e., the belief that, in the long run, wages will be kept at the subsistence level by the population trends, is nothing but a conclusion from the other two assumptions. Thus land plays the role of the devil in the Ricardian system.[2]

If we are right that land is unconsciously identified with the female, the tendency to disparage land implies an unconscious

[1] *Essay on Population*, II, p. 157.

[2] His idea that the rent which the landlord receives for the use of land is the only type of income which will not deteriorate and fall in the long run seems significant in this connection. Ricardo's political and economic antagonism toward the landlords is interrelated with his advocacy of free trade and his fight against the Corn Laws. It is reflected in his beliefs about the long-run trend of rent, which differ from those of the long-run trend of wages and profits, and his belief that the interests of the landlords are in conflict with the interests of the other two classes. The same attitude manifests itself in the idea that the scarcity of fertile lands is to blame for the detrimental long-run results of the free market. It is the landed gentry and their property which cause all this trouble.

tendency to disparage the female. The question, then, arises: Are there any psychocultural reasons for such a tendency in the socioeconomic and cultural situation of the nineteenth century? Some light can be thrown on this by examining the diametrically different attitudes of a critic of the socioeconomic system of that period.

The Antagonists: Friedrich Engels

Friedrich Engels has dealt directly with the interrelations of private property and capitalism, on the one hand, and the family and sex relations, on the other. In his *The Origin of the Family, Private Property, and the State*[1] he established a historical relationship between the patriarchal family dominated by the male and private property.[2]

Accepting the theories of L. H. Morgan,[3] and J. J. Bachofen,[4] he assumed that the monogamous patriarchal family 'was the first form of the family to be based not on natural but on economic conditions.' It was a result of the 'victory of private over the primitive, natural property.'[5] When the male became the owner of property, he wanted to leave it to children who were undoubtedly his own. This led to the establishment of patrilocal marriage and methods of figuring descent in a patrilineal way.[6] Bachofen, Morgan, and Engels believed that the patriarchal, patrilocal, and patrilineal family was the result of a long development. Originally, mankind lived in sexual promiscuity within each tribe. No jealousy, no incest taboos, either between parents and children or between siblings, existed.[7] According to Morgan, the consanguine family developed out of this

[1] I have retranslated some passages.

[2] We are discussing Engels' theory only because Ricardo's and Malthus' attitudes toward land and labour can be better understood after a comparison with Engels' ideas. For the purpose of such a comparison it does not matter that Engels was wrong in many respects. His theories can be treated as projective material. The way writers react to anthropological facts can be used in the same way as the reactions of an individual to a Rorschach or thematic apperception test. What a person sees in a random concatenation of inkblots does not tell us anything about the inkblots, only something about the mind of the reacting person. Similarly, the selection and interpretation of facts by an author tell us something about his attitudes.

[3] *Ancient Society.*

[4] *Das Mutterrecht.*

[5] Engels, *op. cit.*, p. 57.

[6] *Ibid.*, pp. 54 ff.; 'patrilocal' means that the wife moves in with the family of the husband; 'patrilineal' means that descent is figured from father to children, not from mother to children.

[7] Engels, *op. cit.*, pp. 27 ff.

primeval state of promiscuity. In the consanguine family, ancestors and progenitors were excluded from mutual marital relationship, but brothers and sisters and first-, second-, and third-degree cousins were allowed to intermarry.[1] In the next stage, the Punaluan family, not only parents and children but also sisters and brothers are excluded from intermarriage. It was still a group form of marriage; a group of sisters married a group of men, who called themselves *punalua*, i.e., 'comrades', '*associés*'.[2] In all cases of group marriage the old dictum: *pater semper est incertus* applies. Descent can be traced only in matrilinear fashion. The third stage is what Morgan and Engels call the 'pairing family', where one man and one woman live together; however, the children belong, as in all previous forms of marriage, to the mother.[3] Thus the ancient history of the family consists in narrowing down the circle which is kept together by familial ties. However, in all three forms of pre-patriarchal marriage the economic unit of organization was the communal household, which, according to Engels and Morgan, was characterized by the predominance (*Herrschaft*) of women in the house, by matrilinear calculation of descent, and by a great respect for women and mothers in general.[4]

The transition from the pairing family to the patriarchal, monogamous form of marriage was brought about, according to Engels, by socioeconomic forces. Domestication of animals and the breeding of herds created a new type of wealth, which belonged originally to the community (the gens) but soon became the private property of the male heads of families. Together with the domesticated animals, the labour power of slaves became valuable property with the introduction of cattle breeding, metalwork, weaving, and, finally, agriculture; the father became important as the owner of cattle and slaves and, thereby, as the producer of food. This provided the stimulus to change the rules of inheritance in favour of his children and led to a change from the matriarchal to the patrilineal approach toward descent and inheritance and to a decline of matriarchy. 'The defeat of matriarchy [*Mutterrecht*] represents the defeat of the female sex in world history.' Thus Engels concludes his account of the history of the family, which culminated in the emergence of patriarchal monogamy.[5]

In Engels' theories we find an interesting parallel between the

[1] *Ibid.*, p. 32. In the footnote on that page Engels mentions a letter of Marx (spring, 1882) in which he criticized Richard Wagner for representing the marriage between brother and sister in *Die Walküre* as criminally incestuous: 'In primeval times the sister was the wife, and this was quite moral,' writes Marx.

[2] Engels, *op. cit.*, pp. 33 ff.

[3] *Ibid.*, pp. 40 ff.

[4] *Ibid.*, p. 42.

[5] *Ibid.*, p. 50.

antithesis of male and female, on the one hand, and the antithesis of private and communal property, on the other. The female is predominant in the family organization without and before the existence of private property; the male is the one who owns private property. Engels discovers all the characteristics of the society with private property in the monogamous patriarchal family. The latter is supposed to be dominated by class conflict in the form of the conflict between the sexes, previously unknown according to Engels. In 1846, Marx and Engels had already stated that 'the first division of labour is the one between man and woman for the propagation of children', and Engels adds that 'the first class conflict in history coincides with the antagonism between man and woman in monogamous marriage, and the first class exploitation coincides with that of the female sex by the male.'[1] Engels interprets sexual relations as division of labour; this may be nothing but a simile taken from the sphere of production and applied to the undeniable difference in biological roles. However, Engels interprets sexual relations in the monogamous family as exploitation. Thus the sexual act is interpreted in analogy to the production process, with the child as the product. Engels has a twofold exploitation in mind: a sexual and an economic one. Sexually, the woman is enslaved by the patriarchal, monogamous mores which impose fidelity, whereas the men are free to roam the field. Monogamy is, according to Engels, always accompanied by prostitution.

According to Engels, monogamy has nothing to do with romantic love between the sexes. The modern bourgeois marriage is mostly based on convenience. Only in the proletariat can romantic love become the basis of sexual relations, because there is no private property and therefore no reason for patriarchal exploitation of women.[2] The proletarian woman, in contrast to her middle-class sister, is not economically dependent; she has moved out of the house and into the factory and is often the breadwinner for the family. The bourgeois woman, however, is a slave in the house. The middle-class man is the breadwinner, 'he is the bourgeois in the family, the wife represents the proletariat.'[3]

The woman, like the proletariat, can be liberated only by participating, on equal terms, in industrial production for the public good; and this requires the elimination of the family as economic unit as a precondition for the abolition of private and the establishment of public property of the means of production. The socialization of the means of production will remove the male motive to adhere to monogamous patriarchal marriage: the desire to leave his wealth to

[1] Engels, *op. cit.*, p. 58. [2] *Ibid.*, pp. 62 ff. [3] *Ibid.*, pp. 65 ff.

his children. With the abolishment of private property and of the patriarchal family, wage labour and prostitution will vanish (the analogy is important!). Women will not be forced to sell themselves for money: monogamy, based on real love and romantic sexual passion becomes a reality—for men and women.[1] Sexual intercourse will become less repressed under the impact of more emancipated public opinion. With the elimination of private property and the family as an economic unit, marriage becomes a completely free contractual relation based exclusively on mutual attraction and love. Such a marriage requires mutuality and exclusiveness and must, by its very character, be monogamous. Thus monogamous marriage in its ideal form, without any predominance of the male and without exploitation of the woman, will be realized only in socialist and communist societies.[2]

We have presented Engels' views at greater length, because they form an interesting antithetical pattern to the views of Malthus and Ricardo. One can say that Engels, in his analysis of the bourgeois family and society, takes the part of the woman against the male head of the family. She is the exploited part, the 'proletariat' in the family; her position is represented as similar to the one of the wage labourer in capitalist society. Engels establishes a close interrelation between male predominance, private property, and capital, the main targets of his criticism. He is also very intent on proving that real love and sexual passion cannot flourish in bourgeois marriage and have to be liberated by the socialist revolution.

All this is definitely in contrast to the implicit attitudes of Malthus and Ricardo. They consider the female element, land and the woman, as the source of all economic evils. In their overt thought they are, on the whole, apologists of the market economy, the profit motive, capital accumulation, and private property of the means of production which Marx and Engels reject. Thus we arrive at two pairs of antinomies which can be co-ordinated with the thought of Malthus and Ricardo, on the one hand, and of Marx and Engels, on the other: capitalist versus anti-capitalist, and anti-female versus pro-female. This suggests an interconnection between those two pairs of opposites. The apologists are anti-female, the antagonists are pro-female. At the same time, the antagonists are anti-male, at least as far as the father, the head of the bourgeois family is concerned.

The antagonists identify the existing economic political and family system with the male father, against whom they revolt. To the oppressed they attribute a female character. We contend that a

[1] Engels, *op. cit.*, pp. 66 ff.
[2] *Ibid.*, pp. 72–74.

similar unconscious symbolism is at work in the thought of the apologists: they are against the female element, land and earth, because they side with the existing economic system, which has a male connotation.

This situation begs for a psychocultural explanation. As we shall show later, it can be found in an amalgamation of biopsychological, social, and cultural factors. The basic biopsychological antithesis between male and female is projected into and blended with socio-economic antitheses in such a way that the dynamic factors of both spheres support and reinforce one another.

Chapter XIII

PSYCHODYNAMIC AND SOCIOCULTURAL FACTORS

The Male-Female Dichotomy in Ontogenetic Development[1]

ALL schools of psychodynamics have concerned themselves with the male-female dichotomy. In spite of considerable difference in the details of interpretation, they all assume that the purely physiological sex differences alone are psychologically not decisive. Superimposed are social and cultural patterns of what male and female roles are supposed to be. These 'male' and 'female' traits are present in a certain mixture in both sexes, defined on a physiological basis.

The Freudian argument about bisexuality rests upon the assumption of various stages through which the individual has to pass before the genitals become the foremost 'erogenous zone'. During these stages other parts of the body are erotogenetic, such as mouth, lips, thumb, tongue, anus, etc. These phases are common to both boys and girls; during these phases the child does not make a clear distinction between the two sexes. This distinction can obviously be made only when the genitals become important; but, at first, both sexes are supposed to have a penis. Thus in the mind of the child the differences between the sexes play a minor role at first, and the situation is characterized by great uncertainty as to what constitutes this difference.

One of the first love objects of the child is obviously the mother. In this love the father becomes the great rival, who, however, is also an object of love for the little boy. Here we have one of the first sources of ambivalence in ontogenetic development, connected with the male-female antithesis. The boy loves the mother and regards her as his property; he hates the father as an obstacle in this relation; he wants to replace the father, become like him in relation to the mother. But he also loves the father and wants to play the mother's role in relation to him. Thus 'the Oedipus

[1] For the following discussion see P. Mullahy, *Oedipus: Myth and Complex.*

complex offers the child two "possibilities" one active, the other passive.'[1]

Every male will develop both tendencies, which will cause ambivalent drives which may express themselves possibly in neurotic doubts not only about his sex role but also about many other conflict situations. In Western civilization the growing boy is forced, by education and institutional pressures, to give up his attachment to his mother. The result is either an identification with the mother or a more intensive identification with the father, according to the relative strength of active or passive elements in his psychological makeup.[2] Thus the Oedipus complex contains two trends, a 'positive' and a 'negative' one,

> due to the bisexuality originally present in children: that is to say a boy has not merely an ambivalent attitude towards his father and an affectionate object-relation to his mother, but at the same time he behaves like a girl and displays an affectionate feminine attitude towards his father and a corresponding hostility and jealousy towards his mother.[3]

Assuming that Freud is correct in his assumptions, would they not throw some light on the role of the male-female antithesis in nineteenth-century economic thought, especially if the biopsychological factors stressed by Freud were reinforced by a specific sociocultural situation? If the male infant has a psychologically bisexual orientation and if he harbours a conflict between active-passive, male-female patterns, his mind will, unconsciously, seize on similar socioeconomic situations and interpret them in the light of this inner conflict. Unconsciously, latent primordial reminiscences in which similar symbolism represents similar conflicts may contribute to this process.

The complete Oedipus complex consists of a dichotomy: a friendly attitude toward the father combined with a hostile one toward the mother and, vice versa, an attitude in which the mother is loved and the father is hated. Does this not conform precisely to the attitudes of the apologists and of the antagonists, respectively? And is this correlation not quite comprehensible if one substitutes for the father the existing economic system and its institutions, such as private property, the market, and the wage system? Assuming that, in the unconscious mind of Malthus and Ricardo, Marx, and Engels the existing socioeconomic system stood for the father because

[1] Mullahy, p. 25.

[2] S. Freud, *The Ego and the Id*, pp. 41–42.

[3] *Ibid.*, pp. 42–43.

of its patriarchal character; then it would be, from the point of view of the unconscious, quite 'logical' or quite 'psychological' for those who side with the father to disparage the mother and vice versa. This follows not only from the Oedipus constellation but also from the assumption of a 'basic bisexual disposition in man', which, in view of the psychological and sociocultural differences in male and female functions and roles, leads to inevitable inner conflict situations.[1] In the following discussion we shall show how the male-female conflict is interrelated with certain other important antinomies of the period under consideration.

Maleness and Activism

The patriarchal principle was the basis of the Western family and Western society, until recently characterized by the social, economic, and ideological superiority of males. This sociocultural situation found its expression in the fact that character traits and modes of behaviour which were positively evaluated in this culture were considered to be male attributes. Thus the entire value-attitude system which we called the 'economic value complex', with its ideals of acquisitiveness, accumulation of capital and wealth, and competitive, individualistic striving for economic success through active, productive labour, had assumed a masculine character in the minds of middle-class persons. This identification was reinforced by the importance of activism as an eminently desirable trait.

The great emphasis on technology and science in Western civilization is interconnected with a positive evaluation of activity directed toward change and control of the external, physical world.[2] In Western culture man is supposed to devote his time to activities directed toward economic success and aiming at a change in his environment. Being active in successful work has become almost the only legitimate way of passing one's time. It is one of the few methods by which modern man can ward off anxiety.[3] Being active is an attitude and style of behaviour moulded according to the pattern of production and technology in which human effort is applied to physical things. Rational economic behaviour is supposed to change existing conditions and to bring about a new situation. That this is a peculiar culture- and time-bound value attitude becomes

[1] By 'bisexual' we do not mean any purely physical distinction but the inner conflict between the identification with father and mother and, consequently, the inner conflict between the assumption of socially defined male and female roles.

[2] H. Lasswell, *World Politics and Personal Insecurity*, in his *A Study of Power*, p. 268; W. A. Weisskopf, 'Industrial Institutions and Personality Structure', 1.

[3] S. De Grazia, *The Political Community*, pp. 59 ff.

clear when compared with the ultimate goals of Eastern philosophies, where a state of complete withdrawal from the external world and utmost passivity is the supreme ideal. The work ethic implies an activistic attitude toward life.[1] This activistic ideal of Western economic civilization, which formed an essential part of the new economic value complex, acquired in the minds of contemporaries a masculine connotation; activity and masculinity became synonymous.

This is reflected in Freud's conception of masculine and feminine. Freud himself, although he wrote in the twentieth century and was ahead of his time in many of his ideas, was to some extent a typical nineteenth-century middle-class Victorian personality.[2] Some of his ideas are not so much scientific findings as reflections of the value attitudes of his time and culture. This appears to be true also of his definitions of masculine and feminine. He considers this distinction to be mainly identical with the antinomy of active and passive. He believed that the libido, the sexual drive, is 'regularly and lawfully of a masculine nature.'[3] He saw the antinomy of active and passive in the biological mobility of the male semen and the stationary female ovum, but even more so in the sexual act, in which

> the male pursues the female for the purposes of sexual union, seizes her and pushes his way into her. But with that you have . . . reduced the quality of masculinity to the factor of aggressiveness.[4]

This is a rather peculiar approach to sexual activity. The purely physiological mobility and stationary situation of semen and ovum do not necessarily have any influence on the psychological attitudes toward male and female. Furthermore, Freud's description of the act of cohabitation reads rather like one of a rape than of a union of lovers. The male is not necessarily aggressive in this act. He was, however, in the nineteenth century supposed to be the active and aggressive partner in the human and social interrelationship which preceded the sexual act. The female part in the act of cohabitation is not necessarily and physiologically a passive one, not even in the form of intercourse most common in our culture. However, even if one considered the female role in this form of intercourse as physically passive, the question arises: Why has this form become the 'normal' one in our civilization?—a legitimate question in view of the innumerable varieties of sexual techniques found in other cultures.

1 De Grazia, pp. 59 ff.

2 See D. Riesman, *Psychiatry*, XIII (1950), 1 ff., 167 ff., 301 ff.

3 'Contribution to the Theory of Sex,' p. 612.

4 *New Introductory Lectures on Psychoanalysis*, p. 156.

The answer may be that the special variety of intercourse considered normal in Western civilization lends itself better to equating the masculine with the active and the feminine with the passive. The very mode of intercourse may be influenced by cultural attitudes toward activism. Thus in our civilization the 'active' one is the male, and not the female the active one. All this leads to the conclusion that we are projecting our sociocultural value attitudes into our interpretation of sex differences. We evaluate highly the active and the masculine; this is why Freud and others have equated them.

We find the same idealization of active, aggressive masculinity in the psychology of Alfred Adler. His entire theory centres around the idea of maleness. Man has a 'masculine goal'. The wish to be a 'complete man' is the driving force of normal and neurotic persons. The neurotic reacts to 'organ inferiority' through 'overcompensation' in his attitudes and actions. The normal person, however, also suffers from inferiority feelings which are inseparable from human existence; to 'be a human being means the possession of a feeling of inferiority that is constantly pressing on toward its own conquest.'[1]

One is reminded of Malthus when reading Adler's statement:

> Who can seriously doubt that the human individual treated by nature in such a stepmotherly fashion has been provided with the blessings of a strong feeling of inferiority that urges him toward a plus situation, toward security and conquest? And this tremendous enforced rebellion against a tenacious feeling of inferiority is awakened afresh and repeated in every infant . . . as a fundamental fact of human development.[2]

In Adler and in Malthus we find the idea of the niggardliness or stepmotherliness of nature. Both Malthus and Adler believe that this 'stepmotherly niggardliness' provides a necessary stimulus to 'male' activity. From the inevitable inadequacies of human existence arises the desire for superiority, power, and dominance. The individual wants to compensate for this inferiority. This leads to the emergence of the 'masculine goal', symbolized especially in the all-powerful figure of the father, with whom the child identifies.[3] According to Adler, in our civilization we have identified power, superiority, and dominance with masculinity, and weakness with femininity. Much

[1] A. Adler, *Social Interest*, quoted from Mullahy, *op. cit.*, p. 116.

[2] Adler, *op. cit.*, p. 99, from Mullahy, *op. cit.*, p. 117. Cf. Malthus, *Essay on Population*, Vol. II, Book IV, chap. i, pp. 157–58, where Malthus considers the faster increase in population compared with the increase of food as a necessary stimulus, established by the Creator, to produce 'that general activity so necessary to the improvement of human faculties.'

[3] Mullahy, *op. cit.*, p. 119.

of this is caused by the male dominance in Western institutions and society, in the family, and in economic life.[1]

There is a remarkable historical consistency throughout the development of Western civilization from the times of Petty, who called labour the father or active principles of wealth, to Freud and Adler, who identified activism and masculinity.

The Socioeconomic Position of the Sexes

Considering the central role of activism in the value system of Western civilization, it is not surprising that a parallel was established between activism and maleness and that the ideologically required type of economic and social conduct was characterized as male. This corresponded to the socioeconomic and cultural division of labour between the sexes in bourgeois middle-class society, which Engels has described not incorrectly, although in polemically exaggerated terms. Prior to the industrial revolution there existed economic equality between men and women in the sense that economic tasks of equal importance and difficulty were allocated to both sexes. The division of labour was perfectly functional and was determined, not by any particular attitude of discrimination toward women or men, but by the physical conditions of the environment and the particular historical and cultural situation. When labour is divided along sex lines,

> every man or woman not only will know how to do all those things that men and women habitually do among them, but must be able to do them efficiently.[2]

The task of providing for the daily needs and basic requirements, however, was equally distributed between men and women or, in a considerable number of cultures, rested to a large extent on the shoulders of women. The economic inactivity which became the fate of the bourgeois middle-class women was practically unknown in most primitive and later pre-industrial civilizations.

Even during the Middle Ages, which had a distinctive patriarchal and male outlook toward women and family, the economic function of women was very important. From the eleventh to the fifteenth centuries, the women in the English countryside were the universal providers for the household.[3] Since a large part of all goods produced was produced at home, this meant considerable participation of women in the process of production of the subsistence economy.

[1] Mullahy p. 121.

[2] M. J. Herskovits, *Economic Anthropology*, p. 126.

[3] F. W. Tickner, *Women in English Economic History* (1923), pp. 14, 29, 49, 53, 67, 68, 80, from which the following description of female economic activity is taken.

However, there was no clear division of labour between husband and wife; the man often helped in the household and the woman with the farming. In the towns the women participated in the work of the shop in addition to their household duties; both spheres of work were in no way so separated as they became later during and after the industrial revolution and the development of the factory system.

> Much of the detailed work of the house was in fact left to the girls and the housewife was left free to work with her husband in the production of goods for sale; just the opposite to the position nowadays, when the housewife stays at home and does all the household tasks while the daughters are out at work.[1]

Women engaged in practically all the industries of importance at the time, such as spinning, dyeing, silk-weaving, knitting, candlemaking, etc. Women also became members of the merchants' guilds and engaged in various trades.

During the Renaissance and Restoration the increase in wealth brought about an increase in leisure. The women of the upper classes began to turn away from their housework and from business activities, and the idea began to take hold that a life of leisure was the most appropriate life for them. In these social strata marriage became the sole preoccupation, and the attraction of men for the purposes of marriage became the most important goal in life. Here, in the aristocracy and gentry, originated the attitude which later on became prominent in the middle classes.

The industrial revolution, with the introduction of machinery and the emergence of the factory system, had a different effect on the position of the women in the various economic strata. For the middle-class woman the trend which had started within the aristocracy became general. She became an economic liability and was confined to the function of a sex mate and social companion. Within the lower classes the factory system and the poverty which forced women to work had a thoroughly disruptive influence on family life. Previously, except for the upper classes, the family was primarily an economic unit in which all members participated in providing the means of subsistence. Now, the middle-class women's economic value declined.[2] This was partly the effect of growing industrialization and the shift of many productive activities away from the household into the factories; partly the result of the growth of education and schools, which took over a large part of the domestic activities of the middle-class woman. As in the upper classes, marriage also became the main preoccupation of the middle-class woman.

[1] W. Tickner, *op. cit.*, p. 49. [2] V. Klein, *The Feminine Character*, pp. 9–10.

The growing wealth, first of the upper and then of the middle classes, together with the elimination of the peasants, yeomen, and workers from the land, the vanishing of domestic industry, and the shift of many types of production from household to factories changed the character of marriage and of the family and therefore the position of women and the male attitude toward them: the upper- and middle-class women became for the male mainly an object of sexual desire and of luxury. The economic aspects became less important in family relations. Men began to choose their female mates not only for economic consideration but also for sexual attraction and beauty. Purity and romance became important, while the economic motive receded into the background.[1] These economic and cultural aspects of the patriarchal family, i.e., the superiority of the male and the inferiority of the female in primary and secondary institutions, were reflected in the economic thought of Malthus and Ricardo in the inferior role ascribed to the 'female' land.

Solidarity versus Competition

The emergence of the market economy was accompanied by the destruction of social ties and bonds. Large numbers of small peasants, yeomen, cottagers, etc., were uprooted from the soil and driven into the factory towns, where they had to earn their living as labourers. The family structure and the character of family relations were changed. Mobility made permanent, lasting ties more and more difficult. The growing division of labour severed the relationship between the worker and his product and prevented him from finding satisfaction in creation. The market economy tended to disintegrate social relations and to destroy the traditional habitat of people. The industrial system functionalized man, alienated him from himself, and depersonalized his relationships to others. The attitude of competitive acquisitiveness, required and enforced by the market system, is in conflict with the need for primary, warm, close, affectionate personal interrelations.[2] The arguments of economic theory that competition is economically beneficial will not eliminate the fact that the individualistic, competitive value-attitude system led to aggressive interpersonal relations. This hostile attitude toward others, originating in the market place, permeated all spheres of social and human relations. It exercised a disintegrating influence

[1] Briffault, *The Mothers: A Study of the Origins of Sentiments*, II, p. 253 ff.; Vol. III, chaps. xxvii, xxviii, xxix.

[2] A. H. Maslow, 'A Theory of Human Motivation', 'Higher and Lower Needs'; A. Montagu, *On Being Human*; W. A. Weisskopf, 'The Ethical Role of Psychodynamics.'

on all primary social and human ties of solidarity and community.

There are parallels between these developments and the series of separations to which every individual is exposed in his life-history. Fromm points out that individuation means

> emerging from a state of oneness with the natural world to an awareness of oneself as a separate entity, an entity separate from surrounding nature.[1]

This is the same process which, in Western societies, took place during the last three centuries. But every individual has to pass through a series of separations: birth itself separates the child from the mother, and the entire process of education consists of separations of the child from his attendants. The separation from the mother is the earliest and, in all probability, the one that leaves the greatest impact on the mind of the individual. The period before the child becomes aware of his own individuality as distinct from the one of the mother is unconsciously 'remembered' as one of complete bliss and automatic need-satisfaction. It becomes the prototype of all situations of community and solidarity. On the other hand, the separation from the mother becomes the paradigm of all breaking of such ties. In the striving for solidarity and co-operation, the feelings toward the mother are reactivated.[2]

Thus the collective experiences during and after the industrial revolution, on the one hand, and the experiences of individuals during their own lives, on the other, show a common element, in that they both include separation, deprivation, and the breaking of ties. Industrial man was deprived of many traditional social ties and human bonds which were in conflict with the newly emerging socio-economic system. He became isolated and separated from the protection which his group-membership had given him before. He reacted to this experience by identifying the previously existing community and solidarity with his own ties to his mother and to the female in general. In his unconscious and in his life-history, the archetype of separation from community was the separation from the mother.

This renders understandable the fact that the female is disparaged by the apologists and praised by the antagonists. The market

[1] *Fear of Freedom*, p. 24.

[2] Alfred Adler says that 'the first act of a new-born child—drinking from the mother's breast—[is] cooperation.' For Adler, co-operation is psychologically a direct derivative of the mother-child relationship. 'We probably owe to the maternal sense of contact the largest part of human social feelings' (A. Adler, *The Social Interest*, quoted from Montagu, *op. cit.*, p. 56).

economy was inimical to communal ties. If these ties have a female connotation, those who approve of the new economic system must reject the high evaluation of such primary ties and, with it, the female element. This is what the apologists have done in their evaluation of land and nature. Malthus' and Ricardo's conscious tendency was directed toward the justification of the existing socioeconomic system. This system undermined the traditional role of the female in the division of labour and the traditional position of middle-class women as equal partners in the process of need-satisfaction. It also led to a disintegration of social and affectionate ties, which were unconsciously identified with the female. Thus the female element was demoted in the society which Ricardo and Malthus discussed. In order to make these anti-feminist trends acceptable, they had to disparage the female element in their thought. This is exactly what they did in the theory of population and rent and in their ideas about long-run economic dynamics.

The opponents, on the contrary, rejecting the system, approve of everything to which the system is hostile; in this case, solidarity, community, with their female connotations. Therefore, Engels (and Marx) place the mothers, the female, solidarity, community, and co-operation on a pedestal. Thus the actual socioeconomic conditions find their reflections in thought through the intermediary of psychological mechanisms and archetypes. Individual psychological mechanisms, emotions, and feelings lie in wait, as it were, in the unconscious mind and are mobilized by the events of history. The latter provide a cue for the reactivation of the former. However, this should not be interpreted as a one-way, monocausal chain of events. Socioeconomic conditions, psychological configurations, and thought form a syndrome in which every factor is both cause and effect of every other one.

Male Morality versus Female Fecundity

The identification of physiological drives with the female and of intellectual activity with the male is part of the primordial heritage of mankind and is frequently found in symbolic language. In Malthus' discussion of moral restraints as a remedy for the detrimental consequences of overpopulation, we find a similar dichotomy. The inevitable fecundity of the female has to be counteracted by the exercise of moral restraint, in order to bring about a balance between the two forces—the increase in population and the shortage of the means of subsistence. Here again, Malthus shows high moral evaluation of the male. Moral restraints of sexual activity and marriage are considered virtues; they restrict fertility, which would otherwise lead to vice and misery. Fertility and fecundity are female qualities. They operate with the power of nature. They have to be restricted by 'human energy and virtue.' There can be little doubt that Malthus means by 'human energy and virtue' the energy and virtue of the male, who is the one to exercise restraint in order to counterbalance the evils caused by 'female' fertility. This becomes quite clear in the following moral commandment:

> It is clearly the duty of each individual not to marry till he has a prospect of supporting his children; but it is at the same time to be wished that he should retain undiminished his desire for marriage, in order that *he* may exert himself to realize his prospect, and be stimulated to make provisions for the support of greater numbers.[1]

All this refers obviously to the male. According to the mores of the period, he is the one who proposes marriage, who decides if and when to marry, who has to support his wife and children, and who is supposed to exert himself in order to maintain a family. The use of the pronoun 'he' and the adjective 'his' confirms this interpretation.

Thus we find in Malthus' ideas a correlation to the socioeconomic trends of his times in respect to marriage and the position of women. The conflict between the passions and the restricting taboos are identified with the conflict between the male and the female. The supremacy of the male is maintained; he is the one who exercises the beneficial virtues which will save man and society from the dire consequences of the law of population, counteracting the irrepressible fecundity of women. The Malthusian ideas about the importance of moral restraints represent also a justification of the bourgeois middle-class ideal of the self-controlled, prudent, rational man. It represents these virtues as a necessary counterweight against female fecundity and nature's niggardliness. The exercise of these male virtues appears, in his system, as the *deus ex machina* who heals the wounds struck by the female factors, woman and land. Thus a place is assigned to these virtues, and it is shown that, with their exercise, man performs a necessary and beneficial function. It is quite obvious that this line of thought must have brought comfort to the middle-class individual who might be chafing under the restrictions imposed by his internalized pleasure taboos and who viewed with resentment the licentious mode of living of the aristocracy. Now he can sacrifice enjoyment with the pride of a person who knows that he fulfils a function in the cosmos.

[1] Malthus, *op. cit.*, II, p. 159.

Chapter XIV

THE PSYCHODYNAMIC MEANING OF LABOUR

Male and Labour

IN symbolic language, productive work was often interpreted as a male activity. In ancient and preliterate cultures various need-satisfying activities which lent themselves to a comparison with the male part in the sexual act had already been characterized by male symbols. We mentioned earlier the sexual symbols in agriculture and in the making of fire. Thus if, in ploughing, the earth was assigned a female role, the plough, penetrating it, was regarded as a male instrument. The plough assumes a phallic meaning in the same fashion as tools, such as hammer, nails, knives, etc. In Aryan and German mythology the hammer of the god Thor was an instrument for consecrating marriage ties. In many folklores the nail is regarded as an instrument of fertility and a penis symbol.[1] Similar symbolism was used in the making of fire, which was originally made by twirling a stick in a bowl, an obvious analogy to the act of cohabitation.

> The quirling of fire as we find it in the culture of most peoples, represents in ancient India the sexual act. The ancient Indians are not alone in this interpretation. The South Africans harbour the same beliefs. The reclining piece of wood is called by the same name as the female sex organ and the upright one by the same as the male.[2]

In Hebrew the expression for male and female are the drill and the hollow.[3] According to Freud, there is an especially close relation between labour and sexuality. He points to the research of a non-

[1] Hugo Winkler, quoted by O. Rank and H. Sachs, *Die Bedeutung der Psychoanalyse für die Geisteswissenschaft*, p. 15, n. 1; see also S. Freud, *A General Introduction to Psychoanalysis*, p. 146.

[2] Frobenius, *Das Zeitalter des Sonnengottes*, p. 338 (my translation).

[3] See also the many examples of similar symbolism in O. Rank, *Psychoanalytische Beiträge zur Mythenforschung*, pp. 22 ff.

psychoanalytical philologist, H. Sperber, of Upsala, who expressed the following view:

> Sexual needs have the largest share in the origin and development of language. He [Sperber] says that the first sounds uttered were means of communication and of summoning the sexual partner, and that in the later development the elements of speech were used as an accompaniment to the different kinds of work carried on by primitive man. This work was performed by associated efforts, to the sound of rhythmically repeated utterances, the effect of which was to transfer a sexual interest to the work. Primitive man thus made his work agreeable, so to speak, by treating it as the equivalent of and substitute for sexual activities. The word uttered during the communal work had therefore, two meanings, the one referring to the sexual act, the other to the labour which had come to be equivalent to it. In time the word was dissociated from its sexual significance and its application confined to the work.[1]

In the primordial heritage of mankind, labour had a sexual and male connotation; we find the same connotations in the thought of political economists. Economic thought served not only the purpose of explaining and interpreting the economic system. The importance of economic activity in the new society moved economic thought into the centre of the ideological system of the times. It became a sort of surreptitious cosmology, including some of the ideas which have been manifest in ancient mythology. The primeval conflict between the active and passive, the male and the female, is expressed in the conceptions of labour and land, at least in the Malthusian and Ricardian systems of thought.

Sir William Petty gave the clue: labour is the father or active principle of wealth, as lands are the mother. In the passage from John Locke, previously quoted (p. 24), this meaning is also indicated:

> Whatsoever, then, he removes out of the state that Nature has provided and left it in, he has mixed his labour with it, and joined it to something that is his own and thereby makes it his property.[2]

It is not too difficult to read into these and similar passages the meaning that the male, through his labour, mixes something of his own with female nature, so that the act of labouring results in a joint product. All this applies as well to the sexual union between

1 Freud, *op. cit.*, p. 149.

2 *On Civil Government*, Book II, chap. v.

man and wife and to procreation. One can assume that labour had a similar meaning in the writings of the classical economists. It is the male principle on which their labour theory of value rests. It is quite consistent when Malthus and Ricardo, together with their disparagement of the female factor represented by land, elevate the male factor of labour to the sole creator of economic value. This forms the counterpart of their demotion of the female principle. It is interrelated with one aspect of the Oedipus situation in which hostility to the mother is combined with admiration of and identification with the father. It also conforms to a sociocultural situation in which the patriarchal principle is predominant. We have analysed the tortuous method by which Ricardo tried to prove that the female principle, that land and rent, have no influence on value. His conclusion that it is labour employed on the marginal land which determines prices and values can also be interpreted as the attempt to represent economic value purely as a product of male activity. In a society in which the male is the centre and masculine activism an ideal, it is quite logical to assume that a male factor, such as labour, is the source, foundation, and measure of economic value, as of everything else.

Labour in the Thought of Marx

How is this interpretation of labour as the male principle compatible with the idea that the antagonists are pro-female? After all the labour theory of value has been primarily connected with the name of Marx, and he has made it famous. Before we can answer this question, we would like to show with a few examples how the masculine character of labour and its various mythological and biopsychological connotations permeate Marxian thought. This, in turn, will throw some light on the question how the pro-feminine attitude of the antagonists is compatible with their labour theory of value. It will indicate that the equation labour equals male has two possible meanings: (1) labour equals the father; (2) labour equals the son. It is the latter psychological equation which forms the background of the Marxian value theory, in contrast to the Ricardian thought, which refers to the former.

Quite in line with the unconscious tenor of classical economics, Marx tried not only to emphasize the importance of the male element in the creation of economic value but to emphasize it to the exclusion of the female part. Thus, in his definition of what he calls the 'expanded relative form of value' (exchange value), he states:

> that it is not the exchange of commodities which regulates the mag-

nitude of their value; but, on the contrary, that it is the magnitude of their value which controls their exchange proportions.'[1]

Value is the effect of labour used in the production of goods and thereby embodied in them. If we consider labour as the male element, this statement implies that it is the male element alone which creates the value in commodities. Exchange has nothing to do with it. Exchange may be translated into the language of the unconscious as sexual intercourse. Intercourse is definitely an act in which man and woman confer mutual favours upon each other and exchange love and sexual enjoyment. The same can be said of procreation, in which the man exchanges his semen for the child given to him by the woman. The analogy of child and gift has frequently been noted in symbolic language. In Western civilization marriage has often been considered a contract. In a contract both parties bestow a mutual consideration on each other. It is not too far fetched to apply the same analogy to the sexual union.[2] If this interpretation is correct, Marx's idea that value is determined by labour bestowed in production and not by the exchange process means, unconsciously, that only the producing active male procreates and that the woman has nothing to do with it. The role of the female is unconsciously belittled.

Throughout his discussion of value in the first volume of *Das Kapital*, Marx seems to imply an unconscious parallel between the production of commodities and the procreation of children. One can interpret the Marxian theory of value and his explanation of surplus value in terms of what Freud called the 'infantile sexual investigation'—the quest of the child to find an answer to the riddle of procreation and birth.[3] In nineteenth-century Western middle-class culture the causes of pregnancy and birth are obscure to the child. So are, to Marx, the causes of the creation of value, especially of surplus value. To him, the transubstantiation of a physical commodity into a carrier of exchange value is 'enigmatical' and 'mystical':

> Hence the enigmatical character of the equivalent form which escapes the notice of the bourgeois political economist, until this form, completely developed, confronts him in the shape of money.

[1] Marx, *Capital* ('Modern Library' ed.), I, p. 73.

[2] Unconsciously, Marx confirms this when he talks about commodities being 'in love with money' (*ibid.*, p. 121); about 'wooing glances cast at money by commodities' (p. 123); even the Freudian equation, faeces equals money, appears in the passage: 'Hence money may be dirt, although dirt is not money' (p. 123). See S. Freud, *Collected Papers*, II, p. 168.

[3] S. Freud, 'Three Contributions to the Theory of Sex,' p. 594.

He then seeks to explain away the mystical character of gold and silver.[1]

The most enigmatic in the entire process of procreation to the child, as well as to the primitive, is the role of the father. There have been civilizations in which the impregnating role of the male was not fully realized. Marx wanted to stress the importance of the father-role when he explained the transformation of money into capital and the origin of surplus value. The phenomenon to be explained is this: the process of capitalist circulation consists in the exchange of money against commodities and in the resale of these commodities for money. This process would be absurd if the same values were exchanged for each other, if $M=C=M$ (money=commodity=money). But it is a process in which 'something new is added':

> More money is withdrawn from circulation at the finish than was thrown into it at the start. . . . The exact form of this process is therefore: $M-C-M'$; where $M'=M+\Delta M$, the original sum advanced, plus an increment. This increment or excess over the original value I call 'surplus value'. The value originally advanced, therefore . . . adds to itself a surplus value or expands itself.[2]

The question is: How does this surplus value arise? Marx makes the answer to this question difficult because he assumes that the nature of the exchange process requires that only equivalents can be exchanged.[3] With this assumption, it is a real enigma why and how surplus value is created.

This problem is pursued and investigated by Marx with the same ardour with which the middle-class child in Western civilization tries to penetrate the mystery of birth, pregnancy, and the sexual act. The parallels between the problem of the origin of surplus value and the infantile sexual investigation are obvious; both are concerned with answering questions of how something new, something that was not there before, is created. In both situations the overt facts give no clue to the solution of the mystery. The exchange process $M-C-M'$ does not provide any answer, because the magnitudes involved are supposedly all quantitative equivalents. The overt relations between father and mother in the middle-class family also do not provide any clue, because the act which leads to

[1] Marx, *op. cit.*, I, p. 66. [2] *Ibid.*, p. 168.

[3] He took this idea over from Aristotle (*ibid.*, p. 68). This assumption shows also his 'substantial' approach to the problem of value; an equal quantity of a 'value-substance' has to be exchanged against an equivalent quantity of the same 'substance'.

impregnation takes place on the inside, behind closed doors, hidden from the view and knowledge of the child; the mystery which, because of the sex taboos of Western middle-class culture, surrounds all sexual phenomena and activities adds to the riddle. All this is reflected very clearly in the tone and content of Marx's analysis. That he tries to hide behind a wall of sarcasm and pretends that he is merely kidding the capitalist cannot obscure the fact that, to him, the explanation of surplus value appears to be a mystery, which, however, he alone is finally able to solve.

In *Capital*, Volume I, Part II, chapter vii, Section II, Marx affirms, at first, the basic principle: 'The value of each commodity is determined by the quantity of labour expended on and materialized in it.'[1] The problem is what portion of the value of the final product is added to the value of the raw materials by the labour of the worker. When, in the value-creating process of capitalist production, labour power is applied directly in the production of a product,

> the raw material serves now merely as an absorbent of a definite quantity of labour. By this absorption it is in fact changed into yarn [the final product] . . . because labour power. . . is added to it; but the product . . . is now nothing more than a measure of the labour absorbed by the cotton [the raw material]. . . . Definite quantities of product . . . now represent nothing but definite quantities of labour, definite masses of crystallized labour-time. They are nothing more than the materialization of so many days of social labour.[2]

It should be observed how eager Marx is to show that the product is nothing but labour; that the physical reality of the product does not really count; that, ultimately, the product is nothing else but labour-time crystallized and embodied in it. He insists on reducing the process of value-creation to a metamorphosis of the substance, labour. Translated into the language of the unconscious, this means that the factor labour alone, the male factor in the production process, creates economic value in the form of the final product. In his example the raw material is cotton, a product of land and nature. This product of the 'female', for which land and nature stand, has no influence on the value of the final product. The value of the raw material is dissolved into the labour which is used in its production; it becomes crystallized labour-time. In psychodynamic language this means that the female factor is changed into the male factor; the value-creating factor is always 'male' labour. Raw material is

[1] *Ibid.*, p. 208. [2] *Ibid.*, pp. 211–12.

only a transitory stage between labour embodied in it and labour embodied in the final product. The 'female' factor, the raw material, is 'merely an absorbent of a definite quantity of labour.' Could the male-female analogy be made clearer? Is not the woman the 'absorbent' part, the one who absorbs the male substance? With all his mighty powers of reasoning, sharpened by Hegelian training, Marx contrives to eliminate the value-creating effects of everything that is not labour, that is, of everything that does not have a male connotation.

But let us follow Marx's argument. He proceeds to add up the labour-time, evaluated in money, which is embodied in the direct labour,[1] in the raw materials, and in the wear and tear of the tools used in the production of the final product, and considers the sum of these values as the 'adequate' price for that product.[2] Then he starts his ridiculing of the capitalists: 'Our capitalist stares in astonishment,' because thus no surplus value can possibly arise. 'Oh, but I advanced my money for the express purpose of making more money.' However, 'because the value of the product is merely the sum of the value of the commodities that were thrown into the process of production' (pp. 212–14), wherefrom is surplus value derived?

Here Marx seemingly makes fun of the capitalist. But unconsciously he may also be making fun of himself. He is caught in the web of his own assumptions: (1) that only equivalent values are being exchanged against each other in the market; (2) that the value of the final product is equal to the sum of the labour values of the factors which were used in producing it. In the symbolic language of the unconscious: How can the parents produce anything beyond themselves, how can anything be created and procreated? Nothing that the child can openly observe would indicate what causes the 'surplus value'. 'Out of such a simple addition of existing values, no surplus-value can possibly arise!'[3]

Finally, Marx resolves the riddle and presents his own solution, which is that labour power has 'the specific use-value . . . of being a source not only of value but of more value than it has itself.'[4] Marx simply transfers the theory of the Physiocrats from land to the factor

[1] Like Ricardo, he figures the value of labour power in terms of labour requisite to produce the necessaries of life required by the labourer (*ibid.*, p. 212). He takes over from Ricardo the subsistence theory of wages.

[2] Marx, *op. cit.*, p. 212.

[3] *Ibid.*, p. 213. In n. 1 on the same page Marx refers to the Physiocrats, who explained the enigma of surplus value by the fertility of the soil; they considered all labour except agricultural labour unproductive. This had to be rejected by Marx because it would impute productivity only to the 'female' factor.

[4] *Ibid.*, p. 216.

'labour power'. Instead of attributing the special quality of surplus productivity to land, he imputes it to human labour power. The mystery, the secret of productivity, the faculty of being able to produce more than there was before, to create something new, is now attributed to labour. This means that 'fertility' in respect to value is transferred from the 'female' land to the 'male' factor, labour.

Marx has an almost mystical belief in the magical productivity of labour. One has only to listen to the psychological overtones of his language, which always betrays the unconscious meaning of conscious statements: 'the capitalist . . . converts value, i.e., past, materialized and dead labour into capital, into value big with value, a live monster that is fruitful and multiplies.'[1] Does this not sound like a complete analogy to the processes of impregnation and procreation? Does not the male convert the female into a 'live monster big with value, that is fruitful and multiplies'? Does not the experience of the pregnancy of the mother, incomprehensible in the light of his own experience, appear thus to the child?

Marx calls the creation of surplus value a 'metamorphosis'; this conversion of money into capital which

> takes place both within the sphere of circulation and also outside of it; within the circulation, because conditioned by the purchase of the labour power in the market; outside the circulation, because what is done within it is only a stepping stone to the production of surplus value, a process which is entirely confined to the sphere of production.[2]

For the middle-class child, procreation takes place also in two spheres: there are the relations between the parents, which it can observe openly; they do not explain how the mother got pregnant and came to give birth; there are, however, the secret, hidden happenings which are not revealed to the child and which are only dimly surmised. This corresponds to the Marxian statement that the metamorphosis into surplus value takes place inside and outside the sphere of circulation.

The psychodynamic meaning of the productivity of labour power becomes very clear in Marx's discussion of constant and variable capital. Marx states that variable capital is the one 'represented' by labour power; constant capital is 'represented' by the means of production.[3] The main difference between the two is that the value of the non-labour factors are merely preserved and transferred to the final product in the production process; whereas the value of the labour power is not only transferred and preserved but also

[1] *Ibid.*, p. 217. [2] *Ibid.*, p. 217. [3] *Ibid.*, p. 232.

increased. All this is accomplished by the work of the labourer alone; he, and he alone, preserves and adds value to the final product:

> In so far then as labour is such a specific productive activity, in so far as it is spinning, weaving or forging, it raises, by mere contact, the means of production from the dead, makes them living factors of the labour-process, and combines with them to form new products.[1]

Here the physical productivity of labour is clearly extolled. It is considered to be a special magical quality which enables the labourer, 'by mere contact', to bring dead materials and tools to life and to impregnate them with life-giving fecundity. Only variable capital, representing labour power, is productive of value.

Previously, Marx had explained surplus value as the difference between the market value of labour power and the market value of the product of labour (minus the value of the non-labour factors of production). This difference arises because the market value of labour power is, according to the Ricardian and Marxian subsistence theory of wages, determined by the price of the necessaries the worker needs for his support during the period of production. It is smaller than the value of the final product. Now, in his discussion of constant and variable capital, Marx states in general terms and without any specific reference to the market and price system, that labour power increases the value of the final product over and above the value of the non-human means of production. The

> subjective factor of the labour-process, with labour-power in action . . . by the mere act of working, creates each instant an additional or new value.[2]

The labourer reproduces the value of his own labour, which Marx considers to be the creation of new value, although

> this new value only replaces the money advanced by the capitalist in the purchase of the labour-power, and spent by the labourer on the necessaries of life. With regard to money spent, the new value is merely a reproduction; but, nevertheless, it is an actual, and not, as in the case of the means of production, only an apparent, reproduction. The substitution of one value for another, is here effected by the creation of new value.[3]

To the unbiased observer it seems that the two processes are exactly alike and in no way distinguishable from each other. The cost of capital goods (means of production, raw materials, and tools) has to be recovered through the sale of the final product. In precisely the same fashion, the wages of the labourers who worked to produce

[1] Marx, *op. cit.*, p. 223. [2] *Ibid.*, p. 231. [3] *Ibid.*, pp. 231–32.

the same product have to be recovered in the price of the final product. To Marx, however, the two processes are not alike. The first process is only a transfer of value; the value of the means of production is consumed, destroyed in the process of production, and transferred to the final product.

> Their value undergoes a metempsychosis. It deserts the consumed body, to occupy the newly created one. But this transmigration takes place, as it were, behind the back of the labourer.[1]

In contrast to the means of production, to raw materials, tools, etc., labour power does not transfer and preserve, but creates anew. There is nothing in the purely objective facts of the production process which would warrant such a distinction. All these factors, human and non-human, co-operate in the production of the product; their value or, better, their costs have to be recovered sooner or later through the sale of the product.[2]

What is the meaning of this obviously untenable distinction? It is of course, a necessary one from the point of view of the labour theory of value, according to which value is created only by labour expended in production. Like Ricardo, Marx cannot admit any other source and foundation of value except labour. Therefore, non-human means of production must be assigned a secondary role; they do not create value, but their value is only preserved and transferred; moreover, they are consumed and destroyed in this process, whereas labour power stays alive forever. All this is quite logical and necessary, once the basic assumption is established that labour, and labour alone, is the creator and determinant of value.

The distinction under consideration, however, is also closely related to the male-female dichotomy. The male factor, labour, is considered to be the real creator of value. It is represented as creative even in so far as it re-creates its own value by recovering the cost of labour in the price of the product. The means of production are regarded as dying, as being consumed in the process. If the reader's mind is sharpened to psychological undertones, he will have noticed, in the passage quoted last, parallels to the process of birth. The value of the means of production 'deserts the consumed body, to occupy a newly created one.' That could be said of the female body, which

1 Marx, *op. cit.*, p. 230.

2 Today the Marxian terminology, his talk of a transfer, preservation and new creation of value, seems inappropriate; it seems merely a problem of recovering costs. His terminology betrays, however, his 'substantial' approach to the problem of value, which is exactly the same as Ricardo's. Value is, at least implicitly, considered as embodied in a substance, which can be preserved, transferred, and created anew, like physical matter.

provides the substance of the embryo. Marx talks about a 'metempsychosis', a 'transmigration'; this again points to the miracle of birth. And all this 'takes place behind the back of the labourer.' Here again, we see the child, complaining implicitly about the secrecy which surrounds the entire act of impregnation and parturition. It takes place behind his back; there is something secret going on which is kept from him.

Be this as it may, the male element, labour power, is extolled as the only creative element:

> labour-power does, in the process of production, undergo an alteration of value. It both reproduces the equivalent of its own value, and also produces an excess, a surplus value.[1]

In psychological terms: the entire Marxian argument culminates in the conclusion that the masculine element, labour, plays the decisive part in the procreation of economic value.

The Male Father and The Male Son

We are now in the position to return to our initial question: If both Ricardo and Marx, apologists and antagonists, emphasize the male role in the creation of value, how is this compatible with our previous conclusions that the apologists are anti-female and the antagonists pro-female? Or, in other words, how does it happen that, in spite of their common 'male' labour theory of value, Ricardo and Marx arrive at such different political conclusions?

Our analysis of the Ricardian theory of value centred around the idea that he, like his contemporaries, had an ambivalent attitude toward the market economy. His thought is beset with conflicting dichotomies: between the early and rude state and the capitalist system; the static and dynamic type of analysis; pessimism and optimism; male and female. Although he harboured some unconscious hostility toward the economic system, he defended it, whereas Marx attacked it openly. How was it possible that these two diametrically opposed points of view could be based on one and the same labour theory of value?

An answer can be given on the psychodynamic level: it is found in the father-son conflict. We have already pointed out that, to the nineteenth-century mind, the existing economic institutions had a patriarchal character. Therefore, the opposition and revolt against them assumed, in part, a matriarchal or pro-feminine tone. However, there is another psychological mechanism at work in such a situation. We have discussed the two alternative attitudes of the Oedipus

[1] Marx, *op. cit.*, p. 232.

complex: the identification with the father combined with a hostile attitude toward the mother and the female; and identification with and love of the mother combined with a hostile attitude toward the father. The latter is the typical attitude of the revolutionary son. In the neo-Freudian interpretation of the Oedipus complex, the emphasis lies less on the sexual aspect than on the revolt of the new generation against the authority of the father or the father-substitutes. Erich Fromm states that the Oedipus

> myth can be understood as a symbol not of the incestuous love between mother and son but of the rebellion of the son against the authority of the father in the patriarchal family; that the marriage of Oedipus and Jocasta is only a secondary element, and only one of the symbols of victory of the son who takes his father's place with all his privileges.[1]

This situation is reflected in the attitude of the antagonists toward the economic system and is clearly expressed in Marxian value theory. In their minds the entire system, with all its institutions, such as private property, wage labour, the production of commodities for exchange against money on the market, the political state, etc., had a patriarchal character and stood for the authority of the father. They felt themselves to be sons who had revolted against this authority and against this system. In the value theory of the advocates, such as Malthus and Ricardo, the male element, that is, labour, represented the father. Their attempts to prove that it is the exclusive creator of value reflect their identification with the authority of the father and their acceptance of this authority. In their attempts to protect and explain this authority, they had to depreciate the female and motherly elements as of secondary importance. Their pro-masculine and anti-feminine attitude meant: pro-father, pro-authority and, therefore, anti-mother and anti-feminine. In the thought of the Marxians, the male element, labour, means the son; they are pro-female, because they are anti-father. Their 'feminism' does not imply an anti-male attitude, but an opposition to the maleness of the father, which by no means precludes a pro-male outlook as far as the son is concerned.

The antagonists have a hostile attitude toward the father, because they revolt against his authority and therefore take sides with the mother against him. One can find the symbolic fight between father and son reflected in the Marxian theory of surplus value. This surplus value is appropriated by the capitalist, although it is the

[1] E. Fromm, *The Forgotten Language*, p. 262.

product of the labourer. Marx wants to restore this surplus value to its rightful owner, the labourer.

According to Freud, the father prevents the son from having love relations with the mother. In Western civilization this situation was expanded into a general sex taboo; to some extent, all premarital sexual activity of the adolescent is forbidden. The internalized, unconscious sanction of this injunction is the fear of castration. This fear is confirmed in the male child when it discovers the lack of a penis in the woman. Children believe that both sexes are equipped with male genitals. The lack of them in one sex is interpreted as the result of castration, a punishment for forbidden sexual activity. These ideas merge with the general sexual taboos of our civilization. Sex and fear of castration become interrelated in the minds of Western middle-class individuals. In the unconscious fantasy of the child, the one who carries out the castration is the father; the victim is the son.[1] The son, then, hates the father because he is the obstacle to sexual activity, and because he threatens him with castration.

All the elements of this situation can be found in Marx. According to Freud, the son is hostile to the father, because he takes something away from him: the mother, the female in general through the injunction against premarital sexual activity, and the penis through castration as punishment for the violation of these taboos. According to Marxian theory, too, something is taken away: the means of production and the surplus value. Like the Freudian son who considers the mother as his property to whom the father bars his access, the Marxian labourer considers the means of production and the surplus value to be his; it is he who produces both, and, therefore, they are supposed to be rightly his. The Freudian conflict is a conflict about property rights to the mother or the female in general. The Marxian conflict is a similar conflict about property rights to the means of production and to the surplus value. We have pointed out earlier that Marx attributes to the means of production a female character; they only transfer value but do not create it; they do not have the attributes of male creativity. Thus, in his system of thought, the conflict is also about property rights to something female. In the Marxian system the role of the father is played by the capitalist. He owns the means of production, as the father 'owns' the mother. As the father prevents the son from having access to the mother and the female, so the capitalist prevents the worker from having access to the means of production. And as the father deprives the son of his penis, so the capitalist deprives the worker of the surplus value.

[1] S. Freud, 'Three Contributions to the Theory of Sex,' in *Basic Writings*, pp. 594 ff.

The violation of the patriarchal taboos and injunctions are punished, at least in the expectation of the 'sons', by castration. Castration means the removal, the deprivation, of a part. In Freudian thought it means the cutting-off of the male genitals. In Marxian thought it means the taking-away of the surplus value. Marx symbolizes surplus value by the sign prime. In the formula which describes the capitalist process of circulation $M-C-M'$, the prime after the second M represents the surplus value. This is an obvious penis symbol. And this is exactly what the worker is deprived of by the capitalist. It would be difficult to find a clearer case in which the Freudian theories are borne out and his symbols found in socioeconomic thought.

In conclusion, it should be emphasized again that our discussion of psychodynamic factors which have influenced economic thought does not imply that sexual, erotic, and biopsychological factors are prime causes and ultimate determinants of thought and behaviour. They interact with sociocultural and intellectual factors as parts of a total situation. Earlier we emphasized the role of other than biopsychological factors; in this section we are concerned with the latter as determinants of the labour theory of value. This explanation has to be read together with the previous ones, in which other factors are stressed; the entire system of interpretation forms an inseparable whole. The male-female antinomy is only one manifestation of the deep conflicts which confront human existence in general and social thought in particular. As long as man belongs to different realms, physical and spiritual, conscious and unconscious; as long as culture imposes on him restrictions which suppress some of his natural traits, such conflicts will arise and will be reflected in thought. How this is done in the writings of some representative economists of the nineteenth century has been shown in the preceding pages.

Part V

Alfred Marshall's Value and Equilibrium Theory

Chapter XV

ETHICS AND ECONOMICS

The Basic Attitudes and Conflicts

IN the period of the neoclassical and marginalist schools which dominated economic thinking in the Anglo-Saxon countries after, roughly, the last quarter of the nineteenth century, the classical pattern was retained but with a shift of emphasis. The increase in capital equipment and the progress of technology created the problem of finding marketing outlets for the products of an economic system with high productive capacity. The result was a growing concern with consumption and selling.

The marginalist and neoclassical schools partly reflected and partly foreshadowed this trend by moving the subjective element into the centre of thought. Consumers' need-satisfaction is considered the ultimate aim of economic activity, and value is explained in terms of utility to individuals. To the classical economists, economic value was a result of labour applied in the production process, an objective phenomenon. To the marginalists, economic value was the result of subjective evaluation by individuals. Although Alfred Marshall tried to combine both points of view, his emphasis lies on the subjective element.

There were utilitarian elements in the writings of Adam Smith. By interpreting labour as the sacrifice of liberty and happiness, Smith used a utilitarian approach. In the hands of Ricardo, however, labour became a more technological and mechanical concept. And both Adam Smith and Ricardo rejected utility as the basis of value. With the advent of the neoclassical and marginalist schools, the happiness of the individual and the utility of things to him became openly and admittedly the foundation of economic value. Demand moved into the centre of discussion, and consumers' motives and actions were now thoroughly analysed.

The turn toward utility and individual desires brought to the fore problems created by the existence of human inclinations incompatible with the conduct required by the economic system. If need-satisfaction is the ultimate goal, economic activity is endangered by the fact that the existing economic system permits only the satisfaction of a relatively narrowly circumscribed type of needs: those which can be satisfied by the acquisition of money and through exchange in the market, and often in a manner conflicting with some 'non-economic' human propensities. Also no social order is conceivable in which the satisfaction of purely individual aims is the supreme goal; such a system must end in anarchy. The classical economists have avoided this result, not only by the fiction of the invisible hand and of the natural harmony of interests, but also by their rigid adherence to the value system, which stressed as ultimate goals objective factors like labour for production. The shift of the marginalist school toward subjectivity removed this possibility. Alfred Marshall provided for a counterweight against purely relativistic and anarchic subjectivity in his emphasis on economic rationality. He represents economic rationalism as an ideal and, at the same time, as the ultimate result of economic laws. He shows that the behaviour of consumer, firm, and industry can be understood with the help of models of rational economic conduct.

The value symbol of rational economic man becomes the focal point of thinking.[1] It is combined with an idealization of the activistic mode of life.[2] Wants are subordinated to activities. An element of the work ethic is still retained, in spite of the stress on subjective desires. Not only satisfaction of needs but activities directed toward the higher goals in life and toward character formation are the ultimate ends. Rational, deliberate conduct and self-control were considered to be ideals.

Through this emphasis on rationality and character-forming activities, the danger was avoided that non-rational and hedonistic drives would enter through the door of subjectivism and destroy not only the regularity of the economic laws but also the value orientation required by the economic system. Therefore, it had to be demonstrated that rationality dominates all types of economic activity. The consumer, the housewife, the entrepreneur, the saver, etc., are all represented as people who consciously balance opposing forces, values, and interests in such a fashion that they maximize the total of their advantages, utility, profits, etc. In all these cases

1 The much misused term ' economic man' has a history which is often overlooked. The 'economic man' of the classicists was not quite the same as that of the neoclassicists, because of the shift from the objective goals of production to the subjective goals of need-satisfaction, although in Adam Smith's description of the parsimonious and prudent man, the Marshallian ideal of deliberateness is already delineated.

2 For the role of activities in Marshall's thought see T. Parsons, *The Structure of Social Action*, Part II, chap. iv.

the existence of inner conflicts between goals, values, and impulses and between what man wants to do and what the economic system permits him to do is ignored. Human action is represented as directed toward a consciously calculable maximization point at which full satisfaction under given conditions can be reached. Conflicting drives and inclinations of a qualitatively different nature are reduced to a common quantitative denominator, so that conscious comparison of relative quantities of gain and loss can show the way to a clear-cut decision, maximizing benefits and equilibrating opposing forces. Rational economic conduct and maximization of gains and equilibrium become symbols of economic harmony.

Because Marshall accepted subjectivism but combined it with some of the objectivist elements of classical thought, his work lends itself excellently to an examination of the psychological, cultural, and intellectual conflicts of the period as far as they centred around the economic system.

In the *Principles of Economics* Marshall presents a system of economic ethics and a scientific interpretation of economic activity. He tries to interpret the existing economy as a morally acceptable and comprehensible order. These two aspects of his thought are inseparably intertwined: neither can be understood without the other.[1]

Higher Goals and Deliberateness

The opening chapters of the *Principles* present the picture of a titanic inner struggle. It is significant that Marshall feels compelled to start his monumental work with a defence of economics against the frequent accusation that economics is concerned merely with materialistic, selfish competition and neglects the higher goals of life.

In chapter i, Marshall emphasizes the influence of business activity on character formation. He rejects the possession of wealth for its own sake and denies that economics is concerned only with this goal.[2]

He rejects competition as the main characteristic of industrial life. He presents his own ideal, which he assumes to be the fundamental attitude of industrial man:

[1] Our examination will have to follow to some extent the sequence of Marshall's own argument. For a psychocultural understanding, not only the content but also the organization of his thoughts are important. Marshall's organization shows his ambivalence, because it reverts again and again to the same problems, thus betraying his own inner doubts about the validity of his own conclusions. This will cause a certain repetitiveness in our own analysis, for which we beg the indulgence of the reader.

[2] *Principles of Economics*, pp. 4, 22, n. 1.

> . . . a certain independence and habit of choosing one's own course for oneself, a self-reliance; a deliberation and yet a promptness of choice and judgment, and a habit of forecasting the future and of shaping one's course with reference to distant aims. . . . It is deliberateness and not selfishness that is the characteristic of the modern age.[1]

Deliberate rational conduct is considered simultaneously as an ideal, as a fact, and as the main concern of economics. In Book I, chapter ii, Section III, Marshall maintains that economics is specially concerned with the side of life

> in which man's conduct is most deliberate and in which he most often reckons up the advantages and disadvantages of any particular action before he enters on it.

Even habitual conduct and customary behaviour 'have arisen from a close and careful watching the advantages and disadvantages of different courses of conduct.' Earning a living is 'the most systematic part of people's lives.'[2]

Footnote 1 on page 20 reveals Marshall's moral preference. People of 'wayward temperament' and persons who 'could not give a good account even to themselves of the motives of their action' are unfavourably compared with 'steadfast and thoughtful' people, whose 'impulses are the product of habits which [they have] adopted more or less deliberately.' Such individuals are rational and deliberate through and through:

> And whether these impulses are an expression of his higher nature or not; whether they spring from mandates of his conscience, the pressure of social connection, or the claims of his bodily wants, he yields a certain relative precedence to them without reflection now, because on previous occasions he has decided deliberately to yield that relative precedence.[3]

This shows how seriously Marshall took the ideal of the rational, deliberate man. To him it is by no means a hypothetical construct used to arrive at determinate, predictable equilibrium solutions. Conscious, deliberate calculation is considered a virtue, an obligation. And rational man is rational through and through; not only when he is consciously rational but also in his impulses, because of their rational genesis. Deliberate calculation is the prime cause of all his actions:

[1] *Principles of Economics*, pp. 5–6. [2] *Ibid.*, pp. 20–21. [3] *Ibid.*, p. 20, n. 1.

> The predominant attractiveness of one course of action over others, even when not the result of calculation at the time, is the product of more or less deliberate decisions made by him before in somewhat similar cases.[1]

Deliberate, rational economic conduct is contrasted with selfishness, which is rejected. Instead of 'competition', Marshall proposes the use of the term 'economic freedom' for the syndrome of self-reliant habits, forethought, and deliberate and free choice, characteristic of modern business and industry.[2]

Marshall regards competition as an outcome of human imperfection and as being in conflict with virtue:

> In a world in which all men were perfectly virtuous, competition would be out of place. . . . But in the responsible conduct of affairs, it is worse than folly to ignore the imperfections which still cling to human nature.[3]

Competition is not virtuous; this is a far cry from the point of view which considers it beneficial and the competitive pursuit of economic self-interest as morally justified because it results in economic benefits. Or is it? Perhaps Marshall's statement is only the open expression of a thought which is latent in the idea of harmony. If it is necessary to justify the competitive pursuit of self-interest by maintaining that it is at least socially beneficial, it may be because of the underlying feeling that it is ethically unacceptable.[4] And this is exactly what Marshall contends. Competition is an outcome of moral imperfection and would not exist if men were perfectly virtuous. It is made quite clear that Marshall rejects the utilitarian and egotistic interpretation of economic activity. To him the main qualities of industrial man are deliberateness in making decisions based on long-range planning and foresight.

However, Marshall knows that deliberate rationality is only one type of human behaviour, that not all actions are deliberate and the outcome of calculation, and that 'in ordinary life people do not weigh beforehand the results of every action.' He refers to 'that group of gratifications which is sometimes named "the pleasures of the chase".'[5] Thus Marshall recognizes that man is not perfectly rational, not even in business life, where, according to his own observations, the pleasures of the chase play an important part. This is incompatible with his statements about business life being the most systematic part of people's life and his praise of deliberate rationality.

[1] *Ibid.* [2] *Ibid.*, p. 10. [3] *Ibid.*, p. 9.

[4] W. A. Weisskopf, 'Hidden Value Conflicts in Economic Thought'; see also above, pp. 46 ff. [5] *Principles*, p. 20, n. 1.

We find here a conflict between an ethical ideal and factual observation. The conflict is solved by interpreting business behaviour as rational, and habits and customs in business as the residue of past calculation of advantages. Thus the non-rational is reduced to the rational by its alleged genesis.

The Profit Motive Rationalized as Methodological Device

In spite of his rejection of acquisitive selfishness, Marshall points out that economics centres around monetary matters and material rewards:

> The steadiest motive to ordinary business work is the desire for the pay which is the material reward of work. The pay may be on its way to be spent selfishly or unselfishly, for noble or base ends; and here the variety of human nature comes into play. But the motive is supplied by a definite amount of money: and it is this definite and exact money measurement of the steadiest motives in business life, which has enabled economics far to outrun every other branch of the study of man.[1]

The measurement of the intensity of motives by the 'measuring rod of money' is explained by Marshall as a methodological device, used for the sake of mathematical precision. But the first page of the second chapter shows very clearly that it is more than that. It starts out with mentioning higher nature and higher motives which are carried into business. It mentions personal affections, conceptions of duty, reverence for high ideals. It talks about noble emulation rather than love of wealth for its own sake, as a motive for business innovations. But after all these higher elements have been invoked, the desire for pay is mentioned, not merely as a hypothetical, fictitious assumption for the sake of quantification and precision, not merely as a conception of an 'as-if' nature, but 'as the steadiest motive to ordinary business work.' It is considered to be a fact and not a fiction. There is an obvious inconsistency between Marshall's interpretation of the money motive as a fact and as a methodological device.

An explanation of this contradiction will be made easier by examining Marshall's methodological argument. He believes that economics has an advantage over the other social sciences because of its opportunities for using exact methods.[2] The exact method is represented as inherent in the subject matter of economics. 'Its special field of work gives rather larger opportunities for exact

[1] *Principles* p. 14. [2] *Ibid.*, p. 15.

methods than any other branch.'[1] Economics is concerned with subjective feelings,

> desires, aspirations and other affections of human nature, the outward manifestations of which appear as incentives to action in such a form that the force or quantity of the incentives can be estimated and measured with some approach to accuracy. . . . An opening is made for the methods and the tests of science as soon as the force of a person's motives—not the motives themselves—can be approximately measured by the sum of money, which he will just give up in order to secure a desired satisfaction; or again by the sum which is just required to induce him to undergo a certain fatigue.[2]

The assumptions implied in this form of reasoning have become standard equipment of the theory of economic behaviour since Marshall. He does not measure subjective feeling directly, 'but only indirectly through its effect.'[3] He deduces the existence of economic motives from their effect in the sphere of money in the same way as classical mechanics deduces the existence of force from mass and velocity.

The psychological meaning of this reasoning becomes clearer when we see that the result of this method is to eliminate qualitative moral differences in motives and to reduce them to a common quantitative denominator: 'Of course various affections belong to man's higher nature and others to his lower, and are thus different in kind.'[4] Even physical 'lower' pleasures of the same and of different persons cannot be compared. But a basis of comparison can be established, according to Marshall, by studying the amount of money which people are willing to pay for a good or for which they are willing to do an extra hour of work.[5] Thus the qualitatively incomparable is reduced to a quantitative common denominator. Marshall states explicitly that in this way, by reducing motives to the common quantitative denominator of money, the problem of ethical evaluation is eliminated:

> Thus, measuring a mental state as men do in ordinary life, by its motor force or incentive . . . no new difficulty is introduced by the fact that some of the motives . . . belong to man's higher nature and some to his lower.[6]

In this way the conflict which he tries to resolve in his first chapter —the conflict between the higher goals of life and undue concern

[1] *Ibid.*, p. 15.
[2] *Ibid.*, p. 15.
[3] *Ibid.*
[4] *Ibid.*, p. 15.
[5] *Ibid.*, p. 16.
[6] *Ibid.*

with the selfishness of pecuniary acquisition—is now eliminated by the magic of a methodological device.

> He [the economist and the everyday person] does not attempt to weigh the real value of the higher affections of our nature against those of our lower: he does not balance the love for virtue against the desire for agreeable food.[1]

Motivations which lead to equal monetary sacrifices or which are undertaken for the same monetary reward are made to appear equally valuable by the equalizing measuring rod of money. However, Marshall hastens to add the important qualification that 'he does not ignore the mental and spiritual side of life' and that it is important, even for the economist, 'to know whether the desires which prevail are such as to help to build up a strong and righteous character.'[2] One can feel Marshall's ambivalence from sentence to sentence. As soon as he describes the quantifying monetizing method of economics and the resulting ethical neutrality, he takes it back by re-emphasizing the importance of higher values.

Marshall's emphasis on deliberateness and rationality has the function not only of stressing the character-forming effects of economic activity but of making economic behaviour quantifiable and calculable, in order to arrive at uniform laws. If earning a living is the systematic part of people's lives,

> general statements can be made about it . . . and numerical estimates can be framed as to the amount of money or general purchasing power that is required to supply a sufficient motive for them.[3]

It is interesting to observe how the ethical and intellectual functions of thought reinforce each other here. The ideal of rational, deliberate calculation becomes a fact and is supported by observation.[4] If people are rational, their motives can be measured in terms of money. Although Marshall rebels against the purely utilitarian approach, he accepts the utilitarian calculus in the end. He represents it as the ideal of deliberate rationality and, at the same time, as a fact. Thus the ethical and the intellectual world picture of the economy become unified.

However, Marshall's inner doubts force him to revert to the problem of the ethical justification of money-making. In Section IV of chapter ii he states that 'the desire to make money does not necessarily proceed from motives of a low order.' It is 'a means to all

[1] *Principles*, p. 16. [2] *Ibid.*, p. 17. [3] *Ibid.*, p. 21.

[4] 'The work of all those engaged in any one occupation can be carefully observed' (*ibid.*, p. 21).

kinds of ends.'[1] After justifying the use of money measurement of motives on intellectual grounds, Marshall tries his utmost to prove that this procedure is quite compatible with the recognition of higher aims. He attempts to dispel his doubts by declaring money to be merely a means. He reiterates the justification of the money motive as a purely intellectual device for measuring human motives on a large scale. He shows in his enumeration of many non-economic motives that he knows, as well as Carlyle and Ruskin, that there are other goals besides the making of money. He defends the economist against Carlyle's and Ruskin's criticism by pointing to man's consideration of non-pecuniary advantages in the choice of an occupation, to his recognition of the desire for approval by others, to the family motive, and to the desire to accumulate wealth 'to be enjoyed after the death of him by whom it has been earned.'[2] All this shows his eagerness to clear economics from the accusation of being the dismal science concerned only with selfish, egotistic, pecuniary motives.

After that, however, he re-emphasizes why, after all, economists deal with the pecuniary side of life:

> Actions which are due to a feeling of duty and love of one's neighbour cannot be classed and reduced to law and measured . . . and it is for this reason, and not because they are not based on self-interest, that the machinery of economics cannot be brought to bear on them.[3]

The methodological argument makes it possible to justify the economist's concentration on the money motive, although it has been morally condemned.

In the system of Adam Smith, the pursuit of monetary self-interest was interpreted as socially beneficial; the invisible hand led the individual to promote, *nolens volens*, the common welfare. Marshall does not openly adopt this line of reasoning. In his system the confinement of economics to the pecuniary motive is reduced to an intellectual device and is justified as such. This, however, indicates the bad conscience of the Victorian; he has to acknowledge that there are higher aims than the desire for money; he has to admit that people do actually act from other reasons and that money-making as an end in itself is morally indefensible. However, he does not want to condemn an economic system which forces people to act as if they were driven primarily by economic monetary motives. His way out of this conflict is to deny that the pursuit of money and wealth is the main goal; to maintain that the characteristic behaviour

[1] *Ibid.*, p. 22. [2] *Ibid.*, p. 23. [3] *Ibid.*, p. 24.

of business life is not the making of profits but deliberateness and long-range calculation; and to explain and justify the confinement of economics to the monetary and egoistic type of action by a methodological argument.

Thus the first two chapters of this great organon of economics serve as a prelude to the all-pervading themes of Marshallian thought: the conflict between value-attitude systems and the attempt to eliminate it through intellectual constructs. They deal with the antithesis between the higher goals and non-pecuniary motives and the egoistic pursuit of money-making. The recognition of higher goals requires the acceptance of qualitative ethical differences. These, however, are not measurable and, therefore, not subject to the laws of science and of economics.

The money motive, however, can be measured by the yardstick of money. Conduct motivated by money gains is supposedly measurable, verifiable, predictable, and subject to laws, regularities, and uniformities. Marshall's final conclusions are that economists deal with those aspects of life for which the motives are regular, the actions predictable, and the causes verifiable. It deals with observable facts, measurable quantities, and man's conduct under the influence of money prices.[1] Although the restriction of economics to the money motive seems to be completely vindicated on purely intellectual grounds, its combination with deliberate rationality contains an ethical element, because deliberateness is considered by Marshall to be a moral virtue. At the end of his discussion Marshall acknowledges the importance of the ethical: the money measurement is used for the sake of greater exactness; but for practical issues we must 'take some sort of account of our ethical instincts and our common sense.'[2] We see that the dichotomic, dialectical character of Ricardian thought can also be found in Marshall's system.

The Cultural Background

The underlying conflicts are of deep cultural significance. In spite of rationalism and utilitarianism, Christian ideals have never completely been abandoned in the Anglo-Saxon countries. As M. Polanyi has pointed out, English rationalism developed at a time 'when religious beliefs were unshaken and, indeed, dominant throughout the nation.'[3] This situation had not changed much in Marshall's time. 'Evangelical morality was . . . the single, most widespread influence in Victorian England.'[4] Although most Evan-

[1] *Principles*, p. 27. [2] *Ibid.*, p. 28. [3] 'The Logic of Liberty,' I, p. 349.
[4] N. G. Annan, *Leslie Stephen*, p. 110.

gelicals became philosophical utilitarians, they kept their Christian ethical beliefs intact. Even as agnostics, they believed in 'right conduct and in the same ethical standards and in the supreme importance of the individual's relation to God.'[1] Annan characterizes the ethics of Leslie Stephen, who may be regarded as a representative Victorian personality, as follows:

> The power of religion over the very minds of those who denied it is nowhere more subtly instanced than in Stephen's evolutionary ethics. . . . Christianity is dissolved into morality.

As Stephen wrote in 1865: 'I now believe in nothing . . . but I do not less believe in morality.'[2] The essence of this overtly agnostic, but secretly Christian, ethic was that the good should be pursued,

> not for self-satisfaction but for the benefit of society as a whole. The sound society rests on the moral health of the individual whose virtues are self-help, thrift, the sanctity of the family, moral courage, and free moral choice.[3]

Leslie Stephen's moral ideas and intellectual development bear a striking resemblance to Alfred Marshall's.[4] He came from a clerical family. His father was a 'tough, old character, cast in the mould of the strictest evangelicals.' Marshall was intended by his father to become a minister. Even after he abandoned his theological beliefs, he 'sympathized with Christian morals, and Christian ideals and Christian incentives.'[5] In his early university days Marshall 'still looked forward to ordination, and his zeal directed itself at times towards the field of foreign missions.' The clerical background of Victorian intellectuals is clearly shown by the fact that

> until about 1865 . . . Leslie Stephen was an Anglican clergyman, James Ward a nonconformist minister, Alfred Marshall a candidate for holy orders, W. K. Clifford a High Churchman.[6]

Although Marshall, influenced by Sidgwick, dropped many of his Christian beliefs, both were 'as far as possible from adopting an anti-religious attitude.' At the end of his life Marshall said, "Religion seems to me an attitude," and, though he had given up theology, he believed more and more in Religion.'[7] Keynes states that 'it was only through ethics that he first reached economics.'[8] And this ethic

[1] *Ibid.*, p. 123. [2] *Ibid.*, pp. 196 ff. [3] *Ibid.*, pp. 199 ff.

[4] As, indeed, to those of every prominent intellectual figure of the period. Most of them had a Christian background, became utilitarians and agnostics, but retained the basic tenets of Christian morality.

[5] J. M. Keynes, 'Alfred Marshall,' in his *Essays in Biography*, pp. 150, 151, 162.

[6] *Ibid.*, p. 163. [7] *Ibid.*, p. 162. [8] *Ibid.*, p. 165.

was a Christian ethic; it was, to a large extent, the anti-chrematistic ethics of precapitalist times, which, in spite of the growth of the new economic system, had, through a curious trick of history, survived more strongly in those Western countries in which the market economy developed first. This may be more than a historical accident. It is quite possible that the new economic system might have destroyed society unless the individualistic, competitive, acquisitive value system had been counterbalanced by the code of Christian ethics, with its emphasis on self-control and altruistic co-operation. The first century of the industrial economy in England and, later, in America was characterized by an amalgamation of business ethics with Christian morals. These two elements, although contradictory, formed a psychocultural unity which established a historically necessary balance between conflicting tendencies. This combination of value attitudes made the growth and the preservation of the system possible. However, it created grave value conflicts, which are clearly reflected in the dichotomic structure of economics from Adam Smith to Marshall.

The philosophy of the early nineteenth century had a stronger utilitarian tinge than did Marshallian economics. Jacob Viner has pointed to the difference between the Benthamism of the 1820's and Marshall.[1] The 'warmheartedness' introduced into economic thought by J. S. Mill under the influence of the romanticism of the age, especially of Wordsworth, the larger role of feeling, the 'heart-throbbing', are reflected in the attitudes of Marshall. His sensitivity to the ideas of the romanticists can be gathered from his defensive attitude toward Carlyle's and Ruskin's attacks on the dismal science.[2] The humanitarianism of the age had led to a more critical attitude toward purely economic goals. Strong ideological resistance to business aims developed. Humanitarian and aesthetic opposition to the tenets of the economic value complex increased in the nineteenth century. These trends are clearly reflected in the Marshallian statement that the ultimate goal of economic activity is to find 'the material means of a refined and noble life' and in his endeavours to justify economics morally.

[1] J. Viner, 'Marshall's Economics, the Man and His Times.'
[2] *Principles*, pp. 22, 780, n. 1.

Chapter XVI

INDIVIDUAL ECONOMIC ACTION

Wants versus Activities

MARSHALL devotes an entire book, Book III of his *Principles of Economics* to the discussion of wants and their satisfaction. The great stress on wants and on demand represents an obvious shift in emphasis toward the subjective aspect of economic conduct. 'The ultimate regulator of all demand is therefore consumers' demand.'[1] Marshall himself points out that 'the subject of demand or consumption has been somewhat neglected'[2] and explains his treatment by 'the spirit of our age', which

> induces a closer attention to the question whether our increasing wealth may not be made to go further than it does in promoting the general well-being.[3]

This is clearly a reference to what today is called the 'problem of optimum allocation of resources'. Attention shifts from the problems of production, on which Ricardo laid disproportionate stress,[4] to the problems of need-satisfaction and demand. Under the impact of growing wealth the subjective elements become more important than the problems of production. The economy of scarcity, with its primary attention upon production, gives way to an economy of abundance, which, by necessity, leads to a rising interest in the problems of wants, subjective enjoyment, need-satisfaction, and consumption.[5]

However, the satisfaction of wants is not considered to be the only and ultimate aim of economic behaviour. Marshall stresses the importance of efforts and activities.[6] Activities are on a higher plane than wants:

1 Alfred Marshall, *Principles of Economics*, p. 92.
2 *Ibid.*, p. 84.
3 *Ibid.*, p. 85.
4 *Ibid.*, p. 84.
5 See David Riesman, *The Lonely Crowd*, p. 19; Hla Myint, *Theories of Welfare Economics*, Part I.
6 *Principles*, p. 85; cf. also T. Parsons, *The Structure of Social Action*, chap. iv.

> while wants are the rulers of life among the lower animals, it is to changes in the forms of efforts and activities that we must turn when in search for the keynotes of the history of mankind.[1]

Chapter ii of Book III ends on a note of praise for activities as ultimate goals in contrast to the desire for things:

> the desire for exercise and development of activities . . . leads not only to the pursuit of science, literature and art for their own sake but to the rapidly increasing demand for the work of those who pursue them as professions.[2]

New activities give rise to new wants. Leisure and stagnation are morally evil. Leisure is permissible only if it is used as an opportunity not for stagnation but for activities. The Puritan condemnation of sloth, sensual enjoyment, leisure, idleness, and stagnation is manifest in every line. Athletic games and travelling are approved of; sensuous craving is abhorred. Drinks which stimulate the mental activities, like tea, are accepted; 'those which merely gratify the senses . . . the grosser and more immediately stupefying forms of alcohol . . .' are rejected.[3] 'The West Indian negro, using his new freedom and wealth not to get the means of satisfying new wants, but in idle stagnation that is not rest' is condemned, and pride is taken that those parts of the English working classes are lessening

> who have no pride and delight in the growth of their faculties and activities, and spend on drink whatever surplus their wages afford over the bare necessities of a squalid life.[4]

The distinction between 'idle stagnation' and 'rest' is quite significant. Leisure is not considered an end in itself; it is mere stagnation, something bad. As rest, it serves as restoration of strength for new activities directed toward the production of goods and the pursuit of higher things; only as a means to an end is it permissible and accepted. This is a clear reflection of an ideal which puts man under a continuous activistic strain.

Thus we already find in the first, introductory, chapter on wants an interesting symbiosis of the activistic work ethic with a new emphasis on the subjective elements of enjoyment and consumption. It shows clearly a conflict between the two attitudes. It is as if guilt feelings arise immediately after Marshall has announced, in opposition to the classical approach, his new emphasis on demand and consumption. To save his Puritan conscience, he hurries to state

[1] *Principles*, p. 85.
[2] *Ibid.*, pp. 88–89.
[3] *Ibid.*, p. 89, n. 1.
[4] *Ibid.*, p. 90.

that, after all, activities and efforts are the creators of wants and, therefore, are more important than wants. And in the end he feels forced to take back his declaration that wants are ends in themselves:

> It is not true therefore that the theory of consumption is the scientific basis of economics. For much that is of interest in the science of wants, is borrowed from the science of efforts and activities. These two supplement one another . . . But if either, more than the other, may claim to be the interpreter of the history of man, whether on the economic side or any other, it is the science of activities and not that of wants.[1]

Wants, Utility, and Prices

The subjectivistic approach to value made it necessary to interrelate subjective utility, desire, satisfaction, or happiness—whatever the term—on the one hand, and prices, on the other. Prices as they fluctuate on markets often bear no relation to the subjective evaluation of goods by individuals. How can the individual accept the fact that the necessities of life are removed from his reach in times of inflation? How can the one-crop farmer be made to understand why his existence is threatened by a glut in the market for his main product? From the point of view of the individual, prices often seem to be unjustified.

Marshall tackles this problem under the heading of the measurability of utility. Here, as elsewhere, the psychocultural problem is presented as a purely methodological one. If economics is supposed to live up to the precision and exactitude of a science, utility has to be measured. The 'measure is found in the price which a person is willing to pay for the satisfaction of his desire.'[2] Thus a relationship between the basic psychological force (desire, utility) and the main phenomenon of the market system, namely, price, is established. If utility is considered as the *prima causa* of economic behaviour, then such an interconnection between utility and price is essential. The belief in this interrelation makes the price system and the role of prices in the economy comprehensible and meaningful to the individual. Therefore, Marshall has to arrive at the conclusion that prices, in some fashion, reflect degrees of satisfaction and utility. He contrives to reach this conclusion by assuming that subjective utilities conform to prices and to the quantitative scale of money values. It is assumed that if a person is ready to spend more money on a good,

1 *Ibid.*, p. 90.

2 *Ibid.*, p. 92.

that good is more useful to him, more satisfactory, more happiness-procuring, than another one on which the individual is willing to spend less. This assumption is not entirely unrealistic. It may often be correct; but there are many exceptions to this rule, so many that the rule itself may be invalidated. Prices are determined by haphazard situations in markets; sometimes they are the result of conscious policies of sellers, sometimes they are the resultant of many individual decisions which add up to some final effect. An individual cannot choose what price he pays for a commodity. His subjective evaluation (assuming that it is a psychological reality to be distinguished from the mere fact of purchase and spending) may be higher for the cheaper and lower for the dearer good. A person may acquire a fountain pen for $5 which he treasures infinitely more than he does a car which he is compelled to buy for a much larger sum of money because of the insufficiency of public transportation. The identification of the subjective scale of values with the external action of the purchase at a price, dictated by the market and beyond the control of the individual, represents an attempt at moral justification. It is, perhaps unconsciously, intended as a demonstration to the individual that, after all, his feeling that prices often in no way correspond to his subjective evaluations is not borne out by the logic of economic science; that he does, after all, value a more expensive good more highly than the less expensive one. This assumption is supposed to convince the individual that the value scale expressed in money prices has a direct relation to his own subjective value scale.

The Law of Diminishing Marginal Utility

However, a number of problems posed by the shift to a subjectivistic theory of value were still unsolved. One of them was the old paradox of value. As long as necessities are relatively cheap and luxuries relatively dear, it is difficult to maintain that prices reflect in any sense subjective values. The distinction between total and marginal utility made it possible to solve the 'riddle' of the paradox of value by assuming that

> the total utility of a thing to anyone . . . increases with every increase in his stock of it, but not as fast as his stock increases. . . . In other words, the additional benefit which a person derives from a given increase of his stock of a thing, diminishes with every increase in the stock that he already has. . . . The marginal utility of a thing to anyone diminishes with every increase in the amount of it he already has.[1]

[1] *Principles*, p. 93. In n. 1 on the same page it is formulated even more clearly and with more emphasis on 'pleasure' as follows: 'the return of pleasure which a

Thus the cheapness of necessities is explained; it is no longer in conflict with the high evaluation of their utility by individuals; this utility is total utility, which may be high even if the price of the unit is low; what determines the value of the unit, however, is not total, but marginal, utility, which declines and becomes lower when the stock increases. Thus a parallel between prices and individual evaluation is established. The results of the market forces no longer appear to be paradoxical and void of sense and meaning. Another logical step has been taken to make the market system comprehensible.

If need-satisfaction is the ultimate aim of economic activity, full and complete satisfaction must be an attainable goal; otherwise, the subjective approach would be invalidated. This idea, however, is in conflict with the limitlessness of the striving for wealth and the acquisition of riches which is part of the economic value complex and prevents industrial man from ever reaching a point where he can say: 'I have accomplished my goal, I am satisfied.' The law of diminishing marginal utility makes it possible to assume that the individual can reach an equilibrium in respect to the consumption and acquisition of a commodity. If it is possible to reach such a point for every commodity, it must be possible to reach an all-round state of satisfaction.

However, the law of diminishing marginal utility works only under the assumption that no 'alteration in the character or tastes of the man himself' takes place; if we take man as he is, without allowing time for any change in his character, the marginal utility of a thing to him diminishes steadily with every increase in his supply of it.[1] The validity of this law is restricted to a period of time too short to allow for a change in character and tastes. If one assumes that people's tastes and characters change over time, the law could not lead to an equilibrium with a satiation point, especially not over the lifetime of an individual. By restricting its validity to situations of unchanging character and tastes and thereby to short periods of time, Marshall denies implicitly that the individual can reach ultimate satisfaction through acquisition and consumption of goods in the long run.

Nevertheless, Marshall uses the law of diminishing marginal utility and the equilibrium concept based on it to explain consumers' behaviour. This may indicate that he considered an unchanging character as an ideal; such a character would also conform to the

person gets from each additional dose of commodity diminishes till at last a margin is reached at which it is no longer worth while to acquire any more of it.'

[1] *Ibid.*, p. 94.

economic value complex. Economic man is a type of inner-directed character.[1]

One of the characteristics of this type is the orientation toward long-run goals. In the nineteenth century, occupational lines were more stable, careers could be planned in advance, and life-goals pursued with greater consistency than today. Also values were relatively stable: the virtues of thrift, diligence, hard work, sobriety, prudence, and methodical, systematic life- and career-planning were still recognized as supreme ideals, although, toward the end of the century, a process of disintegration had already begun.

Marshall's restriction of the law of diminishing marginal utility to a state of affairs where the tastes and characters of people do not change may indicate that he adhered to the old ideal of long-run consistency and systematic planning and that he believed that tastes, character traits, values, and attitudes should not change. The sternness, the solidity, the consistency of the Puritan and the Victorian are alive in his discussion.

In his reasoning the old and the new ideals are combined. The old ideal is represented by the assumption that character and ideals do not change. The new ideal manifests itself in the idea that satisfaction can be reached. The latter thought is alien to the Puritan economic value system, in which satisfaction is not important. It is again as if Marshall wanted to buy indulgence for advocating such a modern ideal as need-satisfaction, by paying homage to the stern, old-fashioned values. It is as if he wanted to say: 'You can reach full satisfaction only if you do not change your ideals and tastes.' Thus the law of diminishing marginal utility, with its prerequisite of no change of tastes over time, represents an attempt to harmonize conflicting value systems.

The law of diminishing marginal utility also served Marshall to explain the declining demand curve. This is accomplished with the help of the concept of 'demand price', the price which a person is just willing to pay for any unit of a commodity, and the concept of 'marginal demand price', which is the price a person is willing to pay for the last unit of a stock.[2] Having first assumed that prices

[1] Riesman (*op. cit.*) defines as inner-directed a character orientation in which 'the source of direction for the individual is "inner" in the sense that it is implanted early in life by the elders and directed toward generalized but none the less inescapably destined goals' (p. 15). It emerged in a society which 'is characterized by increased personal mobility, by rapid accumulation of capital (teamed with devastating technological shifts), and by an almost constant expansion . . . in the production of goods and people, and extensive expansion in exploration, colonization and imperialism.' These people act as if they followed the direction of a 'psychological gyroscope' (p. 16).

[2] *Principles*, p. 95.

reflect consumers' subjective evaluations and then, through the law of declining marginal utility, that the utility of a unit declines with the size of the stock, he can now arrive at the conclusion that

> the larger the amount of a thing a person has, the less . . . will be the price which he will pay for a little more of it; . . . his marginal demand price for it diminishes.[1]

This explains why the demand schedule of an individual shows an inverse variation between prices and quantities demanded.[2] By tying together individual evaluation, subjective utility, and demand prices, he forged a logical link between subjective values and prices. As we shall see later, the demand curve forms an important basis for Marshall's analysis of market-price determination and market equilibrium.[3]

Rational Economic Conduct

The Consumer

The final conclusions in respect to the equilibrium of the consumer are drawn in chapter v of Book III. There Marshall outlines the pattern which he applies later to all types of economic conduct.

The housewife who has to distribute a limited number of hanks of yarn from the year's shearing among the various domestic wants for clothing is used as a prototype for all rational economic individuals. Supposedly she 'tries to distribute the yarn between them in such a way as to contribute as much as possible to the family well-being.' The aim then, is the maximization of welfare or utility.[4] This maximization is achieved when

> she made just so many socks and vests that she got an equal amount of good out of the last bundle of yarn that she applied to socks, and the last she applied to vests. This illustrates a general principle, which may be expressed thus:—If a person has a thing which he

[1] *Ibid.*, p. 95.

[2] See the definition of the individual demand schedule and curve, *ibid.*, pp. 96 ff.

[3] See below, pp. 194 ff. It is quite significant that modern price theory moves in the direction of a purely behaviouristic explanation of demand. Indifference-curve analysis tries to avoid the psychological pitfalls of the law of diminishing marginal utility. Thereby, it severs the link between subjective evaluations and prices which Marshall took so much trouble to establish. This modern trend betrays a growing doubt not only of the validity of marginal utility analysis but also of the possibility of justifying prices from the point of view of the individual.

[4] *Principles*, p. 117.

can put to several uses, he will distribute it among these uses in such a way that it has the same marginal utility in all.[1]

The description of rational economic conduct is based on the following assumptions: (*a*) a scarcity of means with alternative uses; (*b*) a variety of ends which can be reached by these means; (*c*) maximization of welfare, utility, and happiness as goals; (*d*) to be accomplished by equalization of utilities at the margin; (*e*) the possibility of gradations of satisfactions; (*f*) knowledge of these gradations by the actor; (*g*) the comparability and measurability of these satisfactions and their gradations on a homogeneous quantitative scale.

That the ideal of rational economic conduct is not merely a hypothetical construct for the sake of the logical unification of the system but, in the thought of Marshall, is a living ethical reality can be gathered from the discussion in Book III, chapter v, Section II. Immediately after the presentation of the basic model or pattern in Section I of this chapter, Marshall launches into what could be called moral economic casuistry, giving advice to the Victorian individual on how to behave in line with the propounded ideal:

> And in a money economy, good management is shown by so adjusting the margins of suspense on each line of expenditure that the marginal utility of a shilling's worth of goods on each line shall be the same. And this result each one will attain by constantly watching to see whether there is anything on which he is spending so much that he would gain by taking a little away from that line of expenditure and putting it in on some other line.[2]

It would be difficult to find a better illustration of an attitude which David Riesman has so aptly characterized as treating one's self like a firm and, at the same time, as the firm's auditor.[3] It is a mode of life of continuous watchfulness and economic awareness. Each penny has to be turned around and around before it is spent, until one has made sure that the intended expenditure will really increase total utility and that it is not spent foolishly on something which will turn out to be less important than something else. Maximization is good management; it is judged according to moral

[1] *Principles*, p. 117. [2] *Ibid.*, p. 118.

[3] *Op. cit.*, p. 124; cf. also p. 44. The Freudians have described the same situation in terms of the superego, an internalized agency, something like the conscience, which watches out to see that the feelings, ideas, and actions of the individual conform to moral rules and which punishes the individual with guilt feelings if these rules are violated. The individual trying to live up to the ideal of the rational economic man has guilt feelings if he does not distribute his resources in conformity with the maximization model.

standards. The examples that follow also show clearly the moralistic character of the idea of maximization. Marshall gives indirect advice, like an experienced housekeeper to a young couple, on how to keep account carefully:

> A chief motive of the advice is that they may avoid spending impulsively a great deal of money on furniture and other things; for, though some quantity of these is really needful, yet when bought lavishly they do not give high (marginal) utilities in proportion to their costs. And when the young pair look over their year's budget at the end of the year, and find perhaps that it is necessary to curtail their expenditure somewhere, they compare the (marginal) utilities of different items, weighing the loss of utility that would result from taking away a pound's expenditure here, with that which they would lose by taking it away there: they strive to adjust their parings down so that the aggregate loss of utility may be a minimum, and the aggregate of utility that remains to them may be a maximum.[1]

Who can fail to discern in these words the preaching Victorian moralist? Who can still maintain, in view of this paternal wisdom, that the model of rational behaviour is merely a methodological device for the analysis of a segment of social behaviour? It is obviously an ideal, although represented as a fact. Those who may have their doubts about the ethical validity of the ideal should be persuaded that, by acting like this, they will merely conform to the general pattern.

One should note the injunction against impulsive action because it may cause regret later on. The individual should not feel any regret after allocating a sum of money for an expenditure.[2] The Marshallian equilibrium of the individual cannot be interpreted as changing from moment to moment; it does not mean merely that people prefer what they buy and consume at the moment. They should continue to prefer what they have bought, because regret indicates incorrect allocation. Marshall clearly has in mind an equilibrium of a lasting and stable nature, rooted in long-run life-goals and their consistent pursuit. Regret can be avoided only if the individual does not change his tastes and character and if he acts according to the tenets of an unchanging value system.

[1] *Principles*, p. 119. In the footnote on that page Marshall talks about distributing resources 'wisely', about 'wise action' and 'wise spending', and about the 'sober' portions of the Anglo-Saxon working classes; all this indicates clearly the moral nature of his thought.

[2] 'She will think she has failed if, when it is done, she has reason to regret that she did not apply more to making, say, socks, and less to vests' (*ibid.*, p. 117).

The ideal of rational economic conduct is also incompatible with luxurious consumption. Marshall's young couple is not supposed to spend money lavishly on furniture. In his analysis of working-class budgets, Marshall gives us a clear notion of his moral ideas about spending and consumption. In discussing the meaning of the term 'productive labour' he admits that

> wholesome enjoyments, whether luxurious or not, are legitimate ends of action . . . but . . . the true interest of a country is generally advanced by the subordination of the desire for transient luxuries to the attainment of the more solid and lasting resources which will assist industry in its future work, and will . . . tend to make life larger.[1]

Can it be denied that terms such as 'true interest', 'transient luxuries', and 'solid and lasting resources' express moral judgments? It is clear that Marshall's entire attitude here is imbued with the economic value complex, that he considers luxuries as bad and savings and investment in lasting properties as good and wholesome. This attitude is projected later on into the model of rational economic conduct; impulsive behaviour and lavish spending are irrational; careful budgeting on the basis of a lifetime budget is rational and virtuous.

It may be fitting to end this discussion by pointing to the sometimes somewhat amusing length to which Marshall will occasionally go in his casuistry of rational economic conduct. He examines what types of consumers' goods will be necessary for the efficiency of unskilled labour; without them,

> its efficiency will suffer in the same way as that of a horse that is not properly tended, or a steam engine that has an inadequate supply of coals.[2]

Consumption is legitimate only in so far as it promotes production. However, Marshall admits conventional necessities, such as

> some consumption of alcohol and tobacco, and some indulgence in fashionable dress. . . . The consumption of conventional necessaries by productive workers is commonly classed as productive consumption; but strictly speaking it ought not to be.[3]

The reader will clearly hear the Victorian schoolmaster's voice. The conventional necessities are not quite *comme il faut*; the Puritan spirit does not quite approve of alcohol, tobacco, and fashionable dress.

[1] *Principles*, p. 66. [2] *Ibid.*, p. 70. [3] *Ibid.*, p. 70.

Superfluous luxuries are roundly condemned unless they take the place of necessaries. And here Marshall engages in a moral-economic calculus of clearly compulsive character:

> Thus a dish of green peas in March, costing perhaps ten shillings, is a superfluous luxury; yet it is wholesome food, and does the work perhaps of three pennyworth of cabbage; or even, since variety undoubtedly conduces to health, a little more than that. So it may be entered perhaps at the value of fourpence under the head of necessaries, and at that of nine shillings and eightpence under that of superfluities; and its consumption may be regarded as strictly productive to the extent of one-fortieth. In exceptional cases, as for instance when the peas are given to an invalid, the whole ten shillings may be well spent and reproduce their own value.[1]

Poor Victorian labourer! He may eat only one-fortieth of his dearly bought peas with a good conscience; the enjoyment of the remaining thirty-nine-fortieths will be marred by the bad feeling that he is consuming superfluous luxuries without any productive or reproductive value. Not only this; he is burdened by the difficult task of figuring out how much of his purchase is legitimate consumption and how much is sinful luxury. A very strenuous mode of life, indeed! Very much reminiscent of the behaviour of obsessional neurotics. The analogy is more than a superficial one. Obsessional neurotics suffer from inner conflicts. So did the individual in the economy of the late nineteenth century. He was still under the influence of the Puritan economic value complex and the ideal of rational economic conduct. However, his utilitarian subjectivism pushed him toward regarding enjoyment as a legitimate goal. This conflict between value systems made him the more anxious and led to such hypermeticulous, compulsive calculations as are shown in the Marshallian example.

Present and Future Wants

The rational economic man has to distribute his resources not only between his various present needs but also between present and future needs. The principle for this type of allocation is the same as the one already discussed:

> A prudent person will endeavour to distribute his means between all their several uses, present and future, in such a way that he will have in each the same marginal utility.[2]

[1] *Ibid.*, p. 70, n. 2.

[2] *Ibid.*, p. 119.

The ideal of rational economic conduct has to be made applicable to every situation; otherwise, the unconscious doubts of its moral validity may come into the open. Furthermore, the logical unity of the system requires the general applicability of the maximization principle through equalization at the margin. In respect to future wants, however, this presents ethical and logical difficulties; as so often in the Marshallian system, the ethical problems are implied in the logical ones.

The evaluation of future wants presents the problem of uncertainty, one of the main obstacles in arriving at a consistent equilibrium scheme. Marshall recognizes this:

> But in estimating the present marginal utility of a distant source of pleasure a twofold allowance must be made; firstly, for its uncertainty (this is an objective property which all well-informed persons would estimate in the same way).[1]

Marshall does not deny the uncertainty about the future directly, but he tries to make it less uncertain by asserting that all well-informed persons estimate it in the same way. This implies the possibility of correctly forecasting the future if one is well informed. His approach may reflect in part the greater stability and security of Victorian times; but, even more, it reflects the long-run orientation of the Victorian individual and his faith in the possibility of understanding the laws of society and predicting the future on the basis of this understanding. Uncertainty is minimized intellectually, to alleviate the anxiety which every human being necessarily experiences because he does not and cannot know what the future will bring.

The ethical conflict involved in the evaluation of future wants is the problem of consumption versus saving and the payment of interest as an economic institution. According to the Puritan attitude and the economic value complex, postponement of present enjoyment is a virtue. By saving, one practises self-control. The prudent individual is supposed to deny himself present pleasures and to accumulate for the future. Marshall is still imbued with this attitude. He considers patience, self-control, and the will to postpone enjoyment as virtues.[2] This makes it difficult for him to justify morally the payment of interest, which is supposedly a reward for such a postponement. If the exercise of self-control and the denial of present enjoyment are ends in themselves, the payment of a premium for waiting would not be justified. Therefore, Marshall is caught on the horns of a dilemma; his Puritan Victorian ethic leads him to evalu-

[1] *Principles*, p. 119.

[2] *Ibid.*, p. 120.

ate savings and waiting positively; his desire to explain the payment of interest as an institution leads him to assume that people naturally prefer present to future enjoyment and have to be rewarded for waiting. He decided for the latter approach, although it conflicts with his ethic of denial and self-control. Thus he believes that

> human nature is so constituted that in estimating the present value of a future benefit most people generally make a second deduction (after the discount for uncertainty) from its future value in the form of what we may call a 'discount' that increases with the period for which the benefit is deferred.[1]

His final solution is that 'the rate at which he discounts future [certain] benefits, will be the rate at which he can discount in the money market.'[2] His aim in this discussion has been to explain and justify the paying and taking of interest for the loan of money. However, his ambivalence and his doubts are reflected in the assumptions which he postulates as prerequisites for the validity of his conclusion: he calls this measure of the discount of future benefits 'artificial' and valid only under the following assumptions:

> firstly, that he expects to be about as rich at the future date as he is now; and secondly, that his capacity for deriving benefit from the things which money will buy will on the whole remain unchanged.[3]

These assumptions reflect the tendency to avoid the anxiety-generating effects of uncertainty. To assume that one would be as rich at a later date as one is today looks like a magical wish to exclude the possibility, so obvious and so likely in a dynamic economy, that one's economic fate may change over time. The assumption of unchanging capacity for enjoyment betrays a hidden doubt of the validity of the entire argument: Marshall seems to be doubtful about the justification of the postponement of present wants for the sake of future wants. Is it really worth while to wait? Should we not enjoy life while we have the ability to do so? The entire value syndrome of waiting, postponement, self-control, and saving, the ideal of the rational economic man, is exposed to doubt. The assumption that the capacity for enjoyment will not change or evaporate seems again like a magical formula, comforting economic man in his fears over the impermanence of his fate and of his vitality.

Thus with the help of a number of simplifying assumptions, Marshall manages to arrive at an equilibrium for the consumer, not only for immediate, but also for future, expenditures. By discounting

[1] *Ibid.*, p. 120. [2] *Ibid.*, p. 122. [3] *Ibid.*, p. 122.

future pleasures because of their uncertainty and their remoteness, he can establish their present value and thereby reduce them to the same common denominator as present pleasures. This makes it possible to compare present and future needs and to calculate their marginal utility in the same quantitative terms. Thus the consumer can reach a complete equilibrium, the result at which Marshall wanted to arrive.

The Worker

Not only the consumer and the housewife but also the working individual behave according to the code of rational economic conduct:

> The simplest case of balance or equilibrium between desire and effort is found when a person satisfies one of his wants by his own direct work. When a boy picks blackberries for his own eating . . . after he has eaten a good deal, the desire for more diminishes; while the task of picking begins to cause weariness. . . . Equilibrium is reached when at last his eagerness to play and his disinclination for the work of picking counterbalances the desire for eating. The satisfaction which he can get from picking fruit has arrived at its maximum.[1]

Again, we find here all the elements of the rational model: the balance of opposing forces, gradually diminishing and increasing utility, an equilibrium at the point of maximization.

The same type of reasoning is applied to the broader problem of supply, especially of labour. It 'depends mainly on the overcoming of the unwillingness to undergo "discommodities",' such as 'labour and the sacrifice involved in putting off consumption.' The discommodity of labour increases in intensity with the severity and the duration of labour.[2] This is called the 'marginal disutility of labour', which is supposed to increase with every increase in its amount.[3] Thus 'the disagreeableness of additional work increases . . . as the agreeableness of additional free time increases.'[4] The chief motive of most labour is 'the desire to obtain some material advantage . . . in the form of the gain of a certain amount of money.' Thus, 'the exertions which any set of workers will make, rise or fall with a rise or fall in the remuneration which is offered to them.'[5] Therefore, higher remuneration will call forth more labour, more exertion, and more production. Parallel to the concept of the demand prices and

[1] *Principles*, p. 331. [2] *Ibid.*, p. 140. [3] *Ibid.*, p. 141.
[4] *Ibid.*, p. 142. [5] *Ibid.*, pp. 140–42.

the demand schedule, Marshall develops the concepts of the supply prices and a supply schedule. The supply price is the one which calls forth a certain amount of labour, exertion, and production. The supply schedule is 'a list . . . of various amounts of exertion and therefore of production' and of 'the prices which must be paid to induce the available workers to put forth these amounts of exertion.'[1] Thus the scheme of rational economic conduct is applied to the producing individual and, at the same time, to the supply side of the market. The working and supplying individual balances the pains of labour against the advantages of monetary gain. In order to arrive at an equilibrium, a gradation of subjective feelings of the discommodities of labour and work has to be assumed. Again Marshall establishes a correspondence between the subjective experience of discommodity of labour and the prices paid for labour. Each wage level corresponds to a degree of discommodity; the higher the wage, the greater will be the willingness to undergo such discommodities; therefore, the prices and supply of labour vary directly. Thus he arrives at an ascending supply curve which will enable him later to establish a point of equilibrium on the market.

The Businessman

In Book V, chapter iv, Marshall explains the actions of an investing businessman as a balance between 'two motives, one deterring the other impelling.'[2] The man who builds a house is supposed to weigh the disadvantages of the efforts of his waiting for the finished house against 'the utility of the house to him when finished.' This is the principle which underlies the behaviour of the businessman:

> the efforts and sacrifices which are the real cost of production of a thing underlie the expenses which are its money cost . . . the fruit of the outlay must be expected to exceed the outlay itself by an amount . . . which increases at compound interest in proportion to the time of waiting.'[3]

The activity of the businessman is an equilibrating, maximizing process:

> the aggregate of the incomings would be balanced against the aggregate of the accumulated outlays; and if the two were just equal, the business would be just remunerative.[4]

Marshall then described how the maximization process functions

[1] *Ibid.*, p. 142.
[2] *Ibid.*, p. 352.
[3] *Ibid.*, pp. 352–53.
[4] *Ibid.*, p. 354.

through the application of the principle of substitution, which is nothing but a special case of equalization at the margin:

> Each businessman taking account of his own means, will push the investment of capital in his business in each several direction until what appears in his judgment to be the outer limit, or margin, of profitableness is reached; that is until there seems to him no good reason for thinking that the gains resulting from any further investment in that particular direction would compensate him for his outlay.[1]

This is exactly the same thing the consumer is supposed to do; his outlay consists of the expenditure of his money income, and the result of his equalizing and balancing procedure is the maximization of total utility through equalization of marginal utilities along all lines of expenditure; the investing businessman does the same thing with outlay for productive factors, in order to maximize his money profits.

Marshall quotes again in Book V, chapter iv, the example of the housewife distributing hanks of yarn, and he summarizes the various logical steps which lead to the maximization situation as follows:

> . . . They would include first decisions as to the relative urgency of various ends; secondly, decisions as to the relative advantages of various means of attaining each end; thirdly, decisions based on these two sets of decisions, as to the margin up to which she could most profitably carry the application of each means towards each end.[2]

'She' is here the housewife; but the chain of steps and decisions applies, as Marshall points out, to the problems of the larger business world as well. The speculative builder, for instance, has to decide what houses should be built, how to build them, in what proportion to use various materials, etc.:

> Like her, he has to reflect that the yield of benefit which any particular use gave would be relatively large up to a certain point, and would then gradually diminish. Like her, he has so to distribute his resources that they have the same marginal utility in each use.[3]

Marshall points to the interrelations between the various applications of this principle of rational economic behaviour and the law of diminishing returns:

> This principle of substitution is closely connected with, and is indeed partly based on, that tendency to a diminishing rate of

[1] *Principles*, p. 356. [2] *Ibid.*, p. 357. [3] *Ibid.*, pp. 358–59.

> return from any excessive application of resources or of energies in any given direction. . . . And it is so closely akin to the principle of the diminution of marginal utility that results in general from increased expenditures, that some applications of the two principles are almost identical.[1]

As pointed out before, the idea that diminishing returns can be found in all spheres of economic endeavour makes it possible to arrive at an equilibrated satiation point everywhere. It also serves to establish a systematic unity and an elegance of logical cohesion which is almost unsurpassed in the history of social science.

Against this interpretation the objection may be raised that, after all, the principle is true that returns diminish if one or more factors are held constant and others increased. But is this situation really of such all-pervading importance as neoclassical and modern price theory assumes? Our dynamic economic system will hardly ever let any factor remain constant. It has been pointed out that in plants built with modern engineering methods the principle does not operate.[2] Some investigations seem to indicate that businessmen do not assume that the principle operates and believe that their average- and marginal-cost curve is either horizontal or declining up to the point of full-capacity output.[3] It seems, therefore, that the extensive use which economic theory has made of this principle stems from the desire to arrive at a point of equilibrium, which would be impossible if the principle did not operate.[4]

The principles of substitution and of diminishing marginal utility and the idea of equilibrium through maximization are all concepts

[1] *Ibid.*, p. 356.

[2] W. J. Eiteman, 'Factors Determining the Location of the Least Cost Point.'

[3] A. H. Hansen, 'Cost Functions and Full Employment.'

[4] A case in which the principle of diminishing returns is deduced from the postulated necessity of arriving at an equilibrium solution can be found in Joan Robinson, *The Economics of Imperfect Competition*, p. 95, where Mrs. Robinson discusses the U-shape of the average- (and marginal-) cost curve, which is a consequence of the principle of diminishing returns. She says: 'Full equilibrium [of the firm] can therefore only be attained, under perfect competition, when marginal cost is equal to average cost. Marginal and average cost are equal at the minimum point on the average cost curve. It follows that there must be a minimum point on the average cost curve. . . . It may appear fantastic to deduce a fact about the nature of the costs of a firm from a purely geometrical argument.'

This is less fantastic than the fact that the deduction is based on the postulate of equilibrium. Unless the average-cost curve was U-shaped, no point of equilibrium could be determined; therefore, the cost curves must be U-shaped; definitely a circular type of reasoning, but psychoculturally justified because of the necessity to provide the mental comfort of a determinate point of equilibrium.

reflecting one and the same value system. It is characterized by deliberateness, by conscious rationality, by the thoughtful weighing of the relative size of various benefits against one another, and by the making of decisions after calculating precisely the maximum of gain. The existence of conflicts between goals, values, and impulses is acknowledged, but its importance is minimized. They are reduced to a common quantitative denominator; thereby they are made comparable, and a logical basis for choice is established. By inserting gradations into the attainment of goals and into the satisfaction of wants, they are represented as converging toward an equilibrium point. Thus intellectual constructs provide a method of eliminating conflict. The idea of equilibrium becomes a symbol for the triumph of knowledge, reason, and harmony. Man is not torn by inner conflicts which he can solve only by temporarily cutting through the Gordian knot. There are really no conflicts, which leave him with regret and longing for the potentialities he has sacrificed, between what he wants to do and what the economic system permits him to do. Antinomies are excluded from the world picture.

Marshall considers deliberateness as an ideal; at the same time, he believes that people actually act in this fashion. It is the same amalgamation of facts and values which is indeed a characteristic of modern social thought. The belief in the ideal has to be bolstered by representing it as a fact. Modern man, who has no other way to justify his beliefs, feels secure only in scientifically grounded convictions.

This entire approach, at first applied to individuals, is then projected into the economic system. Not only individuals but also groups are subject to the same laws of conduct. Equilibrium in the market is established in a similar manner as within individuals. To show this in detail, we shall have to examine the Marshallian concepts of market and normal equilibrium. The transition from individual to group rationality, however, is accomplished through the law of large numbers, which we have to discuss in this context.

The Law of Large Numbers

In spite of his emphasis on rational economic behaviour, Marshall knew that human beings are not entirely rational. In view of his subjectivistic outlook, he could not entirely reject and ignore this aspect of human behaviour, which threatened to introduce 'irrationality' and 'irregularity' into the universe of economic discourse.

In Book III, chapter iii, Section V, where Marshall makes the transition from individual demand to market demand, he faces the problem of individual irrationality: 'There are many classes of things the need of which on the part of any individual is inconstant, fitful and irregular.'[1] However, the economist is not so much interested in individual behaviour; he studies the behaviour of an

> industrial group in so far as the motives of that action are measurable by a money price; and in these broad results the variety and fickleness of individual action are merged in the comparatively regular aggregate of the action of the many. . . . The peculiarities in the wants of individuals will compensate one another in a comparatively regular gradation of total demand.[2]

This belief that irrational and irregular elements of individual action and behaviour will cancel out in groups has, as the law of large numbers, been reiterated many times in economic literature and has become an essential tenet of economic theory. Its fallacies have been pointed out recently by a psychologist. Individual differences will cancel out in large numbers only if random factors prevail. 'But if the same factors influence very many people at the same time in the same direction, the deviations add up instead of cancelling out.'[3] It may be that Marshall would have abandoned his belief in the law of large numbers if he had observed the irrational mass movements of our time. However, many economists who have done so still retain their comforting belief that group behaviour is uniform and regular because the irrational factors cancel out. The rational economic man has been and still is often represented as a statistical average:

> One tries to make believe that rational behaviour is, in spite of individual deviations, the normal behaviour. . . . How does one know that the individual 'irrational' deviations which are admitted have such a statistical dispersion that the 'law of large numbers' is applicable?[4]

This assumption would not even be justified if random factors prevail. The tenacity with which the law of large numbers and the belief in the collective cancellation of individual irrationalities is retained in economic theory indicates that these ideas fulfil a psycho-cultural function. An entire series of beliefs and conflicts is involved: (*a*) the conflict between the ideal of rational economic conduct and the irrational impulses of the individual; (*b*) the assumption that only rational behaviour is regular and subject to uniform laws, whereas

[1] *Principles*, p. 98. [2] *Ibid.*, p. 98.

[3] G. Katona, *Psychological Analysis of Economic Behavior*, pp. 21–22.

[4] G. Myrdal, *Der politische Ideengehalt der Nationaloekonomischen Doktrinbildung*, p. 147.

irrational behaviour is not; (*c*) the tendency to interpret group behaviour according to the pattern of rational individual action.

The Marshallian ideal of rational economic conduct is incompatible with impulsive, capricious, spontaneous, emotional attitudes. It requires constancy of life-goals, long-range planning, and consistent realization of such plans. The new trend of the times toward subjectivity, however, does not permit the complete neglect of 'irrational' modes of individual behaviour. Furthermore, the ideal is in conflict with subjective impulses which push the individual toward its violation. This conflict between values and inner drives, between ideal and actual facts, is reflected in the vacillating attitude of Marshall in the interpretation of individual behaviour; on the one hand, he admits that the needs of individuals may be fitful, irregular, and inconstant; on the other hand, he interprets practically all types of economic behaviour according to the code of rational conduct. Thus his thought shows clearly the ambivalance of his time toward the ideal of the economic man and the ensuing conflict between subjectivism and its non-rational elements and economic rationalism. This conflict may be the reason for the rather illogical assumption of the law of large numbers. In this law it is assumed that group behaviour is rational and regular, and individual behaviour to some extent irregular and irrational. This logically and factually untenable assumption reflects the conflict in the (conscious or unconscious) mind of the Victorians, between their individual non-rational cravings and the socially imposed ideal of the rational economic man. The conflict is resolved, at least on the intellectual level, by interpreting an inner dichotomy within the individual as an external difference between individual and group behaviour.

The assumption that only rational behaviour is regular and susceptible to scientific investigation represents an attempt to depreciate non-rational behaviour. In a period in which science is one of the supremely valued forms of cultural activity, anything which does not lend itself to its scrutinity is of inferior value. Without the belief in the ideal of rational behaviour, the idea that irrational individual behaviour lacks regularities and uniformities would not have been conceived. Modern dynamic psychology has shown that one can derive laws of so-called 'irrational' behaviour from the study of the unconscious mind and its effects on human action. The very idea that the irrational is not subject to 'laws' is a preconception born out of the bias of a rationalistic century.

Finally—and this is the most important aspect of this discussion, in view of our following examination of Marshallian equilibrium analysis—the belief in the law of large numbers reflects Marshall's tendency to interpret group phenomena in accordance with the pattern of rational economic conduct. He regards the economic universe as a rational system. Therefore, he has to eliminate irrational elements which conflict with the rational model. The law of large numbers accomplishes just this. If group behaviour conforms to the ideal of rational economic man, the validity of the ideal is proved. If it is actually found to be the rule of the social universe, it is thereby confirmed as valid in the same way as, for medieval man, the belief in good works was confirmed by the statement that they were prescribed by God.

Chapter XVII

EQUILIBRIUM OF DEMAND AND SUPPLY

The Basic Pattern of Equilibrium

IN his analysis of price equilibrium Marshall created a system of thought which represents one of the most impressive and, at the same time, one of the most unreal of intellectual edifices.[1] The basic pattern for the equilibrium of price is the same throughout the entire analysis. It is developed most clearly in Book V, chapter iii, in relation to normal demand and supply. It is the well-known point of intersection of the demand-and-supply curves, the first declining, the other ascending, so that a point of equilibrium will be reached.[2] The point of equilibrium is characterized by stability:

> When the demand price is equal to the supply price, the amount produced has no tendency either to be increased or to be diminished; it is in equilibrium. . . . Such an equilibrium is stable; that is, the price, if displaced a little from it, will tend to return, as a pendulum oscillates about its lowest point. . . . When demand and supply are in stable equilibrium, if any accident should move the scale of production from its equilibrium position, there will be instantly brought into play forces tending to push it back to that position; just as, if a stone hanging by a string is displaced from its equilibrium position, the force of gravity will at once tend to bring it back to its equilibrium position.[3]

[1] His equilibrium theory is found in *Principles of Economics*, Book V; after a definition of markets in chap. i, the temporary equilibrium of demand and supply is discussed in chap. ii, and the normal equilibrium in chaps. iii to v. The same topics are treated from the aspect of the equilibrium of factor employment in chaps. vii to ix. The moral evaluation of equilibrium is contained in chap. xiii. The exceptions disturbing the unified structure are dealt with in chap. xii (increasing returns) and xiv (monopoly). Chapter xv summarizes the entire argument.

[2] Marshall explains the demand curve in Book III, chap. iii, pp. 96 ff.; the supply schedule or curve in Book V, chap. iii, pp. 343 ff.; and the equilibrium situation through their intersection in Book V, chap. iii, pp. 345 ff.

[3] *Principles*, pp. 345–46.

This concept is of crucial importance in economic theory. It is perhaps one of the most influential symbols which the modern social sciences have developed. Its understanding will provide the key for much of what is incomprehensible to common sense in economic thought. It deserves, therefore, a thorough psychocultural investigation.

To anticipate briefly our interpretation of the meaning of this equilibrium concept: (1) It provides a centre of repose and continuance for the fluctuations of prices; thereby it gives comfort to the individual living under the market system and suffering from haphazard changes in market prices. (2) It constructs the effect of market forces in accord with rational economic conduct of individuals: opposing forces, graduated in such a way that they can be represented by declining and ascending curves, are balanced against one another until a satiation point is reached. (3) It is related to the classical idea of harmony, because equilibrium bears traces of beneficiality and ethical justice. (4) It enables the economist to analyse the operation of market forces with scientific precision; as the analogies drawn from physics of the law of gravity and of the swing of a suspended stone, as well as the mathematical appendix, show, Marshall tries to be scientific by emulating the pattern of the natural, especially the physical, sciences.[1] (5) There is definitely an aesthetic side to this line of reasoning. The interpretation of the economy, composed of forces moving toward a stable equilibrium of intersecting curves, presents a beautiful and thereby comforting picture. It contributes to the harmonious interpretation of the economic system. We shall now try to uncover in Marshall's argument these unconscious motivations and shall study the way in which they are intertwined with logic and scientific reasoning.

Inner Balance and Market Equilibrium

Marshall tries to establish an analogy, almost an identity, between individual conduct and the phenomena of the market. He always begins by discussing individual behaviour and applies his findings there to group phenomena as if the two were on the same level. The parallelism of techniques serves to establish the semblance of real unity and conformity.

It may be significant that Marshall assumes, at first, that the 'equilibrium' does not need any special explanation:

[1] This is, of course, a general trend of economists (see above about Ricardo, pp. 52 ff.).

> . . . We have now to examine the general relations of demand and supply; especially those which are connected with that adjustment of price by which they are maintained in 'equilibrium'. This term is in common use and may be used for the present without special explanation. Thus it is not descriptive, nor does it deal constructively with real problems. But it sets out the theoretical backbone of our knowledge of the causes which govern value, and thus prepares the way for the construction which is to begin in the following book. It aims not so much at the attainment of knowledge, as at the power to obtain and arrange knowledge with regard to two opposing sets of forces, those which impel man to economic sacrifices, and those which hold him back.[1]

It is significant that Marshall related the equilibrium concept to a human conflict situation. The conflict between the duty to exert effort and the desire for leisure, between being active and passive, was chosen to explain the meaning of the basic instrument of economic analysis. It would be difficult to find a clearer illustration of the way by which intellectual constructs are unconsciously chosen. The basic inner conflict to which the economic system exposed man is the starting point of Marshall's analysis of the external market forces and of price determination. The conflict is originally an intra-individual one, but it is projected into the economic system and thus becomes the basis of the interpretation of extra-individual situations. The same equilibrium concept is applied to the individual and to the market situation.

The transplantation of this inner conflict to the external collective sphere has little justification in the facts of economic life. Marshall interprets the two aspects of the market—supply and demand—as the two opposing forces which determine prices. However, supply and demand are not opposing forces in the sense that inner drives are. The desire to acquire wealth, income, prestige, or power may impel the individual to work and to strive for economic success; and his desire for leisure, relaxation, enjoyment of the senses, contemplation, passivity, etc., may hold him back from production. These are definitely inner forces which oppose one another. It is, however, impossible to apply this antinomic structure to supply and demand. The individuals who supply goods are identical with those who demand goods. One cannot say that production and consumption, supply and demand, are 'opposing forces'. Buyers and sellers perform conplementary functions; each seller, as a seller, tries to find a buyer, and vice versa. When Marshall tries to construe the entire

[1] *Principles*, pp. 323–24.

economic system according to the pattern of opposing forces moving toward an equilibrium level, he transfers the pattern of individual conduct to the market.

The fact that the equilibrium pattern is represented as a construct and not as a reality indicates an inner doubt of the validity of the concept. By stating that this pattern is applied to price determination merely as a theoretical 'backbone', a device to organize knowledge in terms of opposing forces, the reality value of the entire construction is made to appear doubtful from the very beginning. However, Marshall regards it sometimes as a real phenomenon and contends that prices actually move toward, and oscillate around, the equilibrium level. His own doubts are reflected in his own vacillating attitude as to what 'equilibrium' really means.

Marshall discusses a series of interrelated equilibria: (1) intra-individual equilibrium established according to the code of rational economic behaviour; (2) equilibrium in barter with the distinction between accidental and true equilibrium (Appendix F); (3) temporary equilibrium of demand and supply (chap. ii of Book V); (4) normal equilibrium (Book V, chaps. iii–v). Temporary and normal equilibria are distinguished by the length of the time period involved. 'Temporary equilibrium' is established during a few hours or a day on a market, where stock, already produced and on hand, is offered for sale.

Marshall begins his discussion of temporary equilibrium with a reference to an intra-individual situation.[1] He uses the example (already quoted) of the berry-picking boy who establishes an equilibrium between the disutility of effort and the pleasure of eating berries. Right after analysing this situation he proceeds with a brief discussion of equilibrium in barter (pp. 331–32). This sudden and unexplained transition from an intra-individual situation to one which involves two persons is significant. Obviously, Marshall wants to construe the equilibrium in a barter transaction between two persons in the same way as that in which he interprets the equilibrium between utility and disutility within one person. He pretends that there is no difference between the two situations, because he does not explain why he assumes this parallelism.

Although Marshall does not analyse the barter situation in his main text but relegates it to an appendix, we shall take it up first because it forms an important link in the transition from intra- to interindividual equilibrium.

[1] *Ibid.*, Book V, chap. ii, p. 331.

Equilibrium in Barter

True and Accidental Equilibrium

In respect to barter, Marshall distinguished between a true and an accidental equilibrium.[1] The equilibrium which is arrived at through barter between two individuals possessing a certain amount of two different commodities purely because the law of diminishing utility would make further exchange disadvantageous for both traders is called 'an accidental equilibrium' but not 'the equilibrium.'[2] The true equilibrium rate is defined as the one which 'if once hit upon would be adhered to throughout.'[3] In the barter situation between the owners of apples and of nuts which Marshall discusses, 'there must be some intermediate rate [of exchange of apples against nuts] at which they would be willing to do business to the same extent.' Assuming that both are satisfied with an exchange rate of 6 nuts for 1 apple and assuming that, after 48 nuts have been exchanged for 8 apples, neither of the two traders wants to continue to exchange, even at the same rate, 'this is then the true position of equilibrium.'[4] What makes this situation 'true' and the other 'accidental'? It is not the rate of exchange as such that matters. If the 'true' rate of 6 nuts for 1 apple were merely the last result of a series of consecutive exchange transactions at different rates, after which each trader has reached a maximum of satisfaction and further trading would not increase the satisfaction of either of them, it would simply be an 'accidental' rate of equilibrium.

Nor is it the maximization of satisfaction of either trader which characterizes the 'true' in contradistinction to the 'accidental' one. 'Accidental' equilibrium is defined as the point up to which 'exchange has increased the satisfaction on both sides but can do so no further.' Thus the accidental rate of equilibrium also represents a point at which the satisfactions of both partners are maximized under the special conditions created by the preceding series of transactions.

Perfect Knowledge and the Personification of the Market

The real distinction between accidental and true equilibrium is that the latter 'once hit upon would be adhered to throughout.' It is a rate which could be established without performing a series of exchange transactions and thus accidentally hit upon (which would change it into an accidental rate of equilibrium) if the bartering

1 *Principles*, p. 332 and Appendix F, 'On Barter,' pp. 791–93.
2 *Ibid.*, p. 791.
3 *Ibid.*, p. 791.
4 *Ibid.*, p. 791.

parties had perfect advance knowledge of their mutual scale of preferences or exchange schedules. If both, like the economist who works out the example, had their mutual exchange schedules in front of them, it would be quite clear to them that they both want to exchange 48 nuts for 8 apples. In this case the true equilibrium rate would be hit upon at once and adhered to throughout. No process of development toward equilibrium would have to take place; the partners to the barter would immediately exchange 8 apples for 48 nuts and be done with the entire business. This is possible only if one assumes that they know exactly what they themselves want and what the other one wants. No difference in bargaining skill, no uneven matching, would exist in such a case. Perfect knowledge of each other's intentions would eliminate all these obstacles to the establishment of true equilibrium.

The rest of Marshall's discussion in Appendix F (on barter) makes it quite clear that the true equilibrium rate is one which depends on perfect knowledge. He himself states that 'there is no reason to suppose that it [the true equilibrium rate] will be reached in practice.'[1] This is because the partners do not have perfect knowledge of each other's intentions. First, he assumes that A (the owner of apples) 'induced B [the owner of nuts] to believe that he does not care much to have any nuts.' In this case A exchanges at a better than the true equilibrium rate, and the bargain will end before the latter is reached. Marshall then changes his assumption to suppose that B is the more skilful in bargaining. Again, the rate of exchange will be different from the true equilibrium rate in favour of the owner of nuts. However, as Marshall states, an equilibrium will be reached when, considering the rate at which the two have exchanged and the amount of goods they find in their possession after these exchanges, they are satisfied under the given conditions. Thus, in the first case (A the better bargainer), A will end up with 65 nuts and 13 apples and B with 7 apples and 35 nuts. In the second case (B the better bargainer), A will end up with 7 apples and 44 nuts, and B will have 13 apples and 56 nuts. Both results are accidental equilibrium situations. In both cases the bargainers are satisfied; but the results are different and different from true equilibrium. The latter, then, is the one at which both would be satisfied, regardless of what bargains might have preceded it, and which they would have chosen and adhered to throughout, if once chosen. All this could not happen unless they knew each other's schedules.

The assumption of perfect knowledge, implied in the concept of true equilibrium, serves as a link between the equilibrium of the

[1] *Ibid.*, p. 791.

individual and the equilibrium of the group. The ideal of the rational economic conduct of an individual requires that the individual know his own value scale and the gradations of his various needs and thus can consciously establish an equilibrium by equalizing marginal values. Here self-knowledge is an essential prerequisite. To make this idea applicable to collectivities, the knowledge supposedly available to the individual has to exist also within the group. The assumption of perfect knowledge, which has become so important in price theory, performs this function. Marshall's true equilibrium between bartering parties can be attained only if they have knowledge of each other's demand schedules in the same way that they have knowledge of their own schedules. The assumption of perfect knowledge of each other's intentions is in this case a projection into a group of the assumption of inner knowledge of the individual. The group, in this case the two bartering traders, are, so to speak, considered as one person. If its members have perfect knowledge of each other's inner experiences, the group is welded into one conscious, deliberate, self-knowing organism.[1]

By assuming perfect knowledge in the group, the belief that the individual has perfect knowledge of himself is strengthened. If it is assumed that we know each other's scales of value, it becomes more likely that we know our own. Thus the doubts about our self-knowledge are silenced, and it is possible to deny that the individual is beset with inner conflicts, that he does not know what he really wants, and that he is not able to evaluate his needs in terms of marginal gradations. It will be argued that Marshall uses the concept of equilibrium merely as an intellectual construct and that he himself emphasizes repeatedly that true equilibrium will rarely be established. We shall see that, nevertheless, he attributes to it considerable reality value. Even as a hypothetical construct, however, it may perform a psychological function. The assumption of knowledge serves to interpret the group as an individual, to reinforce the waning belief in the validity of the ideal of rational, deliberate, economic conduct, and to unify the system by subjecting individual and group behaviour to one and the same principle.

Temporary Equilibrium

Next Marshall tries to show that in a temporary market, in which the supply consists of stock on hand or is at least 'in sight', an equilibrium price will be established within a few hours or a day at the

[1] This is in line with Marshall's inclination toward an organismic theory of society (see *Principles*, p. 461).

point at which the declining demand curve and the inclining supply curve intersect and the quantities demanded and supplied are equal. In his famous example of a corn market in a country town he assumes the demand-and-supply situation shown in the accompanying table.[1]

	Price (Shillings)	Quantity for Sale (Quarters)	Quantity Demanded (Quarters)
A...	37	Another 300; total 1,000	600
B...	36	Another 100; total 700	Another 100; total 700
C...	35	600	Another 200; total 900

In this case Marshall makes distinctions similar to those in the case of barter. Either equilibrium is established through perfect knowledge and/or through correct forecasting; this corresponds to the true equilibrium in barter (see Appendix F, p. 791; above, pp. 198 ff.); or it is established without it; this corresponds to the accidental equilibrium of the barter situation (*ibid.*).

Equilibrium with 'Perfect Knowledge'

Marshall does not state explicitly that he assumes perfect knowledge on the part of all the market participants, nor does he define the scope and content of perfect knowledge. However, his implicit assumptions are clearly contained in the following passage:

> The price of 36*s*. has thus some claim to be called the true equilibrium price; because if it were fixed on at the beginning, and adhered to throughout, it would exactly equate demand and supply . . . and because every dealer who has perfect knowledge of the circumstances of the market expects that price to be established. If he sees the price differing much from 36*s*. he expects that a change will come before long, and by anticipating it he helps it to come quickly.[2]

The words 'perfect knowledge of the circumstances of the market' seem to indicate that Marshall means that a dealer knows all the supply-and-demand schedules of every other dealer. If every market participant knows the schedules, he has the same knowledge as the analysing economist who follows Marshall's argument. This assumes an identity between the knowledge of the actor, on the one hand, and

[1] *Ibid.*, pp. 332–33.

[2] *Ibid.*, pp. 333–34.

that of the detached observer, on the other, and is analogous to the same assumption made in the analysis of barter.[1]

The self-knowledge of the individual is spread over the group, and the latter is thereby changed into a unit. The psychocultural motivation is the same as in the case of barter: to reinforce the belief in the universal applicability of the code of rational economic behaviour and to preserve the intellectual unity of the system. That this is so can be gathered from the fact that perfect knowledge and equilibrium are again interrelated: the dealer who has perfect knowledge expects the equilibrium price to be established and, by anticipating it, helps to bring it about. Thus knowledge and equilibrium are correlated and made mutually interdependent in the same way as they are within the individual: only the person with self-knowledge can equilibrate his need-satisfaction. Equilibrium depends on knowledge.

Perfect Forecasting

The second case Marshall discusses in relation to temporary equilibrium is a situation which, although not including perfect knowledge, approaches it very closely:

> Everyone will try to guess the state of the market and to govern his actions accordingly. . . . So the price may be tossed hither and thither like a shuttlecock. . . . But unless they [buyers and sellers] are unequally matched; unless for instance one side is very simple and unfortunate in failing to gauge the strength of the other side, the price is likely to be never very far from 36*s*.[2]

This does not presuppose perfect knowledge. The words 'unless equally matched' imply that both sides gauge correctly the intention of the others, which amounts to a high degree of knowledge. This becomes quite clear from Marshall's analysis of the motives and considerations of buyers and sellers. The seller will be 'unwilling to let slip past him any offer that is well above' 36*s*., if he 'thinks that the buyers will really be able to get at 36*s*. all that they care to take at that price.'[3] This implies correct guessing of the demand-and-supply schedules and of their point of intersection. 'Buyers . . . if at any time the price should rise considerably above 36*s*. . . . will argue that the supply will be much greater than the demand at that

[1] See above, pp. 198 ff. It must lead inevitably to the exchange of 700 quarters for 36*s*. a quarter, because buyers and sellers know that they cannot exchange what they want to exchange at any other price.

[2] *Principles*, pp. 332–33.

[3] *Ibid.*, p. 333.

price,' and wait. This again implies that they make correct guesses about the demand-and-supply schedules. Thus a situation similar to the one with perfect knowledge obtains. In both cases equilibrium will be established at the price at which the market is cleared. It will be a 'true equilibrium' in the sense that 'if it were fixed on at the beginning and adhered to throughout, it would exactly equate demand and supply.' True equilibrium requires perfect knowledge or correct forecasting for its establishment.

Absence of Perfect Knowledge and Correct Forecasting

Marshall, however, abandons these assumptions in the final stage of his argument.

> It is indeed not necessary for our argument that any dealer should have thorough knowledge of the circumstances of the market. Many of the buyers may perhaps underrate the willingness of the sellers to sell [or] sellers had underrated the willingness of the buyers to pay a high price.[1]

The assumption of correct forecasting is thus dropped. In this case:

> 500 quarters may be sold before the price sinks below 37*s*. But afterwards the price must begin to fall and the result will still probably be that 200 quarters will be sold and the market will close on a price of about 36*s*.[2]

600 quarters are demanded at a price of 37*s*. Why must the price begin to fall after only 500 quarters have been sold at that price? Why would not 600 quarters be sold at that price? The answer might be that after 500 quarters have been sold at 37*s*., and only 100 more quarters are in demand at that price, the bids may become scarcer, and it may dawn on the sellers that they cannot sell all they want to sell at 37*s*. Then, underbidding may start, and lower offers may come in. In other words, knowledge may begin to spread, and correct forecasting may be generated by the market developments. Theoretically, this means the reintroduction of correct forecasting as an assumption necessary for the movement of the price toward the true equilibrium level.

However, if Marshall's analysis is understood as a description of reality, such a sequence of events is possible, but by no means inevitable. It could be that the sellers, after 500 quarters have been

1 *Ibid.*, p. 334.

2 *Ibid.*, p. 334. The kind reader is asked to use the table on p. 201 for a better understanding of the following.

sold at 37*s*., do not realize that a large part of what is saleable at 37*s*. has already been sold. In this case not only 500 quarters may be sold at 37*s*., but the full 600 quarters which are demanded at that price. If the assumption of perfect knowledge or correct forecasting is abandoned, the movement toward the equilibrium level does not have to start as early as assumed. The price does not necessarily have to fall after 500 quarters have been exchanged at 37*s*., as Marshall assumes.

However, the real problem begins after 500 quarters have been sold at 37*s*. and 200 at 36*s*., as Marshall assumes. Let us hear Marshall's explanation of why 'the market will close on a price of about 36*s*.':

> For when 700 quarters have been sold, no seller will be anxious to dispose of any more except at a higher price than 36*s*., and no buyer will be anxious to purchase any more except at a lower price than 36*s*.[1]

This conclusion is correct if the various quantities offered and demanded at the three price levels are all demanded and supplied by the same individuals, so that the three quantities supplied and demanded at the three price levels are mutually exclusive alternatives. In this case the schedule (see p. 201) implies that sellers would not sell more than 700 quarters except at 37*s*. and that the buyers would not buy more than 700 quarters except at a price of 35*s*. Therefore, no more exchanges could take place after 700 quarters have been exchanged, because, after that, buyers and sellers could not reach a meeting of minds. The situation would be altered if the various quantities were offered and demanded by different individuals, e.g., each 100 quarters by a different person (see below, pp. 207 ff.).

Marshall does not make it quite clear whether he assumes that all buyers and sellers are involved on all three price levels or whether different persons are offering and demanding at different prices. In respect to the suppliers he states:

> There are not more than 600 qr. the holders of which are willing to accept as low a price as 35*s*., but that holders of another hundred would be tempted by 36*s*. and holders of yet another three hundred by 37*s*.[2]

That seems to indicate that 'the holders of another hundred' are not identical with those whose supply price is 35*s*., and with the

[1] *Principles*, p. 334.

[2] *Ibid*., p. 332.

'holders of another 300 qr.' whose supply price is 37*s*.; in other words, different individuals supply the respective quantities at the three different supply prices.

About the buyers Marshall says:

> For if a holder thinks that the buyers will really be able to get at 36*s*. all that they care to take at that price, he will be unwilling to let slip by any offer that is well above that price.[1]

This seems to imply that the same buyers will take either 600 quarters at 37*s*., or 700 quarters at 36*s*., or 900 quarters at 35*s*.; in other words, these three situations are mutually exclusive alternatives for all buyers. That would mean that Marshall constructed the demand side of the market in a different way from the supply side.

Moreover, Marshall makes a tacit assumption, namely:

> that the sum which purchasers are willing to pay and which the sellers are willing to take, for the seven hundredth quarter would not be affected by the question whether the earlier bargains had been made at a high or a low rate. We allowed for the diminution in the buyers' need for corn (its marginal utility to them) as the amount bought increased. But we did not allow for any appreciable change in their unwillingness to part with money (its marginal utility); we assumed that that would be practically the same whether the early payments had been at a higher or a low rate.[2]

This passage seems to indicate that, in spite of our previous quotation from page 332, Marshall assumed that all buyers (and probably all sellers) are demanding and supplying at all three price levels. The fact that the demand prices will have to be lower when larger quantities are demanded is explained by the diminution of the buyers' (plural!) need for corn. The marginal utility of corn would not decline with increasing quantities unless the same buyers had acquired it. This interpretation is in line with Marshall's method of deriving total (market) demand curves by summing up the quantities demanded in individual demand curves.[3]

By the assumption that all buyers and sellers are demanding and supplying at all three price levels, buyers and sellers become homogeneous groups, who, as a group, would act like one and the same

[1] *Ibid.*, p. 333. [2] *Ibid.*, pp. 334–35.

[3] *Ibid.*, Book III, chap. iii, Sec. V, pp. 96 ff.: 'The total demand in the place for, say, tea is the sum of the demands of all individuals there' (p. 99); 'The demand is represented by the same curve as before' (the demand curve of an individual, see p. 96, n. 2); 'only an inch measured along *OX* [the horizontal axis] now represents ten million pounds instead of ten pounds' (p. 99, n. 1).

individual and would thus bring about the same results as in barter. Marshall's temporary equilibrium without perfect knowledge or correct forecasting, therefore, resembles the accidental equilibrium established in barter which is reached when

> exchange will cease because any terms that the one [barterer] is willing to propose would be disadvantageous to the other. Up to this point exchange has increased the satisfaction on both sides, but it can do so no further.[1]

One can describe the temporary equilibrium in the corn market in the same terms: after 700 quarters are sold, the sellers will ask for 37*s*., the buyers will bid only 35*s*. (*Principles*, p. 334), so that no terms proposed by one group will be advantageous to the other. Therefore, transactions will come to a halt, and accidental equilibrium will be reached. The implied condition, however, is that all buyers and all sellers have already participated in the previous exchange of the equilibrium quantity of 700 quarters. Thus buyers, as one collective individual, and the sellers, as its counterpart, reach maximum satisfaction after 700 quarters have been exchanged, which cannot be increased by further exchanges because of the divergence of the marginal utility curves for both groups. Thus the sequence of exchange transactions becomes a well-ordered process, leading to an equilibrium position which represents a terminal point for price movements. The desire to arrive at such a terminal point was probably the decisive motive for the way in which Marshall explains the process of equilibrium. If he had assumed that buyers and sellers do not participate at all price levels, he could not have arrived at such a centre of repose and continuance.

This assumption may not be unrealistic in a small market where buyers and sellers are physically present and where the market 'closes' literally after a few hours or a day. It becomes unrealistic if applied to larger markets in which many different individuals participate who are not physically present.[2] Therefore, it is important to state that in markets in which many different individuals participate the demand curve may decline not only because the

[1] *Principles*, Appendix F, p. 791.

[2] Or if it takes time for a more or less uniform price to be established. Although Marshall develops his ideas about the establishment of equilibrium in respect to temporary, i.e., short-run equilibrium, he implies similar developments for the long run. The analysis of normal, i.e., long-run, equilibrium runs also in terms of intersecting demand-and-supply curves (see below, pp. 217 ff., and *Principles*, Book V, chap. iii, Sec. VI, p. 346, n. 1). Therefore, the importance of his analysis of the way in which temporary equilibrium is established transcends this particular case. This is also true in view of the fact that it has become a general feature of all textbook economics.

same individuals demand more at a lower price but also because, at a lower price, new buyers will enter the market who could not afford the commodity at a higher price. E.g., it would be quite possible that, in the schedule reproduced above (p. 201), every 100 quarters are offered and demanded by different individuals. In this case, Marshall's conclusion that 'when 700 quarters have been sold, no seller will be anxious to dispose of any more, except at a higher price than 36*s.*, and no buyer will be anxious to purchase any more except at a lower price than 36*s.*' (p. 334) is not necessarily cogent.

It is correct only under the assumption that (*a*) the sellers who have previously sold 500 quarters at 37*s.* and 200 quarters at 36*s.* are the ones whose supply prices are 36*s.* or 35*s.* and (*b*) that the buyers who purchase those 700 quarters are the ones whose demand prices are 36*s.* or 37*s.* It is correct only if the buyers and sellers have been paired off in a very special way: if (referring to the usual diagram of a declining demand curve and an ascending supply curve, intersecting at the point of equilibrium) the buyers represented by the part of the demand curve to the left of the equilibrium point will exchange with the sellers represented by the part of the supply curve to the left of the equilibrium point. There is no reason why this specific kind of pairing should take place.

If different buyers and sellers are involved at the three price levels (i.e., if every 100 quarters are supplied and demanded by a different individual), the following sequence of transactions could take place (see table on p. 201): 300 quarters could have been sold at 37*s.* by sellers with supply prices of 37*s.* to buyers with demand prices of 37*s.* (leaving 300 quarters still demanded at 37*s.*); 100 quarters could be sold by sellers with supply prices of 36*s.* to buyers with demand prices of 36*s.* After 400 quarters have thus been exchanged, there are still 600 quarters for sale. These 600 quarters not yet sold are offered for sale by sellers whose supply prices are 35*s.* (those in group C in the schedule in the table on p. 201). But only 500 quarters are now in demand (the entire quantity demanded according to the schedule is 900 quarters, and 400 quarters have already changed hands). Of these 500 quarters, 300 are in demand at the demand price of 37*s.* (buyers in group A of the schedule in the table on p. 201), and 200 quarters are in demand at 35*s.* (buyers in group C in the schedule in the table on p. 201). Therefore, these last 200 quarters will exchange hands at 35*s.*, because those buyers do not want to spend more than this price. The remaining 300 quarters offered for 35*s.* and demanded for 37*s.* may change hands at any of the three prices, or at any price from 35*s.* to 37*s.*, according to the bargaining skill of the parties involved. One hundred quarters will remain unsold, because the total quantity demanded is only 900 quarters, whereas 1,000 quarters are supplied altogether.[1]

Under these circumstances it is impossible to consider 36*s.* as the equilibrium price. The final result under our assumptions will be: 300 quarters have changed hands at 37*s.*, 100 quarters at 36*s.*, 200 quarters at 35*s.*, and the remaining 300 quarters at any price from 35*s.* to 37*s.* Which one of the three prices can rightly be called the equilibrium price? Obviously, no equilibrium price exists in this case. In this case, 36*s.* is not even a floor under which the actual price cannot fall. The actual market prices are determined, under our assumptions, by the accidental sequence in which the various transactions take place. None of these prices has any special distinction which would justify calling it an equilibrium price. All one can say is that various quantities will be exchanged at various prices within the limits of the highest and the lowest demand-and-supply prices.[2]

Thus the equilibrium price would be reached only if there is perfect knowledge (or correct forecasting) or if all buyers and all sellers are involved at all price levels. Without these conditions, especially if various quantities are offered and demanded by different individuals, equilibrium could be established only through the right pairing of buyers and sellers. This, again, could be brought about only by perfect knowledge. In this case no seller would sell below the equilibrium price, and no buyer would pay more than the equilibrium price (if they all knew the total demand-and-supply schedules). Only perfect knowledge would induce the right kind of pairing (of buyers and sellers to the left of the equilibrium position), and only this would exclude from exchange those sellers whose supply prices are higher and those buyers whose demand prices are lower than the equilibrium price. Without perfect knowledge, however, there is nothing which would justify the assumption that this right kind of pairing would take place and that transactions would come to a stop when the equilibrium price and quantity had been reached. If not all market participants are involved at all price levels and in the absence of perfect knowledge, there is nothing which would make such a movement toward the equilibrium position inevitable. However, Marshall wants to arrive at an equilibrium

[1] In this entire discussion we assume, with Marshall, that the supply-and-demand schedules do not change; that is, the buyers and sellers do not change their demand-and-supply prices or the respective quantities demanded and supplied at these prices (*ibid.*, Book V, chap. ii, Sec. III).

[2] Our example shows only one among many possible results of a situation without perfect knowledge or correct forecasting and with a multiplicity of buyers and sellers at all price levels. All such situations, however, will be characterized by the absence of an equilibrium price.

position; it is postulated because it is a psychocultural necessity. It serves as a point of repose and continuance, as an analogy to the action of the individual who balances opposing inner forces, as a last remnant of the idea of harmony, and as a seemingly rigorous method of analysing market developments. Therefore, his assumptions are chosen in such a way that the equilibrium position can be derived from them, whether they are realistic or not. The real element in this situation is the psychoculturally needed result and not the applicability of the construct to observable phenomena.

Later equilibrium theory has tried to evade these difficulties in its concept of perfect competition. Perfect competition requires

> perfection in many other respects than in the absence of monopoly. It may imply . . . an absence of friction in the sense of an ideal fluidity or mobility of factors such that adjustments to changing conditions which actually involve time are accomplished instantaneously in theory. It may imply perfect knowledge of the future and the consequent absence of uncertainty. . . . If a purely competitive market is also perfect, deviations from equilibrium cannot, strictly speaking, occur even momentarily. The general proof, that no price other than the equilibrium one could maintain itself must then be regarded as a proof that no such price could appear even for an instant. There would be neither movement towards an equilibrium nor oscillations about it. The equilibrium price would not be 'worked out' by the play of supply and demand; it would coexist with the market through the realization of stability at a single stroke the moment the market came into existence.[1]

Here we have expounded lucidly what Marshall wanted to accomplish: the equilibrium situation established without any necessity to explain how it is brought about. There is a close analogy between this model of perfect competition and the Marshallian equilibrium analysis of the individual. In both cases it is the passing of time and the changes wrought by it which create difficulties. Equilibrium is made possible by the Chamberlinian model of perfect competition through the elimination of time and change, which is implied in the assumption of frictionless adjustment. This construct has to be correlated with the idea that, for the completely rational, conscious individual with perfect knowledge, unchanging character, and long-run life-goals, who knows all his needs and marginal utilities with instant clarity, the establishment of equilibrium is no problem; he will establish it at once with the lightning-like insight of a superconscious demiurge. The model of perfect competition, used

[1] E. Chamberlin, *The Theory of Monopolistic Competition*, pp. 6, 26.

by Chamberlin and implied by Marshall, is a projection of this ideal into the market. The assumptions of perfect knowledge and instantaneous adjustment do away with the disequilibrating actions of buyers and sellers in the same way as the assumptions of rationality and of unchanging character do away with impulses which could disturb the equilibrium of the individual.

It is interesting to observe the difference in the Marshallian and Chamberlinian intellectual techniques. Marshall tries to be realistic. Therefore, he describes the functioning of the market in which persons with perfect knowledge participate as if it were a realistic picture. Nobody who reads carefully Book V, chapter ii, can avoid the impression that this is meant to be, on the whole, an analysis of what actually occurs on a corn market in a country town. The abstract, symbolic scheme is hidden. Chamberlin, belonging to a period with less faith but with more intellectual sophistication, abandons all attempts to be realistic; for him, perfect competition is a purely hypothetical construct. However, the fact that he and others use this model shows that there are still remnants of the old faith in economic rationality hidden behind the entire system of equilibrium theory; otherwise, it would not make any sense whatsoever to construct such a perfect model.

Because it will be vehemently denied by orthodox economists, we reiterate our conviction: models, constructs, and hypothetical fictions in socio-economic thought are not chosen arbitrarily; they fulfil a psychocultural function. In the case under consideration, the reason for the belief in the perfect model—implicit in Marshall and made explicit by Chamberlin—is the desire to arrive at an equilibrium. Logically, equilibrium is simply postulated. However, as an arbitrary postulate it does not make sense. It does make sense, however, if one assumes that we believe in a meaningful economic system which is governed by the laws of rationality and will lead to an equilibrium, a point of satiation, a centre of repose and continuance. As so often, the 'irrational' belief is more rational than the logical assumption. In a rationalistic civilization it is not 'irrational' to believe in a rational economic system. This belief makes life under this economic system easier, and it is, therefore, an aid for living. It is senseless to interpret such a belief merely as an intellectual construct, an arbitrary assumption. Such an interpretation betrays contempt for the meaningfulness of life. It assumes that thinking can take place divorced from life and without connection with it. This approach is the misbegotten creation of an overcerebrated philosophy; it is as if the life-negating intellect has touched one with the cold finger of death.

Chapter XVIII

EQUILIBRIUM OF NORMAL SUPPLY AND DEMAND

The Time Element

IN contradistinction to temporary equilibrium, normal equilibrium refers to a longer period of time. Marshall states that time plays an essential part on all markets and that 'the equilibrium price is affected by calculations of the future relations of production and consumption.'[1] Therefore, he is, in his analysis of normal equilibrium,

> concerned with movements of price ranging over still longer periods than those for which the most far-sighted dealers in futures generally make their reckoning; we have to consider the volume of production adjusting itself to the conditions of the market, and the normal price being thus determined at the position of stable equilibrium of normal demand and normal supply.[2]

Thus it is his intention to consider long-range developments in time. But, from the very beginning, the time element is excluded by assumptions. This is done by confining equilibrium to a unit of time and by abstracting from the changes wrought by the passage of time:

> The unit of time may be chosen according to the circumstances of each particular problem: it may be a day, a month, a year, or even a generation: but in every case it must be short relatively to the period of the market under discussion. It is to be assumed that the general circumstances of the market remain unchanged throughout this period; that there is, for instance, no change in fashion or taste, no new substitute which might affect the demand, no new invention to disturb the supply.[3]

The periods of time under consideration are split up into small units. Thus, the time element is actually eliminated. Time is a continuous flow; if it is dissected into units and if the situation pertaining to such a unit is considered regardless of what happened in other time units

[1] *Principles of Economics*, p. 337. [2] *Ibid.*, p. 338. [3] *Ibid.*, p. 342.

before and afterward, the flow of time is ignored, and a timeless, static type of analysis is applied.

This is a problem with which philosophers have struggled for ages. The Greek philosopher Zenon of Elea had already demonstrated the impossibility of dividing the infinite flow of space and time into infinitesimally small parts. The problem of interrelating the infinite and the finite is involved in infinitesimal calculus and has occupied Descartes and Leibniz. It is not an accident that calculus is so widely used in economics, because it seemingly makes possible a synthesis of the finite and the infinite. It makes possible the dissection of the infinite flow of time into static, timeless, infinitesimally small moments of time and the synthesis of these timeless units again into an aggregate by integration. The methods of calculus are legitimate in mathematics. However, their application to real situations in economics and elsewhere leads to the negation of the basic existential dichotomy of the finite and the infinite. The attempt to combine both has a psychocultural motive, namely, to establish a harmony where none exists. By trying to analyse the flow of time and of change in terms of timeless units, economists have excluded the very phenomenon which they wanted to analyse.

Marshall assumes further that conditions remain unchanged in spite of the fact that events take place in time. Thus the main problem which time creates, namely, the problem of change, is avoided. The conditions which are assumed to remain constant cease to be variables, and thus cease to have any influence on the events under consideration. The factors mentioned in the last quotation (fashions, tastes, substitutes, inventions) cause the most important changes over time. By assuming them to be constant, the changes caused by time are excluded. At first, Marshall intends to take the long-run changes in time into consideration; then, however, he excluded the change brought about by time by using the *ceteris paribus* clause.

The same procedure is obvious in the definition of the long-run equilibrium situation. 'When . . . the amount produced (in a unit of time) is such that the demand price is greater than the supply price,'[1] there is no equilibrium. 'When the demand price is equal to the supply price, the amount produced has no tendency either to be increased or to be diminished; it is in equilibrium.'[2] In this definition of the equilibrium position the passage of time is excluded by the explicit statement that the analysis refers to a unit of time. Thus the equilibrium position does not exist within a range of a flow of time but is confined to a small, indivisible unit of time, in spite of the fact

[1] *Principles*, p. 345. [2] *Ibid.*

that Marshall purports to deal with a long-run time period and that he considers such an equilibrium position as stable in time under certain conditions.[1] The very idea of a stable equilibrium is a way of evading the influence and the obstacle of time. Marshall realizes this quite clearly:

> For indeed the demand and supply schedules do not in practice remain unchanged for a long time together, but are constantly being changed; and every change in them alters the equilibrium price, and thus gives new positions to the centres about which the amount and the price tend to oscillate.[2]

This admission gives the concept of a stable equilibrium a very specific meaning. Logically, the idea of stability can be maintained only if it is confined to a 'unit of time'. Only for such a unit or moment will the curves remain constant and unchanging. Everything Marshall has said about the forces which will drive the market back into the once accomplished and established equilibrium position holds true only under the assumption of unchanging curves, that is, for a timeless moment, unless one excludes change by assumption, which again eliminates time by eliminating its essential characteristic.

The extent of the Marshallian and, after him, neoclassical ambivalence in respect to time and change is revealed in a passage in which he talks about the meaning of long-run, normal, natural value:

> This is the real drift of that much quoted and much misunderstood doctrine of Adam Smith and other economists that the normal or 'natural' value of a commodity is that which economic forces tend to bring about in the long run. It is the average value which economic forces would bring about if the general conditions of life were stationary for a run of time long enough to enable them all to work out their full effect.[3]

On the one hand, it is the passage of time which will bring out the normal, natural value of the true equilibrium price in the long run. On the other hand, it will come about only 'if the general conditions of life were stationary for a run of time long enough to enable them to work out their full effect.' That means the exclusion of change and, thereby, of time. Time and change are identical phenomena: they are inseparably interrelated, and abstracting from one means abstracting from the other. If change is excluded by assumption, time is assumed not to pass; a stationary state is a timeless one.

[1] *Ibid.* [2] *Ibid.*, p. 346–47. [3] *Ibid.*, p. 347.

Therefore, what Marshall asserts in one breath he takes back in the next. First, he makes the establishment of the equilibrium position dependent on the passage of time; then he postulates that during that period of adjustment nothing should change; otherwise, the position could not be established. This is meaningful only from the point of view of 'psycho-logic': as an expression of an ambivalent attitude toward (inner and outer) change and toward the concept of equilibrium.

In Book V, chapter v, Marshall finally gets around to deal overtly with the problem of time, although he has dealt with it implicitly throughout his entire analysis of normal equilibrium in Book V and, indeed, throughout his entire work.

> The element of time is a chief cause of those difficulties in economic investigations which make it necessary for man with his limited powers to go step by step; breaking up a complex question. . . . In breaking it up, he segregates those disturbing causes, whose wanderings happen to be inconvenient, for the time in a pound called Cæteris Paribus.[1]

Here the implicit aim of the 'other things being equal' clause is clearly expressed: the inconvenient factors are, for the time being, eliminated. Marshall hastens to state that 'the existence of other tendencies is not denied, but their disturbing effect is neglected for a time.'[2] However, for the time being, the difficulty is avoided and the model-building economist can rejoice in the feeling that, for the moment, the difficulty is overcome.

The argument that this method has proved 'successful' in the natural sciences does not make this psychological interpretation invalid. First, in many such cases in the physical sciences, the elimination of certain factors is actually possible in the laboratory. Thus it loses its abstract character and becomes something real. Other unrealistic concepts, such as the idea of a vacuum, can be used in the discovery of laws applicable to reality, because the physical universe is structured differently from the human universe. In the former, the elimination of factors often leaves the remaining ones unaltered. In the latter, the parts form a whole; the separation of one of them alters the whole and changes it into something entirely different. Human behaviour and action conceived outside the flow of time are non-existent and impossible. So are the results of cutting the flow of time into segments and the assumption of a time period without change. The stream of time forms a unity, and everything in it operates all the time; the mere distinction between long and

[1] *Principles*, p. 366.

[2] *Ibid.*, p. 366.

short run, between constant and variable factors over time, is fallacious; the former is composed of the latter, and everything changes in a continuum. The long run becomes a useful concept only if one assumes the constancy of certain factors which allow the 'long-run factors to work themselves out'; that means, however, stopping the flow of time and change in order to explain their effects—an inherently contradictory procedure. That does not mean that there is no such thing as laws of long-run development. But they cannot be discovered by excluding the influence of certain factors. A different type of model-building has to take place here. The model must be of the 'ideal-type' variety which comprises all the essential traits of the phenomenon under consideration. By leaving out essential factors, such as time and change, one will only arrive at a completely distorted picture of reality.

The crowning idea in Marshall's treatment of time is the 'fiction of the stationary state.'

> In it the general conditions of production and consumption, of distribution and exchange remain motionless; but yet it is full of movement; for it is a mode of life. The average age of the population may be stationary; though each individual is growing up from youth towards his prime, or downwards toward old age. And the same amount of things per head of the population will have been produced in the same ways by the same class of people for many generations together; and therefore this supply of the appliances of production will have had full time to be adjusted to the steady demand.[1]

Ambivalence permeates this description of the stationary state. One could call it a masterpiece of synthetic combinations of opposites; it is motionless, but full of movement; the average age is stationary, but people are born, grow up, and die.

In such a stationary state,

> the plain rule would be that cost of production governs value. . . . Each element of cost would be governed by 'natural' laws. . . . There would be no distinction between long-period and short-period normal value.[2]

However, Marshall himself admits that 'nothing of this is true in the world in which we live.'[3]

Marshall recognizes the abstractness of his model; at the same time, he attributes to it a realistic character. In his description of the stationary state he has already called it 'a mode of life', which is

[1] *Ibid.*, p. 367. [2] *Ibid.*, p. 367. [3] *Ibid.*, p. 368.

not the same thing as a hypothetical construct. And now, after he has stated in no uncertain terms that it is unrealistic, that 'in this world therefore every plain and simple doctrine as to the relations between cost of production, demand and value is necessarily false,' he proceeds to apply the model of the stationary state to reality by assuming that it is, after all, not so unrealistic:

> The stationary state has just been taken to be one in which population is stationary. But nearly all its distinctive features may be exhibited in a place where population and wealth are both growing, provided they are growing at about the same rate, and there is no scarcity of land; and provided also the methods of production and the conditions of trade change but little; and above all, where the character of man himself is a constant quantity.[1]

Here the hypothetical construct is changed into the description of a real situation. If we want reality to conform to a certain pattern, it will be possible to make it appear in the desired light. It is obvious that Marshall considers the new assumptions of an equal rate of growth of population and wealth and of the absence of scarce lands as realistic possibilities. They are, however, nothing but another device to eliminate the uncertainties brought about by time and change. If change is, by assumption, reduced to such predictable regularities, its disturbing character is toned down, and uncertainty of the future is transformed into foreseeable certitude. These assumptions merely make the stationary state appear as more realistic, because they admit of some changes, although in unrealistic form. They render time and changes innocuous by assuming regularity and predictability.

What is more important, however, is that the realization of the stationary state is tied in with the constancy of human character! Do we need a more conclusive proof of our thesis that the entire problem of equilibrium is originally a problem of ethics and character formation? In the statement quoted above, Marshall states clearly that constancy of character will bring about a situation closely approximating a stationary state. If we keep in mind that this state is the prerequisite for the establishment of equilibrium, the moral skeleton of his system becomes crystal clear. What Marshall means to say is:

> If man obeys the code of rational economic behaviour, if he has a steady scale of values and pursues constant life-goals, the market forces will establish an equilibrium such as the equilibrium which rational economic man can establish within himself.

[1] *Principles*, p. 368.

By making constancy of character a prerequisite for the stationary state and, with this, for the establishment of an equilibrium price, Marshall has unified his system and assured its ethical justification with one stroke. To see this clearly, the content and meaning of normal equilibrium has now to be examined.

The Content and the Meaning of Normal Equilibrium

Normal equilibrium shows the same characteristics as those of all other kinds of equilibrium: intersection of declining and ascending curves, equality of amounts exchanged, balance of opposing forces. Its distinctive characteristic is that it refers to longer periods of time during which the prices are supposed to become equal to the cost of production.

> The remainder of the present volume will be chiefly occupied with interpreting and limiting this doctrine that the value of a thing tends in the long run to correspond to its cost of production.[1]

Marshall connects cost of production with supply price and supply price with the discommodities of labour: effort and waiting. He defines supply price as 'the price required to call forth the exertion necessary for producing any given amount of a commodity.'[2] This price reflects the discommodity of labour and the exertions of the workers in such a way that 'the exertions which any set of workers will make, rise or fall with a rise or fall in the remuneration which is offered to them.'[3] Not only does this enable Marshall to draw inclining supply curves of labour and of goods,[4] a prerequisite for arriving at a point of equilibrium; but also establishes a direct relation between money price and exertion; the money prices reflect the 'real' cost of production. This makes possible the identification of exertion, production, and supply prices.

This interrelation is used in the analysis of normal long-run equilibrium. The real costs of production are described as follows:

> The exertions of all the different kinds of labour . . . together with the abstinences or rather the waitings required for saving the capital used in making it: all these efforts and sacrifices together will be called the real cost of production of the commodity. The sums of money that will have to be paid for these efforts and

[1] *Ibid.*, Book V, chap. iii, p. 348.

[2] *Ibid.*, Book IV, chap. i, Sec. II, p. 142; see above, pp. 186 ff.

[3] *Ibid.*

[4] He derives the ascending shape of the supply curve of goods from the labour supply curve, by assuming for 'the moment . . . that production depended solely upon exertion of . . . workers' (*ibid.*, p. 142). The concept of a supply schedule is developed in Book V, chap. iii, Sec. V, pp. 343 f.

> sacrifices will be called either its money cost of production or . . . its expenses of production; they are the prices which have to be paid in order to call forth an adequate supply of the efforts and waitings that are required for making it; or, in other words, they are its supply price.[1]

Thus money expenses correspond to real efforts, and sacrifices to work and waiting. This enables us to understand why the long-run normal price must 'tend to correspond to its cost of production.' It means that the long-run effects of the market forces lead to a just result: to a price which corresponds to the efforts and sacrifices in production, a just reward for those efforts and sacrifices.

We find here a revival of the ethical idea of the labour theory of value which has often been interpreted as being a special version of a cost-of-production theory. This is only partly correct, in view of the mechanistic character of Ricardian theory, in which labour is, to some extent, regarded as a mechanical force which creates value in the same way as a force moves a body.[2] However, the Marshallian cost-of-production theory has the same ethical basis as Ricardo's. Prices are justified because they conform to efforts and sacrifices. Correspondence between money cost, supply price, efforts, and sacrifices, however, exists only under certain conditions. It is here that the time element and the vacillating attitude of Marshall toward it play an important role. The

> doctrine that the price at which a thing can be produced represents its real cost of production, that is, the efforts and sacrifices which have been directly and indirectly devoted to its production, [has a] great many different limitations. . . . For in an age of rapid change such as this the equilibrium of normal demand and supply does not thus correspond to any distinct relation of a certain aggregate of pleasures got from the consumption of the commodity and an aggregate of efforts and sacrifices involved in producing it. . . .[3]

And then follows the passage already discussed,[4] in which he limits the establishment of a natural, normal value and price to the long run, but only if the general conditions of life were stationary for a long run of time.

Here we have the very essence of the equilibrium concept! Ideally, the long-run equilibrium price should represent the balance of an aggregate of pleasures from consumption with an aggregate of efforts of production. Production and consumption, supply and demand, efforts and pleasures, are all parallel and correlated magni-

[1] *Principles*, pp. 338–39.
[2] See above, pp. 52 ff.
[3] *Ibid.*, p. 347.
[4] P. 213; *Ibid.*, p. 347.

tudes. They are all functions of the amounts produced, consumed, acquired, and enjoyed. They form pairs of opposing forces. They all supposedly decline or increase continuously by small marginal quantities. Thus it becomes possible to reach an equilibrium point which balances efforts and pleasures (within the individual), supply and demand (on the market), and production and consumption (on markets and within the whole economy). The pattern is taken from the code of rational economic behaviour. In the individual sphere it perhaps makes some sense to talk about a balance of opposing tendencies, because the individual can at least try to establish such a balance. However, the same pattern is projected into the market and into the economy. Thus Marshall arrives at an equilibrium price which seems just, because it balances subjective efforts and sacrifices against subjective pleasures. It represents a just reward and a rational harmony between those opposing forces which are the basic prime movers in the Marshallian system.

However, this equilibrium is, even in Marshall's system, only a chimera, only a mirage. It will be established only in the long run. This in itself is an important qualification. The long run, in economic thought, plays a role similar to the belief in life after death in many religions. Its role is one of a compensatory fantasy gratification. What we are lacking now is promised to us, in the one case after death, in the other in the long run. That this is so and that very little reality value can be attributed to it can be gathered from the fact that the attainment of the equilibrium of supply and demand with a balance of efforts and pleasures is not only dependent on the passage of a long period of time but also qualified by the prerequisite that 'the general conditions of life were stationary for a run of time long enough to enable them all to work out their full effect.'[1] What is first postponed and projected into the long run is then made quite unattainable by this requirement. Repeatedly, Marshall states that things do not remain stationary, that demand-and-supply schedules do not remain unchanged, that we live in an age of rapid change; therefore, this requirement of a stationary state makes the realization of the ideal long-run, normal equilibrium wellnigh impossible.

The method of first constructing an equilibrium model and then making it unattainable by surrounding it with impossible prerequisites is an expression of ambivalence toward equilibrium. It is the same procedure which we have observed before in the case of Ricardo and in the reasoning of Marshall: an argument is developed, only to be taken back again in the form of qualifications. At first, Marshall tries to universalize the ideal of rational economic conduct

[1] *Ibid.*, p. 347; see above, p. 213.

by projecting it into the market and into the economy as a whole. He constructed an equilibrium concept which, if at all, makes sense only if applied to the rational behaviour of individuals. In order to be able to apply it to markets and to the economy, he introduces a host of fictitious assumptions, albeit in such a way as to make this projection appear as a close approximation to reality. Finally, however, he destroys, so to speak, his entire structure by making it dependent on a prerequisite impossible to realize—the fiction of a stationary state. It is as if he were to say:

> It would be desirable for prices to be determined by rational action, and to be able to prove that market forces bring about just prices. But this is a mere wish dream; prices could be just if we had the powers of Joshua and could make time stand still; but as we all know, we do not have such powers; our interpretation of price determination is, therefore, a mere wish dream.

The important role which Marshall attributes to cost of production in the determination of long-run normal value is in conflict with his utilitarian subjectivism. This is the same conflict as the one between classical political economy and the marginalists. Marshall takes an intermediate stand. He states that utility and cost of production determine value in the same way as the upper and the lower blade of a pair of scissors cut a piece of paper.[1] However, he does not really attribute equal roles to both in the determination of value. They have a different influence on price according to the time period under consideration. In temporary markets when the stock is practically fixed, price is governed by demand and utility. In the longer run, price will fluctuate around the cost of production, especially in the case of goods produced under the law of constant returns (where the expansion of production will not tend to increase unit costs). The upshot of his discussion is

> that, 'as a general rule, the shorter the period which we are considering, the greater must be the share of our attention which is given to the influence of demand on value; and the longer the period, the more important will be the influence of cost of production on value.'[2]

This could be accepted as a realistic statement; it has, however, psychocultural implications. His confinement of the effects of demand and utility to the short time period and the association of a cost-of-production price with the long run seems to indicate a some-

[1] *Principles*, p. 348.

[2] *Ibid.*, p. 349.

what higher evaluation of the latter. That this is so can be seen from the continuation of the statement just quoted:

> The actual value at any time, the market value as it is often called, is often more influenced by passing events and by causes whose action is fitful and shortlived, than by those which work persistently. But in long periods these fitful and irregular causes in large measure efface one another's influence; so that in the long run persistent causes dominate value completely.[1]

Here we find the synthesis of many ideas. Previously, Marshall had assumed that the fitfulness and irregularity of individual action would be cancelled out in group action because of the law of large numbers (see above, pp. 190 ff.); now he assumes that the fitfulness and irregularity of day-to-day phenomena will cancel out in the long run; and this latter statement also implies that the fitfulness and irregularity of demand and utility will cancel out in the long run and leave only the stable and just cost of production as a regulator of prices and value. Short run here becomes identical with subjectivism, fitfulness, and irregularity; long run with efforts, sacrifices, and cost of production. Here, at least, Marshall's sympathies are on the side of the efforts and sacrifices and the cost-of-production theory of value, which he projects into the long run and by which he tries to get rid of the disturbing fitfulness of subjective utilities. In this long run, which is, as we have said, the Marshallian kingdom of heaven, demand and utility play a small role, and cost of production reigns supreme as the determinant of value. Price will correspond to effort, and rewards will be commensurate with sacrifice; the model and ideal of the labour theory of value is restored.

Normal Equilibrium and Maximum Satisfaction

The establishment of an equilibrium by the individual presupposes the possibility of maximizing utility, satisfaction, happiness, etc. In order to apply this pattern to long-run value and price determination, it would be necessary to prove that aggregate satisfaction is being maximized in the market in the long run. Therefore, Marshall sets out (in Book V, chap. xiii, Sec. V) to examine 'a little more closely . . . the general doctrine that a position of (stable) equilibrium of demand and supply is a position also of maximum satisfaction.'[2] He refers to Bastiat's *Economic Harmonies* as one of the sources of this doctrine, which he defines as

[1] *Ibid.*, pp. 349–50.

[2] *Ibid.*, p. 470.

> the doctrine that the free pursuit by each individual of his own immediate interest, will lead producers to turn their capital and labour, and consumers to turn their expenditure into such courses as are most conducive to the general interest.[1]

He distinguishes two versions of the theory of maximum satisfaction.

> There is indeed one interpretation of the doctrine according to which every position of equilibrium of demand and supply may fairly be regarded as a position of maximum satisfaction.[2]

He illustrates this case by describing a situation in which two parties are confronted in exchange: a buyer and a seller, the former with a declining demand curve, the latter with an ascending supply curve.[3] Marshall assumes that the demand price at first exceeds the supply price, that is, that the quantities exchanged are to the left of the equilibrium position. In this case, further exchanges at any price between the supply and the demand prices will

> give a surplus of satisfaction to buyer or to seller, or to both. The marginal utility of what he receives is greater than that of what he gives up, to at least one of the two parties.[4]

That implies that the demand-and-supply curves are marginal utility curves and that the various demand-and-supply prices indicated by these curves precisely reflect changes in the marginal utilities of the two traders which are brought about by the changes in the volume of their stock. In this case the two traders will continue to exchange until an equilibrium is reached:

> So far then every step in the exchange increases the aggregate satisfaction of the two parties. But when equilibrium has been reached, demand price being now equal to supply price, there is no room for any such surplus: the marginal utility of what each receives no longer exceeds that of what he gives up in exchange.[5]

In respect to such an equilibrium Marshall arrives at the final conclusion:

> It is true that a position of equilibrium of demand and supply is a position of maximum satisfaction in this limited sense, that the aggregate satisfaction of the two parties concerned increases until the position is reached; and that any production beyond the equili-

[1] *Principles*, p. 502.

[2] *Ibid.*, p. 470.

[3] This conforms to the accidental equilibrium of the barter situation (see *ibid.*, Appendix F, p. 791, and above, pp. 108 ff.).

[4] *Principles*, p. 470.

[5] *Ibid.*, p. 470.

> brium amount could not be permanently maintained so long as buyers and sellers acted freely as individuals each in his own interest.[1]

This equilibrium, however, merely means that both traders will find it disadvantageous to continue the exchange beyond the equilibrium point, because this would not increase their own individual satisfaction or utility. This is, in all probability, what Marshall wants to say. The interpretation of his argument hinges on the meaning of the term 'aggregate satisfaction of the two parties', which he uses in both the previous quotations. He probably means the aggregate totals of their individual satisfactions, each total considered separately and not added up to form a total of social, supra-individual utility.

Nevertheless, in this way Marshall interrelates equilibrium and maximum satisfaction. Although he uses as an example a situation in which two traders confront each other, one gains the impression that he is inclined to apply the same reasoning to a market with a plurality of buyers and sellers. When the equilibrium position is reached on such a market (from a point at which the demand prices are higher than the supply prices to a point where the two are equal), those buyers and sellers who have not yet exchanged cannot increase their satisfaction by exchanging, because they would not find any partners who would want to exchange at mutually satisfactory prices. Thus such an equilibrium implies 'maximum individual satisfaction' under the given market conditions.

There is, however, another version of the doctrine of maximum satisfaction which assumes that

> a position of equilibrium of demand and supply is one of maximum aggregate satisfaction in the full sense of the term: that is that an increase in production beyond the equilibrium level would directly . . . diminish the aggregate satisfaction of both parties.'[2]

Marshall considered this not to be universally true because of the differences in wealth which cause differences in the marginal utility of money to the poor and to the rich. If the producers were much poorer than the consumers, aggregate satisfaction could be maximized by reducing the supply and thereby increasing the equilibrium price, so that the aggregate satisfaction would be increased by increasing the satisfaction of the poorer producers; the position of maximum satisfaction would be to the left of the previous point of equilibrium. The opposite would be true if the consumers were the poorer class.[3]

[1] *Ibid.*, p. 471. [2] *Ibid.*, p. 471. [3] *Ibid.*, p. 471.

This reasoning implies the possibility of a concept of social supra-individual welfare. This concept forms the basis for the discussions about optimum allocation of resources and becomes the central theme of welfare economics. It requires the assumption that the feelings, emotions, satisfactions, and marginal utilities of different individuals are standardized, homogeneous, comparable, and can be added and aggregated to arrive at a social interindividual maximum. Marshall believes that maximum, aggregate, total satisfaction in a social sense can be increased either by voluntary or by compulsory action. If supply is increased to increase the satisfaction of the 'poorer consumers' total aggregate social satisfaction is increased (p. 471). Such reasoning is implicitly based on the assumption that the marginal utilities of the poor and of the rich can be measured by a common quantitative denominator and added up. Marshall talks explicitly about increasing aggregate satisfaction of consumers and producers as a group (p. 471, fourth paragraph), and not of individuals alone. That this is so becomes crystal clear when he uses the term 'total happiness', which will not always be increased by mere self-interested action.[1]

The attempt to arrive at a formula for social maximization again shows Marshall's tendency to personify economic collectivities. The individual can perhaps maximize by equalizing utilities from various activities at the margin. If one talks about an increase in aggregate social satisfaction or about social maximization, one assumes implicitly that the social organization or institution acts like an individual. Marshall implies that equilibrium can be accompanied by maximum social satisfaction if income and wealth are equally distributed and if, therefore, the marginal utility of money is the same for everybody. In this case there would be no qualitative differences between feelings of different individuals, if one assumes that unequal distribution of wealth is the only cause of such differences. Feelings, however, may be qualitatively homogeneous at best only within one and the same individual. The difficulty arises mainly from the problem of comparison of feelings of different individuals. When individual subjective feelings are homogenized and added, to accomplish maximum social satisfaction, the economy is assumed to act like one individual.

Marshall deals here with one of the basic problems of economic ethics: how to justify social goals in spite of an individualistic philosophy. If the good of the individual is the ultimate goal, the concept of a common good has to be derived from the idea of individual welfare. This was done by the philosophers of the Enlightenment by

[1] *Principles*, p. 474; for full quotation, see below, p. 225.

assuming that the individual needs the community for his own ends and has to surrender some of his autonomy in order to receive protection and co-operation from others. Marshall and neoclassical economists, however, betray their ambivalence in respect to the problem of individual versus society by trying to operate with the idea of individual utility, on the one hand, and aggregate satisfaction or common welfare, on the other. They try to combine an individualistic and a collectivistic ideal within the same conceptual framework. This method cannot succeed, because subjective satisfaction and social welfare are not always in harmony with each other. According to Marshall, the main causes of this situation are the inequality of income distribution and the fact that not all types of production have a character-improving effect. Maximum social satisfaction is not always 'attained by encouraging each individual to spend his own resources in that way which suits him best,' because

> if he spends his income in such a way as to increase the demand for the services of the poor and to increase their incomes, he adds something more to the total happiness than if he adds an equal amount to the incomes of the rich, because the happiness which an additional shilling brings to the poor man is much greater than that which it brings to a rich one; and that he does good by buying things the production of which raises, in preference to things the production of which lowers the character of those who make them.[1]

Thus economic liberty does not necessarily lead to a maximum of social welfare. This is why Marshall has to deny that equilibrium, the result of economic liberty and of the free pursuit of self-interest, is accompanied by maximum social satisfaction, and that is why he talks about compulsory action (p. 471) and government interference (p. 475) in this context. He criticizes the existing economic system because it does not bring about an equilibrium with maximum social satisfaction; that means implicitly because inequality of income distribution and character-corrupting economic pursuits do exist. This implies that equilibrium ought to be accompanied by maximum social satisfaction; Marshall's basic ideological scheme requires this identity. That it is not established in reality leads to a condemnation of reality, thus again betraying Marshall's ambivalence toward the existing economy. This ambivalence arises because of the conflict between ethical ideals about the ultimate good and the effects of the economic system. Marshall tries, throughout his entire work, to harmonize the two. Sometimes he succeeds in

[1] *Ibid.*, p. 474.

explaining away the conflict, but, on many occasions, the dichotomy of economics and ethics breaks through. This is the case in the foregoing passages. The conflict we found in the initial chapters in the analysis of wants is clearly reflected here: economic activity and the results brought about by the market forces are not necessarily good in a moral sense.

Increasing Returns

The law of increasing returns may be worded thus: An increase of labour and capital leads generally to improved organization, which increases the efficiency of the work of labour and capital.[1] This law formulates a condition for economic progress. It contains an element of optimism in respect to the increase in labour supply and capital accumulation; it is assumed that they will increase efficiency through the improvement in organization. At the same time, the law implies that the increasing size of business organization has beneficial effects. Thus the law constitutes, to some extent, a justification of large-scale enterprise, in spite of its tendency toward monopoly. It represents an optimistic approach to long-run economic dynamics, in contrast to Malthusian and Ricardian pessimism.[2]

Marshall ascribes the law of increasing returns to man and blames nature for the law of diminishing returns:

> In other words, we say broadly that while the part which nature plays in production shows a tendency to diminishing return, the part which man plays shows a tendency to increasing returns.[3]

Here we again find the Malthusian bias against 'female' nature and the predilection for the 'male' activity in production.

The law of increasing returns, however, is a disturbing element in the Marshallian system. For one, it presents another obstacle to the attainment of maximum social satisfaction in an equilibrium brought about by the free interplay of market forces.

[1] *Principles*, p. 518.

[2] It is interesting to observe how Marshall vacillates between the admiration of economic progress and anti-economic romanticism. When he introduced an optimistic note in pointing out that a growing population can be a blessing under certain conditions and can lead to the benefits of large-scale production and result in 'new opportunities of getting social enjoyments and the comforts and luxuries of culture in every form,' he added as a note of caution: 'No doubt deduction must be made for the growing difficulty of finding solitude and quiet and even fresh air: but there is in most cases some balance of good' (*ibid.*, p. 321; see also n. 1 on the same page).

[3] *Ibid.*, p. 318.

> Even if we assume that a shilling's worth of happiness is of equal importance to whomsoever it comes . . . we have to admit that the manner in which a person spends his income is a matter of direct economic concern to the community.

He should not spend it on things which obey the law of diminishing returns, because

> he makes those things more difficult to be obtained by his neighbours . . . while in so far as he spends it on things which obey the law of increasing return, he makes those things more easy of attainment to others.[1]

Therefore, the unrestricted pursuit of self-interest will not necessarily lead to the same increase in the common interest.

Second, the law of increasing returns is an obstacle in the path of long-run equilibrium, because it results in downward-sloping, long-run supply curves. Such curves will not intersect the demand curves (except in the special cases in which the slope of the demand curves is steeper than the slope of the supply curves). Without intersection, there will be no equilibrium. Marshall has to admit

> that the term 'margin of production' has no significance for long periods in relation to commodities the cost of production of which diminishes with a gradual increase in the output . . . in the problems in which the tendency to increasing returns is in effective force, there is no clearly defined marginal product.[2]

That means that, in such cases, no point of equilibrium can be clearly defined. A declining supply curve may prevent the establishment of a determinate equilibrium position. Nevertheless, Marshall tries to arrive at some kind of equilibrium which includes the law of increasing returns. The marginal cost of a representative firm[3] will

[1] *Ibid.*, pp. 474–75.

[2] *Ibid.*, Appendix H, p. 805.

[3] *Ibid.*, p. 367. The concept of the representative firm plays an important part in Marshallian thought on normal equilibrium. It is another device to eliminate the irregularities of reality caused by individual differences between firms. It is also an attempt to freeze the structure of an industry by eliminating changes in time. If the representative firm remains of the same size and structure in the long run, many inconvenient changes are avoided. The representative firm is a construct which serves to eliminate individual differences and to bridge the gap between the individual and the group, at least in the relations of the single firm to the industry. Marshall realizes that 'the history of the individual firm cannot be made into the history of an industry any more than the history of an individual man can be made into the history of mankind' (*ibid.*, p. 459). And yet he tries to do just this by his concept of the representative firm, 'which has had a fairly long life and a fair success, which is managed with normal ability, and which has normal access to the economies, external and internal, which belong to that

rise in the short-run with an increase in demand and output. Thus its short-run supply curve will be a rising one, allowing for an equilibrium position at the point of intersection with the declining demand curve. However, in the long run a gradual increase in demand will increase the size and efficiency of this firm and lead to internal and external economies. Thus,

> when making a list of supply prices (supply schedules) for long periods in these industries, we set down a diminished supply price against an increased amount of the flow of goods: meaning thereby that a flow of that increased amount will in the course of time be supplied profitably at that lower price, to meet a fairly steady corresponding demand . . . and we look towards a position of balance and equilibrium between the forces of progress and decay, which would be attained if the conditions under view were supposed to act uniformly for a long time.[1]

What Marshall means is that, in the long run, the forces bringing about diminishing returns and rising marginal costs and supply prices may be offset by forces causing increasing returns, falling costs, and falling supply prices. He attempts to construct a long-run equilibrium which balances the effects of the laws of increasing and diminishing returns, represented as 'forces of progress and decay.' Long-run dynamic forces are thus pressed into the Procrustean bed of static equilibrium analysis. This idea, however, is vitiated immediately by the prerequisite that the same conditions would have to act uniformly for a long time in order to bring about such an equilibrium. Thus the dynamic element and the time factor are

aggregate volume of production' (*ibid.*, p. 317). Marshall himself calls this firm an average firm, but 'a particular sort of average firm' (*ibid.*, p. 318). It is a mixture of a statistical average and an ideal norm. The concept of the representative firm enables Marshall to condense the industry into a firm, and to treat the behaviour of a group as the behaviour of an individual firm. It is the same tendency which we have encountered before, namely, to reduce group action to individual action. At the same time, the representative firm is an individual which has none of the deviating, irregular, abnormal characteristics of a physical person. It is a normal, representative 'individual'. This type of procedure is, of course, logically quite legitimate; the social sciences would be entirely frustrated if it were not possible to use types of one sort or another. However, the use of types should be confined to situations where it does not lead to unrealistic results. In the case of long-run price determination within industries, the spread of cost differentials among firms is perhaps more important than the cost situation of a representative, average firm which may not exist in reality. The construct of the representative firm enables Marshall to arrive at a determinate point of long-run equilibrium of supply and demand, determined by the cost of production of a representative firm. Thus it becomes an auxiliary construction of an ideological character.

[1] *Principles*, p. 460.

again excluded because the long-run continuation of the same conditions implies actually a stationary situation and the elimination of change and, thereby, of time.[1]

Finally, Marshall has to admit the incompatibility of the static equilibrium theory and the dynamic long-run approach. He states that there is an essential difference between the theory of stable equilibrium of normal demand and supply on the one hand, and the problems of organic growth on the other. The first

> helps indeed to give definiteness to our ideas. . . . But when pushed to its remote and intricate logical consequence it slips away from the conditions of real life. . . . For the statical treatment alone can give us the definiteness and precision of thought, and is therefore a necessary introduction to a more philosophical treatment of society as an organism; it is yet only an introduction.[2]

Thus he ends with the recognition of a basic antithesis between equilibrium analysis, based on diminishing returns, and long-run economic development and progress, connected with increasing returns. In this antithesis an inner conflict of industrial man is reflected. The law of increasing returns, the belief in economic progress, and the moral duty to strive for unlimited acquisition are psychoculturally synonymous ideas. They are in conflict with the desire for satisfaction and rest. In order to eliminate this conflict, Marshall tries to construct a long-run stable equilibrium model in which the laws of increasing and diminishing returns, the forces of progress and decay, are balanced. In the end, however, he has to admit to the failure of these attempts.

[1] See above, pp. 215 ff.

[2] *Ibid.*, p. 461.

Chapter XIX

VALUE AND EQUILIBRIUM OF FACTORS OF PRODUCTION

Distribution in an Imaginary World

IN Book VI, Marshall deals with distribution. He starts out with constructing a simplified model of an imaginary world, in which (*a*) everyone owns the capital that aids him in his labour (but little capital is used); (*b*) gifts of nature are free and unappropriated; (*c*) everybody has an equal capacity for work and shows an equal willingness to work; (*d*) all work is unskilled and unspecialized; (*e*) everyone produces directly for sale without the co-operation of others and without any middlemen.[1] It is not difficult to see in this model the traces of the early and rude state of Adam Smith and Ricardo, where no accumulation of stock and no appropriation of land existed. This connection is confirmed by the conclusion which Marshall draws from this model: 'Things exchange for one another in proportion to the labour spent in producing them,' earnings will be 'normal', and 'everyone's earnings will be equal to those of everyone else.'[2] It is hard to avoid the impression that this model represents an ideal state in the same way as did the prelapsarian state of Smith and Ricardo. Marshall's model does not contribute anything to his following analysis of the real world, in which conditions are obviously different. And even if one interprets this type of model-building as an application of the method of gradual approximation to reality, the choice of abstractions is significant. Marshall abstracts from those features of reality which, in his period and in ours, have given cause for criticism of the existing system.[3] In his imaginary world incomes are determined by efforts, and economic equality is attained—a result deemed highly desirable by some social reformers. It is likely that, consciously or unconsciously, Marshall was influenced by these thoughts when he constructed this model.

[1] *Principles*, Book VI, chap. i, Sec. III, pp. 510–11. [2] *Ibid.*, p. 511.

[3] See W. A. Weisskopf, 'Psychological Aspects of Economic Thought,' where Professor Knight's abstractions, which are, to some extent, similar to Marshall's, are analysed.

The Ethics of Marginal Productivity

That Marshall starts his discussion of wages, interest, and distribution with a model which leads to the same result as the labour theory of value seems surprising, in view of the fact that his is basically a subjectivistic and utilitarian theory of value. However, as we have seen, he still believes in the activistic work ethic of the classical period and tries to combine it with his subjectivistic emphasis on need-satisfaction.

The ethical principle which determines factor prices, incomes, and distribution is, according to Marshall, 'in close harmony with such common sayings of everyday life as that "everything tends to find its own level", that "most men earn just about what they are worth", and that "if one man can earn twice as much as another, that shows that his work is worth twice as much."[1] The national dividend is distributed among the various agents of production according to their quantity and according to the services that each agent renders.[2] Thus the costs of each agent in its marginal application will become 'proportionate to the additional net product resulting from its use.'[3] The wages of labour 'tend to be equal to the net product due to the additional labour of the marginal labourer.'[4] Distribution is governed by marginal need,

> the need at that point at which people are indifferent whether they purchase a little more of the services . . . of one agent, or . . . of other agents. The supply of each agent will be closely governed by its cost of production.[5]

The differences in the earnings of the various agents of production reflect differences in efficiency. Efficiency, rewards, incomes, and money costs are interrelated.

> The efficiency of human agents of production on the one hand, and that of material agents on the other, are weighed against one another and compared with their money costs; and each tends to be applied as far as it is more efficient than the other in proportion to its money cost.[6]

These principles form the ethical basis of the marginal productivity theory. The marginal value product determines the price of a unit of a factor of production. This is in conformity with a moral

1 *Ibid.*, Book V, chap. viii, Sec. II, p. 404.
2 *Ibid.*, Book VI, chap. i, Sec. VII, p. 514.
3 *Ibid.*, p. 515.
4 *Ibid.*, p. 518.
5 *Ibid.*, pp. 536–37.
6 *Ibid.*, p. 662.

principle, at least in an ordinal sense: a high reward corresponds to a higher degree of efficiency of this factor than the lower price of another factor. At the margin of indifference between the employment of two factors, 'their prices must be proportionate to their efficiency.'[1] The underlying principle is: 'to each according to his productive contribution', which is essentially a moral principle destined to make the determination of incomes in the market economy appear morally acceptable.

However, the ethical principle involved in the marginal productivity theory is not based merely on justice to the individual. The individual supposedly receives the equivalent of his net product as reward; but it is not the value of his own productive contribution which determines his compensation; it is determined by the net product of the marginal labourer or factor unit. This marginal product of the marginal labourer depends on the size of the labouring group; no member of such a group is worth more than the contribution of the marginal labourer, whatever his actual product is. Thus reward is commensurate with productive contribution, but productive contribution is measured in social terms; one's product as a member of a group is interchangeable with the one of the marginal worker. This represents an important deviation from the ethical principle of the labour theory of value, where, ideally, an equality is established between effort, product, and reward. This identity and correlation of product and reward is, to some extent, maintained by the marginal productivity theory, where wages and incomes supposedly tend to become equal to the net marginal product. The difference between the two theories, however, consists in the introduction of a social or group element into the marginal productivity theory.[2] This theory allocates individual rewards according to efficiency and productive contribution, thereby making them appear just to the individual; but it combines this with a social element by making the reward conform to the marginal product which is determined by the size of the group. The introduction of this social element disturbs the correspondence between reward and individual effort; efficiency is not defined entirely in terms of individual effort but in terms of the group's contribution to the social product. This is another attempt

[1] *Principles*, p. 406.

[2] 'This dependence of the wages of each group of workers on the numbers and efficiency of others is a special case of the general rule that the environment (or Conjuncture) plays a part at least co-ordinate with a man's energy and ability in governing that net product to which his wages ever approximate under the influence of competition' (*ibid.*, p. 667). Environment includes the fact that every individual is a member of an occupational group, the size of which determines his net marginal product.

to harmonize the conflict between individual and society. It cannot be successful, however, unless people feel that their occupational status, which determines their marginal product, is a deserved one. As this is often not the case, the marginal productivity theory cannot serve generally as an ethical justification of incomes.

However, Marshall's ideal is, to some extent, a reward which corresponds to effort, as can be seen from his distributive model of an imaginary world. In order to establish more close-knit ties between reward and effort, he proceeds to prove the ethical homogeneity of labour and capital. This tendency is obvious in his treatment of interest as a form of income. Polemizing against the socialist idea that the surplus produced by labour should be received by the labourer and not by the capitalist, he emphasizes that 'capital itself is the product of labour and waiting.'[1] He underscores this point by reformulating it:

> if it be true that the postponement of gratifications involves in general a sacrifice on the part of him who postpones, just as additional effort does on the part of him who labours . . . then it cannot be true that the value of a thing depends simply on the amount of labour spent on it.'[2]

Although he rejects here the labour theory of value, he reaffirms its basic ethical principle. By reducing both waiting and labour to the same common denominator, namely, sacrifice, he establishes their ultimate moral homogeneity. Both the saver and the labourer do the same thing; they both sacrifice. Thus the effort or sacrifice which determines the real cost of production becomes the source of just reward. Interest is justified as the reward of the sacrifice of waiting.[3] The justification is not merely a utilitarian one, because otherwise no loanable funds would be forthcoming in an economic system in which people are motivated mainly by monetary gain. Sacrifices and efforts, such as those involved in work and in the postponement of gratifications, have to be rewarded for moral reasons. All this shows clearly the ethical nature of Marshall's discussion of factor price determination and distribution.

There is, however, another reason why labour and capital have both to be interpreted as sacrifice. Equilibrium in the employment of productive factors is again viewed as a balance of opposing forces.[4]

[1] *Ibid.*, p. 587. [2] *Ibid.*, p. 587. [3] *Ibid.*, p. 588.

[4] Here again Marshall's description abounds with physical analogies: see the references to the keystone of an arch, to the balls lying in a bowl, to a weight suspended from a string (*ibid.*, p. 526); all this points to one of the psychocultural roots of the equilibrium concept; to achieve, for reasons of psychological security, the certainty of the physical sciences.

The same forces which bring about equilibrium in prices of consumers' goods are at work in the establishment of the equilibrium of prices of productive agents: the pleasures of consumption are balanced against the efforts and sacrifices of production. In order to make this scheme applicable to factors of production, Marshall has to explain all productive agents as sacrifices (of efforts or waiting). Not only does this interpretation justify their respective rewards (wages and interest) in a moral sense, but it also makes it possible to assume that factors of production are 'the result' of effort and sacrifices:

> Another thread of continuity . . . connects the various agents and appliances for production, material and human; and establishes fundamental unity between them . . . wages and other earnings of effort have much in common with interest on capital. For there is a general correspondence between the causes that govern the supply prices of material and personal capital: the motives which induce a man to accumulate personal capital in his son's education, are similar to those which control his accumulation of material capital for his son.[1]

Thus labour skills and capital are created and allocated by the sacrifices of the parents and traced back to the same common source.

Substitution and Factor Equilibrium

In equilibrium every factor unit receives the equivalent of its marginal product, and thus rewards correspond to efficiency. Furthermore, rewards are proportional to the sacrifices of labour and waiting. Thus distributive equilibrium represents a morally appropriate situation. It is brought about by the rational action of entrepreneurs, by the

> alert businessman [who] is ever seeking for the most profitable application of his resources, and endeavouring to make use of each several agent of production up to that margin, or limit, at which he would gain by transferring a small part of his expenditure to some other agent.[2]

The employment of labour is determined in the same way. The alert manager of a railroad is referred to as one who

> is constantly weighing the net product in saving of time and of annoyance to passengers, that will accrue from the aid of a second guard on an important train, and considering whether it will be worth its cost.[3]

[1] *Principles*, pp. 660–61. [2] *Ibid.*, pp. 514–15. [3] *Ibid.*, p. 515.

In a similar fashion, a farmer confronted with the problem of how many shepherds he should employ

> reckons that the net product of an additional man will be twenty sheep. If he can be got for much less than the equivalent of their price, the alert farmer will certainly hire him; but, if only for about that price, the farmer will be on the margin of doubt; and the man may then be called a marginal shepherd, because his employment is marginal.[1]

All these are examples of the application of the principle of substitution. This principle itself is nothing but a special formulation of the code of rational economic behaviour.[2] The businessman, the employer, the farmer, act like any other individual who balances the marginal utilities of various expenditures for the purpose of maximization. Such rational behaviour of individuals, however, is supposed to bring about the same type of maximization in the economy by allocating resources rationally through the competitive process:

> To sum up the whole in a comprehensive, if difficult statement: Every agent of production . . . tends to be applied in production as far as it profitably can be. If employers, and other businessmen, think that they can get a better result by using a little more of any one agent they will do so. They estimate the net product . . . that will be got by a little more outlay in this direction, or a little more outlay in that. . . . Thus, then the uses of each agent of production are governed by the general conditions of demand in relation to supply: that is, on the one hand, the urgency of all the uses to which the agent can be put . . . and, on the other hand, by the available stocks of it. And equality is maintained between its values for each use by the constant tendency to shift it from uses, in which its services are of less value to others in which they are of greater value, in accordance with the principle of substitution.[3]

Marshall's problem in respect to the equilibrium of the factors of production is the same as it was in his previous equilibrium analysis: to show how rational action of individuals will lead to a social equilibrium situation which has the same characteristics as the equilibrium established within the individual, namely, balance of opposing forces and maximization of utility through equalization of marginal values. The equilibrium of factor employment established by the process of substitution is therefore constructed in this image.

[1] *Ibid.*, p. 516.

[2] See above, pp. 197 ff.

[3] *Ibid.*, pp. 521–22.

We have shown that a balance of opposing forces, of efforts and sacrifices of production, on the one hand, and of pleasures of consumption, on the other, is involved. The maximization is accomplished in the same way as within the individual, through equalization at the margin; the marginal product of a factor will, in equilibrium, have to be equal in all its uses. If this process works smoothly within the entire economy, an optimum allocation of resources will be attained.[1]

It is significant that the maximizing allocation process is carried out in the same way within the individual and within the entire economy, namely, by the rational action of individuals. Entrepreneurs, by applying the principle of substitution, bring about the optimum allocation of productive agents in the same way as the individual maximizes his total utility by allocating his own income and his own resources to various uses until marginal values are equalized. Thus, again, Marshall tries to interpret events which take place within the entire economy as in individual behaviour. However, individual rationality does not necessarily lead to socially rational results. Therefore, the process of substitution carried out by independent individuals has to be supplemented by a process of social interaction, namely, competition. Through 'vertical' competition between workers with different skills within the same industry, and through 'horizontal' competition (movement between occupations), factor equilibrium is attained.[2] Competition is the social counterpart of individual rational action. What the individual accomplishes for himself by consciously maximizing behaviour, competition is supposed to accomplish for the economy. Through competition, the personified economy, the invisible hand of the deity, establishes an equilibrium in which resources are optimally allocated and social utility thereby maximized.

However, Marshall has his doubts about the results of this system, especially about the efficient allocation of the factor entrepreneurship:

> For while it is through their conscious agency that the principle of substitution chiefly works in balancing one factor of production against another; with regard to them it has no other agency than

[1] The idea of optimum allocation of resources and the formulation of the conditions of a general optimum for the economy as a whole were developed on the Continent (by Walras and Pareto). However, Marshall's analysis of factor equilibrium contains the basic idea of an optimum allocation approach which was then applied to Anglo-Saxon welfare economics by A. C. Pigou (see Hla Myint, *Theories of Welfare Economics*, pp. 89–93).

[2] *Principles*, pp. 662–63.

> the indirect influence of their own competition. So it works blindly, or rather wastefully . . . it strengthens those who are strong, and hands over the business of the weak to those who have already obtained a partial monopoly. But on the other hand, there is also a constant increase in the forces which tend to break up old monopolies.[1]

Whereas all other factors of production are allocated by the actions of entrepreneurs, the factor entrepreneurship itself is not consciously allocated by anybody, except by competition. Thus the element of rational allocation represented by conscious substitution of the more efficient factor for the less efficient is lacking in entrepreneurship.

Marshall exaggerates the differences in the allocation of entrepreneurship and of other factors. From the fact that entrepreneurs consciously maximize profits, he concludes that they become a 'conscious agency' of substitution. However, from the fact that each individual enterpriser substitutes consciously the cheaper for the dearer factor, it does not follow that an optimum allocation will be brought about for the whole economy. The same blindness and wastefulness which he admits in the allocation of the factor 'entrepreneurship' also operates in the allocation of all other factors by entrepreneurs. Certainly, allocation would not function merely with substitution alone, unless competition between entrepreneurs for factors of production spread the effects of substitution throughout the economy. Competition is a necessary prerequisite for the allocation of all factors, not only of entrepreneurship. Marshall's argument is unconsciously motivated by the endeavour to restrict this haphazard working of all allocating forces to the smallest possible segment of the economy, namely, entrepreneurship. And even here he qualifies his criticism by showing how monopoly tends to be broken up and by concluding that

> on the whole the work of business management is done cheaply—not indeed as cheaply as it may be in the future when men's collective instincts, their sense of duty, and their public spirit are more fully developed. . . . But yet it is done so cheaply as to contribute to production more than the equivalent of its pay. For the business undertaker, like the skilled artisan, renders services which society needs and which it would probably have done at a higher cost if he were not there to do them.[2]

Could one be more vacillating in one's opinion than Marshall is here about the services rendered to society by enterprisers? It is done

[1] *Ibid.*, p. 663.

[2] *Ibid.*, p. 664.

cheaply; but entrepreneurs should have more collective instincts and sense of duty; but they give more than they receive; etc. In the sentence 'The ablest businessmen are generally those who get the highest profits, and at the same time do their work most cheaply,'[1] the ambivalence reaches its apex by culminating in a logical contradiction: high profits make the work of the ablest businessmen expensive to society, and not cheap, even if one assumes that they have earned them. To summarize: in respect to the most important socioeconomic group in our economy, the entrepreneurs, Marshall has to admit that the principle of substitution does not work and that competition may not always lead to optimum allocation, although, as an expression of his ambivalence, he tries to make the entrepreneur appear in a favourable light.

Optimum allocation of resources through substitution and competition depends again on the principle of diminishing returns: 'the notion of the marginal employment of any agent of production implies a possible tendency to diminishing return from its increased employment.'[2] The process of substituting units of different factors for one another, until equal marginal productivity between two factors is reached, cannot take place unless the marginal physical product declines with the increasing employment of each and every factor. Marshall makes a distinction between the application of this principle to the action of individual enterprisers and farmers in case they apply resources in undue proportions, on the one hand, and to the country as a whole when an increase in the total amount of capital applied to agriculture causes diminishing returns of produce, on the other hand. However, he states that the two cases are akin to each other.[3] The distinction has to do with his tendency to show the beneficiality and ethical validity of factor prices and income distribution. The law of diminishing returns in agriculture, as it works for an entire country, has, as we have seen, a pessimistic implication. In respect to rational economic action of enterprisers who substitute the more efficient for the less efficient factor, however, Marshall interprets the working of the principle as beneficial and as leading to just prices and incomes. Rational economic behaviour in connection with the principle of diminishing returns is supposed to lead not only to just factor prices and incomes but also to a beneficial optimum distribution of factors and resources. Therefore, the law in its pessimistic application to the whole economy has to be distinguished from its optimistic effects in respect to the action of individual entrepreneurs, factor prices, incomes, and rewards. The main function of this law, as applied to factor prices and distribution,

1 *Principles*, p. 665. 2 *Ibid.*, p. 407. 3 *Ibid.*, pp. 408–9.

however, is that it makes possible the establishment of factor equilibrium, that is, optimum allocation. Distributive equilibrium and optimum allocation are psychoculturally necessary. They serve to show that the market forces lead to an 'ideal' situation. This will reduce the anxiety of the individual who is exposed to the effects of these forces. The 'anarchy' of the market is thus again transubstantiated into harmony.

Part VI

The Disintegration of Economic Rationalism

Chapter XX

REASON AND RATIONALISM

IN Part V we have interpreted Marshall's thought as a manifestation of economic rationalism. His model of rational economic behaviour is so well defined that it did not require a general discussion of the term 'rationalism'. However, before concluding our analysis with a brief glance at the disintegration of this type of rationalism, a short excursion into its broader meaning is in order.

The terms 'rational' and 'rationalism' can be used in an absolute sense or in a relative, historical sense. In the former meaning reason (*ratio*) is a universal human faculty; in the latter sense, rationalism is a historical phenomenon peculiar to modern Western civilization and it is related to the economic value complex.

In an absolute sense, reason means the ability of the human mind to be logical, to classify, to analyse, to super-, sub-, and co-ordinate logically well-defined entities; it represents the ability to think discursively and grammatically. It is definitely a conscious type of activity. It has to be distinguished from the intuitive intellect, which comprehends through passive, receptive, mental 'impregnation', through mere 'looking', through what German philosophy called *Anschauung* ('vision'). In this sense, *ratio* is a universal general human quality. The term 'rational', used with an absolute meaning, refers to an ultimate, self-evident human experience which exists prior to, and goes beyond, the realm of discursive thinking and is, therefore, impossible to define. Reason must exist in some sense before rational, discursive thought can take place. Therefore, its essence cannot be clearly defined by the methods of rational, discursive thought, and such definitions will always remain tautological. One can understand the absolute meaning of reason only through individual, direct, intuitive experience of 'rational' thought and action.

Reason, as a universal human faculty, is only a part of the human person, only one of the human faculties, and shows only one aspect of human existence. Reasoning is conscious activity; but there is also unconsciously motivated action. There are emotional, capricious, erratic, impulsive, spontaneous motivation and behaviour. Reason perceives, orders, and classifies the results of perception in a logical way; but there is also intuition, the direct, lightning-like comprehension of the essence of things, which is different from logical, discursive, and analytical understanding. The latter operates in an active way; but there is also the mood of passive, silent, intuitive receptivity as an instrument of acquiring knowledge. But reason is an instrument for dealing with, and for adapting one's self to, the social and cultural conditions of life. The harmonizing function of reason is one of the most important weapons of man to make the burden of his life more tolerable.

Western Rationalism

Reason in an absolute sense is common to all human beings of all periods and cultures. The role, however, which reason and rationality play, the importance attributed to it, and the degree to which other aspects of existence and other faculties of the mind are recognized or neglected vary considerably from culture to culture and from period to period. Modern Western civilization is characterized by a prevalence of rationalism. In the main stream of Western thought of the eighteenth and nineteenth centuries—in spite of differences in philosophy and exceptions—man is identified with his reason and his ego. Reason and consciousness are highly emphasized and positively evaluated. Being rational and acting rationally are considered as virtues and supreme values. The ideal of human conduct is the deliberate, conscious planning of life based on well-defined, clear-cut, long-range goals. Not being rational is considered a negative, 'bad' type of behaviour. One is not supposed to behave in an irrational way, and the existence of irrational motives is only reluctantly admitted.

In the ideological systems of the seventeenth and eighteenth centuries, in which the foundations of our present ideas, creeds, and institutions were laid, man, society, and the universe were interpreted in terms of reason alone. The rationalistic elements of Christian theology were taken over and separated from the theological and metaphysical framework in which they were imbedded during the Middle Ages. The laws of reason were secularized and separated from their divine origin. Man was seen mainly as conscious, rational, and able to understand these laws. Human relations and social institutions were to be ruled by reason alone. It was assumed that every human being was able to govern his own actions by rational insight. Hence the great emphasis on education and government by rational persuasion. It was believed that as soon as everybody was sufficiently wellinformed to understand these laws, an ideal society could be established. The dominant institutions of this period—political democracy and the free-market system—were justified by the laws of reason conforming to a purely rational, egotistical human nature.

This rationalism attempted to eliminate the irrational from the world picture. The world is viewed as a coherent, reasonable structure. Modern Western rationalism, as a historical phenomenon, has embraced the logical and mathematical approach to nature and has attempted to discover self-evident and universal rational principles which apply to nature as well as to human conduct. Intuition and sense-impressions are considered unreliable; this rationalism refuses to accept the world as our senses present it to us. The idea that chance and fate have any influences on social and individual life has been discarded. The instinctive, the customary, the traditional, are criticized and rejected; so is everything which is incompatible with the general laws allegedly discovered by rational reflection.[1]

Scientific Rationalism

The rationalistic element in our culture is related to the trinity of economics, technology, and science. The scientific method is rationalistic par excellence. The approach of Western science is positivistic, analytical, segmental. Reality is dissected logically instead of being comprehended in its essence through insight, empathy, and intuition. Science divides reality instead of integrating it and trying to understand it in its totality. The goals of science are to discover laws and uniformities of general validity. This makes science blind to the unique and to the qualitative. Uniformities of a scientific nature are usually established through quantification, which makes phenomena calculable and comparable. Science in this sense is a peculiar phenomenon of modern Western civilization and one of the characteristic manifestations of Western rationalism in the limited, historical sense. This interpretation of science as a culture-bound phenomenon in no way belittles its results. Many laws of the natural sciences are undoubtedly 'true' in the sense that they enable man to predict and control. That does not mean that they include all the truth and all reality. To the utilitarian mind, prediction and control may be the only possible goals of knowledge. There is, however, a different type of knowledge which attempts to penetrate to the essence of things, to establish an intuitive connection with the qualitative aspect of their existence. This type of knowledge is neglected by scientific rationalism.

[1] B. Grothuysen, 'Rationalism.'

Economic Rationalism

The rational element is of special importance in the social and economic sectors of our culture. As Schumpeter has pointed out, the economic pattern is, at least in modern Western civilization, the matrix of logic:

> The rational attitude presumably forces itself upon the human mind primarily from economic necessity; it is the everyday economic task to which we as a race owe our elementary training in rational thought and behaviour—I have no hesitation in saying that all logic is derived from the pattern of economic decision.[1]

However, Schumpeter uses an example taken from the field of technology to demonstrate how economic behaviour fosters rationality. In order to get results in physical production, rational methods will have to be used instead of magical formulas. The projection of rationality from production technology into economic conduct and from there into all other compartments of life is a peculiar Western development. It is connected with the great emphasis of this civilization on the economic and the production side of life.

The quantifying and mathematical method, an important characteristic of rationalism, is closely interrelated with the use of monetary calculation in business. The use of money as a unit of accounting; the acquisitive attitude, with its precise profit-and-loss calculation; the use of double-entry bookkeeping as a method which makes the rational, systematic pursuit of economic gains possible; the capitalist form of enterprise, which distinguishes itself from previous kinds of enterprise by the use of this type of accounting—all these phenomena emerged together and simultaneously with rationalism, science, and technology as characteristics of modern Western civilization.[2]

The Decline of Rationalism

Although predominant in modern Western thought and culture, rationalism did not develop unchallenged. The cultural and intellectual development during the eighteenth and nineteenth centuries could be interpreted as a struggle between a classical rationalism and a romanticism which emphasized emotional and non-rational aspects. These trends were intensified toward the end of the nineteenth century. A general turn to subjectivism and toward intro-

[1] A. Schumpeter, *Capitalism, Socialism, and Democracy*, pp. 122–23.

[2] *Ibid.*, pp. 123–24; Max Weber, *General Economic History*, Part IV.

spection took place, manifesting itself in different fields: the subjectivism of the marginal utility school of economics, Kantian and neo-Kantian subjectivism, the individualistic type of Christianity in the writings of Tolstoy and Kierkegaard, the Russian and French novel, impressionism and expressionism in painting—all these trends were manifestations of a turn toward the subjective, of a new interest in the psyche, with all its unconscious, emotional, and non-rational aspects. Moreover, the importance of non-rational forces in history and in the universe was stressed. Marx's materialistic and dialectic interpretation of history pictured man as subject to transpersonal economic forces; Schopenhauer found in an almost unconscious transcendent will the creator of the external and internal world; Henri Bergson and his disciples discovered the creative aspects of a transcendent, biological force called 'life'. The seeds of the romanticism of the nineteenth century and of the *fin de siècle* atmosphere blossomed in the twentieth century into cultural products of a non-rational character and into the irrationality of two world wars. Totalitarian mass movements, nihilistic, relativistic philosophies, the adoration of the instinctive, and irrational schools of art are some of the symptoms of this trend.

We have given account of the various forms which rationalism has taken in the thought of some classical economists and in the thought of Marshall. The decline of rationalism is equally reflected by economics. It manifests itself in modern economic thought in the slight reality value attributed to the postulate of rationality. The rationalistic models are now interpreted as methodological devices, as hypothetical, heuristic principles. The rationalistic ideal has become diluted and is demoted to a mere box of tools. Thus a hidden doubt of its validity is unconsciously expressed. The Enlightenment really believed in the purely rational character of man, nature, and the universe. Modern man has abandoned this belief. The use of rationalistic models as ideal types or as instruments of economic analysis represents a last bastion of exaggerated rationalism. Why are these models retained? Because they still perform a sociocultural function. We have to assume that man is perfectly rational and that his rationalism leads him to act as industrial civilization requires him to act. The belief in perfect rationality and in maximization is necessary to make life under the industrial system intellectually tolerable. The repressed non-rational aspects of the human personality are continuously knocking at the door of our consciousness. They strive for realization. They cannot attain it, because under the present system personality traits which do not conform to the rationalistic and acquisitive ideal of modern industrialism cannot be developed successfully. The constructs of economic theory help to silence these disturbing forces. They tell the individual:

> You are as industrial society wants you to be. You are a completely rational, conscious being, whose main purpose in life is the satisfaction of known needs, which are satisfied by industrial production. You are trying to maximize utility by equalizing expenditures at the margin. The mode of life which industrial society imposes on you is what you really want.

This can be proved by the laws of economic conduct derived by economic analysis from 'irrefutable' premises. The aims of the individual are represented as identical with the aims of industrial civilization. Economic theory comforts the individual, who is torn apart by the conflict between economic rationalism demanded by society and the desire to develop all the potentialities of his personality. However, by representing its rational models as hypothetical constructs without any counterpart in reality, modern economic theory has ceased to perform this psychocultural function. It has implicitly admitted that the economy is rational only in thought, not in reality.

Ethical Relativism

The uneasiness of modern man in respect to the acquisitive ideal and its gradual disintegration is reflected in the tendency of more recent economic theory to avoid a discussion of ultimate values. Although economic rationalism represented a moral attitude and was imbued with a clear-cut ethical ideal, at least in the writings of Alfred Marshall and some of his followers, it contained an element of ethical relativism which became more important in the twentieth century.[1] Utility is supposed to be maximized, but no criterion is given to distinguish the useful from the useless, the good from the bad. Modern economics assumes 'randomness of ends.'[2] It is not concerned with ethical values:

> So far as we are concerned our economic subjects can be pure egoists, pure altruists, pure ascetics, pure sensualists. . . . Our deductions do not provide any justification for saying that caviar is an economic good and carrion a disutility. . . . Individual valuations . . . are outside the sphere of economic uniformity . . . from the point of view of economic analysis these things constitute the irrational elements in our universe of discourse.[3]

[1] W. A. Weisskopf, 'Individualism and Economic Theory.'

[2] T. Parsons, *The Structure of Social Action*, pp. 59 ff.

[3] L. Robbins, *An Essay on the Nature and Significance of Economic Science*, p. 106.

Thus the most important problem of human action, the search for guiding norms for behaviour, is excluded from 'rational' consideration by the economist. He has become satisfied to state that the deliberate maximization of utility, based on extra-economically given values, constitutes a sufficient ideal as well as a tool of economic analysis. That it is also an ideal, a normative value system, has been clearly expressed by Robbins:

> And thus, in the last analysis, economics does depend . . . on an ultimate valuation—the affirmation that rationality and ability to choose with knowledge is desirable. If irrationality, if the surrender to the blind forces of external stimuli and unco-ordinated impulse at every moment is a good to be preferred above all others, then it is true that the raison d'être of economics disappears.[1]

Conscious maximization is an ideal, although a purely formal one, devoid of ethical content: every action which maximizes subjective utility to the individual—regardless of what the individual considers to be useful—if undertaken 'with complete awareness of the alternatives rejected', conforms to the norm. Thus economic rationality becomes a symbol for two conflicting tendencies of the age: to relativize ethical concepts, on the one hand, and to idealize formal rationality of choice and action, on the other.

Economic Non-Rationality

The trend toward the disintegration of the economic value system and its symbols continued in modern economic thought in imperfect or monopolistic competition theory[2] and in recent trends in the theory of the firm. A new element which one might call, lacking a better term, 'economic non-rationality' is discovered in the behaviour of the consumer and the entrepreneur. The old type of purely rational consumer (the consumer under pure competition) distinguished between homogeneous, standardized products merely on a price basis; he acts like a rational economic man, buying as cheaply as possible. He has no preference for the products of different sellers, except for their cheaper price. A commodity is to him something unequivocal, a thing with definite objective qualities, defined and circumscribed by physical characteristics, and clearly delimited from other goods.

The newly discovered consumer of monopolistic markets develops a psychological attitude toward goods which makes possible

[1] *Ibid.*, p. 157.

[2] Inaugurated by J. Robinson, *The Economics of Imperfect Competition*; and E. Chamberlin, *The Theory of Monopolistic Competition.*

modern advertising and selling methods, that is, 'product differentiation' in modern economic parlance. This consumer does not see a commodity as a definite physical object. He has a feeling for the nuances and differences in products caused by the 'conditions surrounding its sale.' The retail buyer considers

> the seller's location, the general tone or character of his establishment, his way of doing business, his reputation for fair dealing, courtesy, efficiency, and all the personal links which attach him either to the seller himself or those employed by him.[1]

All these 'intangible' elements become part of the 'product', differentiating similar physical goods from one another in the minds of the consumers. The consumer has become interested in things which previously may have been considered accidental and extraneous, such as patented features, trade-marks, packaging, design, colour, style, etc.[2]

Economists have always considered economic processes as interrelations between inanimate and abstract objects like labour, commodities, money, etc. Therefore, product differentiation has been discussed under the disguise of a redefinition of the concepts of 'commodity' and 'industry'. What has been discovered here, however, is a new psychological attitude of consumers, a type of motivation for economic behaviour. We would like to leave open the question whether this attitude represents a twentieth-century development or whether it has existed all along and was overlooked in economic theory because it did not conform to its rationalistic interpretation of economic conduct. There is probably some truth in both interpretations. The attitude of consumers that makes 'product differentiation' possible has probably developed since the beginning of the twentieth century, with its roots in the nineteenth; the history of advertising, which requires for its effectiveness a corresponding receptive attitude on the part of consumers, seems to support this contention. However, only in the 1930's did economic theory begin to acknowledge and to analyse this type of motivation. The fact that consumers may prefer to pay a higher price because they are attracted by the colour of the package or the looks of the salesgirl does not fit into the picture of economic man which neoclassical economics had presented. The final recognition and admission that consumers do not act merely on the basis of purely economic advantages but that they are also motivated by a host of capricious, impulsive, spontaneous, emotional, and habitual factors

[1] Chamberlin, *op. cit.*, pp. 56 ff.   [2] *Ibid.*

represents the introduction of a new 'irrational' element into economic analysis—'irrational' only because it is extraneous to its traditional conceptual framework.

Something similar happened to the economic interpretation of entrepreneurial behaviour. In addition to the traditionally accepted motivation of profit maximization, which corresponded to the ideal of rational economic man, a host of other motives for managerial action was discovered. It was pointed out that businessmen and managers strive for security, for the power position of their firm in the industry, for liquidity and retention of control of the firm, for the establishment and maintenance of morale of staff and line, for a balance between the various interests of corporate departments, for favourable publicity, for a balance between the interests of the labour force, the suppliers, the customers, and the government, and so on.[1]

Although some of these aims are 'economic' in the traditional sense, others are not; and their multiplicity and qualitative peculiarities preclude the possibility of applying the maximization principle because of the absence of a common quantifiable denominator. The model of economic rationality becomes inapplicable where conflicting tendencies cannot be measured on a homogeneous, continuous scale.

Indeterminateness

This situation has been recognized by monopolistic competition theory in the oblique way of admitting that there are situations of 'indeterminateness' in the market. The model of rational economic behaviour fails to lead to a determinate equilibrium solution in 'oligopolistic' situations, that is, when a small number of large firms compete with one another, because, then, the action of individuals becomes important. In the words of R. Triffin, oligopolistic markets are characterized thus:

> [If] a seller has such an influence upon one or several competitors that his own price-output decisions are capable of influencing the price-output decisions of this, or these, competitors, this

[1] These ideas are found mostly in periodical literature and are not yet in the stage of systematic codification. The following is by no means a complete list: A. A. Alchian, 'Uncertainty, Evolution, and Economic Theory'; S. Enke, 'On Maximizing Profits'; M. W. Reeder, 'A Reconsideration of Marginal Productivity Theory'; J. S. Duesenberry, *Income, Savings, and Consumers' Behavior*, esp. chaps. iii, iv; W. W. Cooper, 'A Proposal of Extending the Theory of the Firm,' 87; R. A. Lester, 'Marginalism, Minimum Wages, and Labor Markets,' and 'Shortcomings of Marginal Analysis for Wage-Employment Problems,' K. W. Rothschild, 'Price Theory and Oligopoly.'

> influence will be a factor to be taken into account. . . . This would not be so troublesome if this influence were perfectly definite. . . . But the other sellers may also have an influence on the first one. . . . It is this mutual but indecisive influence that opens the door to an infinitely varied pattern of possibilities. The oligopolist may be afraid of unleashing unpredictable reactions. . . . No doubt there is a sense in which the solution is always determinate: it all depends on the number of variables considered. But it is clear that the variables that would have to be considered to determine the solution might be of a different type from the ones generally used by pure economics of the equilibrium brand. Such considerations as financial backing, political influence, prestige, psychology, optimistic or pessimistic slant, enterprising or routine-like attitudes in business, etc. may well play an overwhelming role in determining the solution.[1]

Thus the importance of 'non-rational' factors is admitted for a specific type of market. Marshallian neoclassicism had to admit that individuals act occasionally in a 'non-rational' way. It assumed, however, that 'non-rational' elements would cancel out in group and mass behaviour because of the law of large numbers.[2] Monopolistic competition theory went one step further. It enlarged the sphere of effectiveness of 'non-rational' factors by admitting that they exercise an influence under oligopoly. In this way these disturbing elements were tied in with a form of market which has always been condemned by a majority of economists. This implies a hidden condemnation not only of monopoly and oligopoly but also of 'non-rational' factors and behaviour. Everything that economists have rejected is combined here in one intellectual syndrome: monopoly and non-rational individualism prevent the economist from arriving at a neat, determinate equilibrium solution. On the other hand, it is still believed that under pure competition, where the number of participants is large and where the influence of 'non-rational' elements is excluded by definition (no product differentiation), economic forces will lead to a 'rational' and determinate equilibrium solution.

Perhaps the most significant phenomenon in recent economic thought, however, may be the application of the rules of games of strategy and warfare to economic behaviour.[3] In the statements that

[1] R. Triffin, *Monopolistic Competition and General Equilibrium Theory*, p. 71.

[2] See above, pp. 190 ff.

[3] G. V. Neumann and O. Morgenstern, *Theory of Games and Economic Behavior*; Rothschild, *op. cit.*

> in a social exchange economy . . . each participant attempts to maximize a function . . . of which he does not control all the variables. . . . This is certainly no maximum problem but a peculiar and disconcerting mixture of several conflicting maximum problems,[1]

the application of the maximization principle to a group like the industry or the economy as a whole is rejected. Equally rejected is the contention that the

> zones of indeterminateness which exist when the number of participants is small, because of the circular interdependence of individual expectations, actions and volitions will disappear as the number increases.[2]

This implies the abandonment of a determinate equilibrium concept, based on maximization, even for large groups and purely competitive markets. What remains is rules of probability and logistics of strategic warfare. Economic behaviour, at least of business firms, is interpreted as warfare:

> The oligopoly-theorist's classical literature can neither be Newton and Darwin, nor can it be Freud; he will have to turn to Clausewitz's Principle of War.[3]

Thus economics has come a long way: from the symbols of labour value, harmony, and equilibrium, through the stage of rational, economic man and markets, to an interpretation which uses strategy and warfare as analogies for economic behaviour and represents economic laws as probabilities. A picture of the individual, the economy, and the universe emerges, full of uncertainties, without ethical guideposts, relativistic, probabilistic, and appropriate to the precarious situation of mankind in mid-twentieth century.

[1] Neumann and Morgenstern, *op. cit.*, p. 11.
[2] *Ibid.*, p. 14.
[3] Rothschild, *op. cit.*, p. 307.

Bibliography

ADLER, A. *The Social Interest.* London, Faber and Faber (1938).

ALCHIAN, A. A. 'Uncertainty, Evolution and Economic Theory.' *Journal of Political Economy*, LVIII (June, 1950), p. 220.

ANNAN, Noel G. *Leslie Stephen.* Cambridge (Mass.), Harvard University Press: London, Chatto and Windus (1952).

AQUINAS, Thomas. *Summa Theologica Secunda Secundae.*

ARISTOTLE, *Politics*, Book I.

ASHLEY, W. A. *English Economic History and Theory.* (London, Longmans Green.)

BACHOFEN, J. J. *Das Mutterrecht.* Basel, Benno Schwabe (1897).

BARNETT, L. *The Universe and Dr. Einstein.* London, Victor Gollancz: New York, William Sloane (1948).

BORKENAU, F. *Der Übergang vom Feudalen zum Bürgerlichen Weltbild.* Paris: Felix Alcan (1934).

BRIFFAULT, R. *The Mothers: A Study of the Origins of Sentiments* (3 vols.). London, Allen and Unwin: New York, MacMillan (1927).

BRYSON, Gladys. *Man and Society, the Scottish Enquiry of the Eighteenth Century.* Princeton, Princeton University Press (1945).

BUNYAN, John. *The Pilgrim's Progress.*

CANNAN, E. *A Review of Economic Theory.* London, P. S. King (1929).

CANTILLON, R. *Essai sur le Commerce* (in Sewell, 1901).

CHAMBERLIN, E. *The Theory of Monopolistic Competition.* Cambridge, Harvard University Press (1942).

CHILD, A. H. *Problems of Sociology of Knowledge.* University of California dissertation (1939).

COOPER, W. W. 'A Proposal of Extending the Theory of the Firm.' *Quarterly Journal of Economics*, LXV (February, 1951), p. 87.

DAHLKE, Otto H. in *Contemporary Social Theory.* Barnes and Becker (eds.), New York, Appleton-Century (1940).

DIETERICH, A. *Mutter Erde* (2nd ed.). Leipzig, B. G. Teubner (1913).

DUESENBERRY, J. S. *Income, Savings and Consumers' Behavior.* Cambridge, Harvard University Press (1949).

EITEMAN, W. J. 'Factors Determining the Location of the Least Cost Point.' *American Economic Review* (December, 1947), pp. 910–18.

ENGELS, Friedrichs. *The Origin of the Family, Private Property and the State.* London, Lawrence and Wishart: New York, International Publishers (1942).

ENKE, S. 'On Maximizing Profits.' *American Economic Review*, XLI (September, 1951), p. 567.

FREUD, Sigmund. *Collected Papers.* II. London, Hogarth Press and Institute of Psychoanalysis (1948).

——*The Ego and the Id.* London, Hogarth Press and the Institute of Psychoanalysis (1947).

—— *A General Introduction to Psychoanalysis.* Garden City, Garden City Publishing Co. (1943).

—— *Group Psychology and the Analysis of the Ego.* London, Hogarth Press (1946).

—— *New Introductory Lectures on Psychoanalysis,* trans. by W. J. H. Sprott. London, Hogarth Press (1933).

—— *Leonardo da Vinci, a Psycho-sexual Study of an Infantile Reminiscence.* London, Kegan Paul: New York, Moffat Yard (1922).

—— *Moses and Monotheism.* London, Hogarth Press: New York, A. A. Knopf (1939).

—— *Three contributions to the theory of Sex,* in Basic Writings of S. Freud, New York, Modern Library (1938).

—— *Totem and Taboo.* London, Routledge and Kegan Paul: New York, in Basic Writings of S. Freud, Modern Library (1938).

FROBENIUS, L. *Das Zeitalter des Sonnengottes.* Berlin (1904).

FROMM, Erich. *Fear and Freedom.* London, Kegan Paul. (*Escape From Freedom.* New York, Farrar and Reinhart, 1941.)

—— *The Forgotten Language.* London, Victor Gollancz: New York, Rinehart (1951).

GORER, G. *The American People, A Study in National Character.* London, Cresset Press: New York, W. W. Norton (1948).

DE GRAZIA, S. *The Political Community.* Chicago, University of Chicago Press (1948).

GROTHUYSEN, B. 'Rationalism,' in *The Encyclopaedia of the Social Sciences,* Vol. XIV. New York, MacMillan (1934).

GROTIUS. *De jure Belli et Pacis* (1623).

GRUNWALD, Ernst. *Das Problem einer Soziologie des Wissens.* Wien and Leipzig, Braumueller (1934).

HALEVY, Elie. *The Growth of Philosophic Radicalism.* London, Faber (1934).

HANSON, A. H. 'Cost Functions and Full Employment.' *American Economic Review,* XXXVII (September, 1947), pp. 552–65.

HARE, A. J. C. *Life and Letters of Maria Edgeworth.* London, Constable: New York, Houghton Mifflin (1894).

HERSKOVITS, M. J. *Economic Anthropology.* New York, A. A. Knopf (1952).

HOLLANDER, J. *David Ricardo, a Centenary Estimate.* Baltimore, Johns Hopkins Press (1910).

JACOBI, J. *The Psychology of Jung.* London, Kegan Paul: New Haven, Yale University Press (1943).

KARDINER, A. *The Psychological Frontiers of Society.* New York, Columbia University Press (1945).

KATONA, G. *Psychological Analysis of Economic Behavior.* New York, McGraw-Hill (1951).

KEYNES, J. M. 'Alfred Marshall' in his *Essays in Biography*. London, MacMillan : New York, Harcourt Brace (1933).

KLEIN, V. *The Feminine Character*. London, Kegan Paul: New York, International Universities Press (1946).

KNIGHT, F. H. *Risk, Uncertainty and Profit*. Reissue by the London School of Economics (1933).

LASSWELL, H. 'World Politics and Personal Insecurity' in his *A Study of Power*. Glencoe, The Free Press (1951).

LAUDERDALE, Earl of. *An Inquiry into the Nature and Origin of Public Wealth*. London, Longman and Rees (1804).

LESTER, R. A. 'Marginalism, Minimum Wages and Labor Markets.' *American Economic Review*, XXXVII (March, 1947), p. 135.

—— 'Shortcomings of Marginal Analysis for Wage-Employment Problems.' *American Economic Review*, XXXVI (March, 1946), p. 63.

LOCKE, John. *On Civil Government*. Everyman's Library.

—— *Essay on Human Understanding*.

—— 'Some Considerations of the Lowering of Interest and Raising the Value of Money.' *Works*, II (6th ed., London, 1759).

LOWIE, R. H. *The History of Ethnological Theory*. New York, Farrar and Rinehart (1937).

MALTHUS, T. R. *Essay on Population*. Everyman's Library.

MANNHEIM, Karl. *Ideology and Utopia*. London, Kegan Paul: New York, Harcourt Brace (1936).

MARSHALL, A. *Principles of Economics*. 8th ed., London, MacMillan (1920).

MARX, K. *Capital*. Modern Library edn.

MASLOW, A. H. 'Dynamics of Personality Organization.' *Psychological Review*, L (1943), pp. 514 ff., 541 ff.

—— 'Higher and Lower Needs.' *Journal of Psychologv*, XXV (1948), pp. 433–36.

—— 'A Theory of Human Motivation.' *Psychological Review* (1943), pp. 370 ff.

MAYO, Elton. *The Social Problems of an Industrial Civilization*. Boston, Division of Research, School of Business Administration, Harvard University: London, Kegan Paul (1945).

MERTON, R. K. *Social Theory and Social Structure*. Glencoe, The Free Press: London, Allen and Unwin (1949).

MONROE, A. E. *Early Economic Thought*. Cambridge, Harvard University Press (1927).

MORGAN, L. H. *Ancient Society*. London (1877).

MONTAGU, A. *On Being Human*. New York, Henry Schuman (1950).

MULLAHY, P. *Oedipus, Myth and Complex*. London, Allen and Unwin: New York, Hermitage Press (1948).

MYINT, Hla. *Theories of Welfare Economics*. Cambridge, Harvard University Press: London, Longmans Green (1948).

MYRDAL, G. *Der Politische Ideengehalt der Nationalökonomischen Doktrinbildung*. Berlin (1932). English Translation: *The Political Element in the Development of Economic Theory*. Cambridge, Harvard University Press: London, Routledge and Kegan Paul (1953).

NELSON, S. *The Idea of Usury*. Princeton, Princeton University Press (1949).

NEUMANN, J. v. and MORGENSTERN, O. *Theory of Games and Economic Behavior*. Princeton, Princeton University Press (1944).

PARSONS, T. *The Structure of Social Action*. Glencoe, The Free Press (1949).

PETTY, Sir William. 'Political Arithmetic' in *Economic Writings* (ed. by C. H. Hull). Cambridge, at the University Press (1899).

—— 'Taxes and Contributions' in *Economic Writings* (ed. by C. H. Hull). Cambridge, at the University Press (1899).

POLANYI, K. *The Great Transformation*. New York, Farrar and Rinehart (1944).

—— 'The Logic of Liberty.' *Measure*, I (Fall, 1950), p. 349.

PRIBRAM, K. *Conflicting Patterns of Thought*. Washington, Public Affairs Press (1949).

PUFENDORF, S. *Of the Law of Nature and Nations*. Oxford (1710).

—— *Devoir de l'Homme et du Citoyen*.

RANK, O. *Das Inzestmotiv in Dichtung und Sage*. Leipzig and Wien (1912).

—— *Psychoanalytische Beiträge zur Mythenforschung*. Wien, Internationaler Psychoanalytischer Verlag (1922).

——, and SACHS, H. *Die Bedeutung der Psychoanalyse für die Geisteswissenschaften*. Wiesbaden (1913). (Eng. trans. by C. H. Payne, *The Significance of Psychoanalysis for the Mental Sciences*, in 'Nervous and Mental Diseases Monograph Series,' No. 23, 1916.)

RANULF, S. *Moral Indignation and Middle Class Psychology*. Copenhagen, Levin and Munksgaard (1938).

REEDER, M. W. 'A Reconsideration of Marginal Productivity Theory.' *Journal of Political Economy*, LV (October, 1947), p. 450.

RICARDO, David. *Principles of Political Economy and Taxation* (Everyman's Library).

—— *The Works and Correspondence of David Ricardo*, Vol. IV, ed. by P. Sraffa Cambridge, at the University Press (1951).

RIESMAN, D. 'Authority and Liberty in the Structure of Freud's Thought.' *Psychiatry*, XIII (1950), pp. 167 ff.

—— *The Lonely Crowd*. New Haven, Yale University Press (1950).

—— 'The Themes of Heroism and Weakness in the Structure of Freud's Thought.' *Psychiatry*, XIII (1950), pp. 301 ff.

—— 'The Themes of Work and Play in the Structure of Freud's Thought.' *Psychiatry*, XIII (1950), pp. 1 ff.

ROBBINS, L. *An Essay on the Nature and Significance of Economic Science*. London, MacMillan and Co. (1946).

ROBINSON, Joan. *The Economics of Imperfect Competition*. London, MacMillan and Co. (1933).

—— *Economics is a Serious Subject*. Cambridge, at the University Press (1932).

ROTHSCHILD, K. W. 'Price Theory and Oligopoly.' *Economic Journal*, LVII (1947), p. 299.

SCHUMPETER, A. *Capitalism, Socialism and Democracy.* New York, Harper (1942).

SEWALL, H. R. *The Theory of Value before Adam Smith.* 'Publications of the American Economic Association,' Vol. II, No. 3. New York, MacMillan (1901).

SISMONDI, S. de. *Nouveaux principes.* Paris (1819).

SOMBART, W. *Die Juden und das Wirtschaftsleben.* Leipzig, Duncker and Humbolt (1911).

SMITH, Adam. *The Theory of Moral Sentiment.* London, H. C. Bohn (1835).

—— *Wealth of Nations* (Modern Library edn.).

STEELE, Richard. *The Tradesman's Calling.*

TAWNEY, R. *Religion and the Rise of Capitalism.* Harmondsworth and Baltimore, Penguin (1947).

TICKNER, F. W. *Women in English Economic History.* London, J. M. Dent: New York, E. P. Dutton (1923).

TRIFFIN, R. *Monopolistic Competition and General Equilibrium Theory.* Cambridge, Harvard University Press (1940).

TROELTSCH, E. *The Social Teaching of the Christian Churches.* London, Allen and Unwin (1931).

VINER, J. 'Marshall's Economics, the Man and his Times.' *American Economic Review,* XXXI (June, 1941), p. 228.

WALKER, Ronald. *From Economic Theory to Policy.* Chicago, University of Chicago Press (1943).

WEBER, Max. *General Economic History,* trans. F. H. Knight. Glencoe, The Free Press (1927).

—— *Gesammelte Schriften zur Religions-Soziologie.* Tübingen, J. C. B. Mohr (1923).

—— *The Protestant Ethic and the Spirit of Capitalism.* London, Allen and Unwin: New York, Scribners (1930).

WEISSKOPF, W. A. 'The Ethical Role of Psychodynamics.' *Ethics,* LXII (April, 1952), pp. 184 ff.

—— 'Hidden Value Conflicts in Economic Thought.' *Ethics,* LXI (April, 1951), p. 195.

—— 'Individualism and Economic Theory.' *American Journal of Economics and Sociology,* IX (April, 1950), p. 317.

—— 'Industrial Institutions and Personality Structure.' *Journal for Social Issues,* VII (1951).

—— 'Psychological Aspects of Economic Thought.' *Journal of Political Economy,* LVIII (August, 1949), p. 309.

WOODWORTH, R. S. *Contemporary Schools of Psychology.* London, Methuen: New York, The Ronald Press (1931).

INDEX

For Product Safety Concerns and Information please contact our EU representative GPSR@taylorandfrancis.com
Taylor & Francis Verlag GmbH, Kaufingerstraße 24, 80331 München, Germany

www.ingramcontent.com/pod-product-compliance
Ingram Content Group UK Ltd.
Pitfield, Milton Keynes, MK11 3LW, UK
UKHW022110190926
475702UK00013B/1370
9780415868860